The Smart
Money Method

The Smart Money Method

How To Pick Stocks Like A Hedge Fund Pro

Stephen Clapham

HARRIMAN HOUSE LTD
3 Viceroy Court
Bedford Road
Petersfield
Hampshire
GU32 3LJ
GREAT BRITAIN
Tel: +44 (0)1730 233870

Email: enquiries@harriman-house.com
Website: www.harriman-house.com

First published in Great Britain in 2020
Copyright © Stephen Clapham

The right of Stephen Clapham to be identified as the author has been asserted in accordance with the Copyright, Design and Patents Act 1988.

Paperback ISBN: 978-0-85719-702-3
eBook ISBN: 978-0-85719-703-0

British Library Cataloguing in Publication Data
A CIP catalogue record for this book can be obtained from the British Library.

Whilst every effort has been made to ensure that information in this book is accurate, no liability can be accepted for any loss incurred in any way whatsoever by any person relying solely on the information contained herein.

No responsibility for loss occasioned to any person or corporate body acting or refraining to act as a result of reading material in this book can be accepted by the Publisher, by the Author, or by the employers of the Author.

To Max and Finn.
Aim high.
Take the first step.
Have fun.

CONTENTS

About the Author	ix
Preface	xi
Introduction	1
1: What Makes a Good Investment?	5
2: Finding Ideas	8
3: Testing the Hypothesis	33
4: Understanding the Industry	53
5: Quality	60
6: Analysis of Company Quality	74
7: Management	90
8: Company Financials	112
9: Valuation	150
10: Communicating the Idea	182
11: Maintaining the Portfolio	193
12: Macro-Economic Analysis	224
13: Looking Forward	238
14: COVID-19 Postscript	258
Acknowledgements	275
Index	277

ABOUT THE AUTHOR

STEPHEN CLAPHAM is the founder of Behind the Balance Sheet, a professional investor training consultancy and online school. Stephen trained as an accountant before joining the equity research department of Hoare Govett, one of London's top stockbrokers. Stephen had a successful career as a sell-side analyst, working for various investment banks and consistently being rated as one of the top analysts in his sector in the leading surveys.

In 2005, he joined Toscafund to cover non-financial stocks. He has held positions as a partner and head of research at two multi-billion hedge funds and one smaller fund. He has been responsible for international equity selection and for managing portfolios as a consultant to one of London's top wealth managers, where he was also a member of the firm's Investment Committee.

In 2018, he set up Behind the Balance Sheet as a training business, initially dedicated to helping professional investors improve their skills. His flagship product, the Forensic Accounting Training Course, had over 250 professional students in its first 18 months, and hundreds more have taken his other courses, webinars and online programmes.

Stephen is recognised as one of the leading commentators on fraud and aggressive accounting in quoted companies, and he regularly appears or is cited in the press, including BBC Radio 4's *Today* programme, *The Sunday Times*, *Financial Times* and specialist financial media such as the *Investors Chronicle*, The Acquirers Podcast and Real Vision.

PREFACE

WHAT THIS BOOK COVERS

In this book I present my research process over an investment's lifecycle, from finding the original idea, through to pulling the trigger to buy the stock and then how to monitor it, and when to sell. We cover assessing the quality of the business, valuing the company, and thinking about how the stock will fit in the overall portfolio.

The book spends little time on investment theory – I don't consider the theory to be particularly relevant or helpful to people trying to make money in the stock market. Investing is common sense and academic content can be confined to understanding a few valuation multiples and financial ratios (which I do explain).

I have tried to make the book as jargon-free and non-technical as possible.

WHO THIS BOOK IS FOR

This book is for investors of any experience level. It will probably be of most benefit to intermediates, the equivalent of people who have started to do parallel turns in skiing. But even complete beginners should find this book accessible and I hope that many experienced and indeed professional investors will find a few nuggets which will help them improve their game.

HOW THIS BOOK IS STRUCTURED

The structure of the book follows the chronological sequence of my research process. I start by finding a stock idea, so I first explain several methods to do this. I then explain how to test the hypothesis – I usually think something is worth buying for one specific reason, so I check that this is valid.

I then explain how to evaluate the quality of the business model and of the company, how to evaluate its financial performance and assess the valuation of the stock, before explaining how I make the final decision to buy – how much and at what price.

Finally, I explain how to monitor the investment, including watching the macro-economic environment, and then when to sell.

I finish off with some thoughts about how the pandemic may change my investment approach.

INTRODUCTION

Picking winning stocks is a key objective of every investor. There must be thousands of newsletters claiming to do exactly that, sometimes run by failed hedge fund managers.

Myself, I am a former hedge fund equity analyst. The difference with this book is that I am not going to offer you stock tips. Instead, I offer a methodology which will help you develop your stock-picking skills and give you the tools and techniques to find great stocks which will beat the market.

Methodology and process are essential to successful investment. In this book, I explain the process I followed when I was a hedge fund analyst making huge investments in companies, with positions often well over $100m each.

When you are investing such significant sums, of course it's necessary to do a huge amount of due diligence, beyond the capabilities of the average investor. The good news is that, as with most of such endeavours, the Pareto rule applies: 20% of the work will take you 80% of the way. And that's enough for 99% of stock decisions. Even better, I shall show you some of the shortcuts the professionals employ in evaluating an investment.

You might well wonder what qualifies me to write a book like this. I was an analyst at various investment banks, top-ten rated in my sector by investors every year. I then moved to join one of my clients and I have been a partner and head of research at two multi-billion-pound hedge funds based in London. I have picked international equities and run portfolios for a £5bn asset wealth manager. And I now run a business training institutional analysts at some of the UK's largest and most successful investors (and an online investor school).

For a few of my clients, I also do bespoke research. One called me in 2019 and asked me to review CK Hutchison, the Hong Kong quoted conglomerate, controlled by Li Ka-shing. It's an incredibly complicated business. My client (which has a team of 40 analysts) did not have the time nor the forensic skills to do an in-depth analysis.

CK Hutchison looked cheap – it was trading on a P/E multiple of 7–8x, an extremely low valuation multiple. And it owns some fantastic assets: ports in Hong Kong and around the world; safe assets like Northumbrian Water, a regulated UK utility; and a string of renewable electricity generation assets. Other positive factors which attracted my client included:

- Li Ka-shing is a billionaire and one of the world's most successful businesspeople.

- Many of the assets owned by the holding company would command multiples of twice or three times the parent, if separately quoted.

- The group had a spread of interests, both geographically and across sectors, which should make it highly resilient to a downturn, reducing investment risk.

At the time, CK Hutchison was quoted in Hong Kong, where local unrest was then a factor in undermining the valuation of the local stock market. My client was naturally intrigued – could they buy this high-quality portfolio of international assets at a discount? Perhaps the market disliked the stock because it was quoted in Hong Kong, although its business was not significantly exposed to the local unrest? I was asked to find out.

My normal modus operandi with a new complex company is to do an initial review to determine the scope of work and agree a framework with the client – this can take a couple of hours or a day in the case of a complex business like this one. In four hours, I emailed the client to suggest abandoning this project.

Why? How could I do this so quickly?

The reason is simple – I found a huge amount of debt (over $10bn!) in a structure which removed it from the group balance sheet, a consequence of CK Hutchison's use of complex ownership structures. Its debt looked lower than the economic reality and its valuation more attractive than it really was.

I found this quickly because I have developed my research process over the last 25 years. That is the subject of this book. Sometimes, when a business is this complex, it's a bit like detective work, but without the weapons. Most of the time, it's straightforward.

In this book, I have distilled all these years of experience, thousands of hours reading thousands of company releases and annual reports, countless meetings with company managements and likely tens of thousands of research reports. For sure, I surpassed Malcolm Gladwell's 10,000 hours to become an expert many years ago, and hopefully this book will save you having to make the same mistakes and spend as much time learning as I did. After reading it, you should be a better investor.

1
WHAT MAKES A GOOD INVESTMENT?

INTRODUCTION

A GOOD INVESTMENT, in my view, is any stock which beats the market over a short or long period. In my professional career as an equity analyst at hedge funds, I looked for stocks which I believed either:

- would appreciate by 50% or more over an 18–30 month period, or

- had 20% or more absolute downside in a prevailing bull market.

Of course, when you buy (or sell) the stock, you can only hope for the right outcome – my actual results fluctuated wildly. But there are a huge number of equities globally in which you can invest, and selection criteria such as this are a useful way of narrowing your field of endeavour.

ROUTES TO PRICE APPRECIATION

For a stock to outperform (or do better than) the market – active managers are generally measured on their performance relative to a market benchmark, hedge fund managers are measured in absolute dollars – one of three things generally has to happen:

1. The stock has to be rerated, i.e., market participants are prepared to pay a higher multiple of earnings or cash flow.

2. The company has to generate high returns on capital and strong cash flows, and reinvest those cash flows at similarly high rates.

3. The company's earnings have to increase, or consensus estimates of those earnings have to increase.

Anticipating a rerating is possible, but difficult to time. An example of the type of rerating opportunity I look for is an orphan stock on its own in a sub-sector, and a competitor with a stronger story coming to the market. This is likely to drag up the rating of the incumbent. A rerating sometimes happens because of a fashion or new trend, but such opportunities tend to be rare. Without such catalysts, it can take a considerable amount of time for the patient investor to be rewarded with a higher multiple, as you wait for the market to recognise the quality of an investment. I tend to avoid this approach, unless there is this type of catalyst.

High-quality cash compounders are, generally, fantastic long-term investments, but they are often highly valued. In recent years, the prevalence of ultra-low interest rates and low growth made such companies inherently more valuable. They have also become much more highly rated. They remain suited to a long-term investment portfolio, rather than my special situation strategy.

My focus has been the exploitation of overly conservative profit forecasts by 'the Street', looking for companies which can beat consensus expectations of earnings over a two- to three-year period. (The consensus is generated by taking an average of the sell-side brokers' forecasts for the company.) Usually, when companies beat expectations they also enjoy a rerating, which makes such investing highly profitable. Conversely, for shorts, I look for stocks likely to miss forecasts.

If the stock with the forecast anomaly is a high-quality business, or is in an industry undergoing a rerating, or enjoys some other benefit, so much the better.

That's what I am looking for in an investment. The next thing to think about is *where to look?*

2
FINDING IDEAS

P ROBABLY THE greatest practical constraint for most investors is lack of time, especially in the context of multiple stock opportunities (a portfolio to assemble and thousands of stocks to choose from). It is not possible to research everything. Idea-generation strategies are therefore critical. It's no surprise that a popular question from potential clients of the hedge fund I worked for – mainly consultants and institutional investors – was "Where do you get your ideas from?"

What they would love to hear is that you have a screening system which mathematically produces guaranteed results. The truth, at least in my case, is that although some processes are scientific, my really good ideas are often somewhat conceptual in nature. I don't have a formula for generating ideas. Instead, I focus on areas which are *likely* to reveal investment opportunities.

While sometimes thematic, my best ideas have tended to be fairly random, although they generally have one factor in common – change a variable and work out the implications for a company's profitability. This is how my best investment ideas are created, as I shall explain.

I believe investors spend far too much time reading information which will expire worthlessly today, tomorrow, next week, or next month. We generally don't spend enough time thinking about bigger issues. This focus on the now is a distraction from the long-term fundamentals.

Rather than worrying about which TV company was acquired last week at what price, it's much more important to ask why the TV industry is consolidating. The price and valuation is always important, but I always try to remind myself to ask *why* as well as *how much*.

In this chapter, I outline the sources from which I tend to generate stock ideas, and discuss some of the advantages and disadvantages of each.

AREAS OF EXPLORATION

If you are going fishing, you need to go where the fish are, and I have listed below a range of sources which drive my idea selection, grouped under the following headings:

- Asymmetric pay-offs
- Own knowledge
- Market action
- External sources
- Thematic investing
- Macro factors
- Random inputs

The classifications or groupings are not important, nor do I bother much about the source of an idea, the important thing is to produce enough ideas to populate the portfolio, and to keep it refreshed.

ASYMMETRIC PAY-OFFS

My favourite opportunities are those with asymmetric pay-offs. Here there is potential for considerable upside, but not a lot of downside (or vice versa for shorts). Sometimes, a share will have fallen out of favour with the market. It usually takes a catalyst – an event such as a change in management – for the market to become more enthusiastic, and for the share price to factor in the recovery opportunity. Whatever the idea, and wherever the source, this concept of a reward which is not commensurate with the risk is a critical objective.

OWN KNOWLEDGE

LATERALS

Laterals are how my best investment ideas have been created. I take a good stock idea, or theme, and apply it to a different stock, industry, or geography. Here are some examples:

- Lidl and Aldi destroyed the valuation of UK food retailers – let's watch the same thing happen in Australia.

- Uber is gaining ground across America – let's sell the stock of the company which finances New York taxi medallions (Medallion Financial, ticker TAXI).

- Car sales are increasing, and miles driven are up because of low fuel prices – let's buy the tyre manufacturers, or sell FirstGroup, the owner of Greyhound.

- Oil prices are falling – let's sell the oil services companies, as they will see a faster and steeper deceleration in earnings than the oil companies.

The number and diversity of ideas is limitless. The common theme is that you take a change in a variable and work out the implications.

SCREENS

Screens are a useful way to identify valuation anomalies and find over- or undervalued stocks, especially when using out-of-the-mainstream valuation parameters. I often use screens to filter ideas and develop a universe of potentially interesting stocks. The topic of screens probably merits a book in its own right, although there are many resources available on the web.

Screens have several advantages. For me, the key advantage is that they help stratify investment opportunities in order of attraction. Reviewing multiple screens, attractive opportunities will stand out as being cheap (or dear) on a number of different relative measures. Often a stock you are already interested in, for a thematic or micro-economic reason, can jump out as being cheap on a number of screens. Companies found by several screens become a higher priority.

Valuation is only one screening tool. Quantitative (or quant) research is another form of screening. It helps me understand which markets or themes (e.g., momentum) quantitative investors are currently attracted to, or what they dislike. This helps categorise a stock into a particular style, which is useful not only for identifying possible investment opportunities, but for understanding factor risk if the stock is eventually added to my portfolio.

Sometimes a stock will fit a theme, will have a particular quantitative factor which looks desirable, and will emerge as interesting from a valuation perspective by looking at a screen. This would be three strong ticks, so the stock becomes a priority for further work.

PERSONAL OBSERVATION - KEEPING YOUR EYES OPEN

Peter Lynch, the legendary investor and manager of the Fidelity Magellan Fund, wrote the brilliant book, *One Up on Wall Street*, in which he described how he watched shoppers in malls to see which carrier bags were most popular.

Certainly, ideas do come to me when I am out and about. Shopping in the Spanish department store, El Corte Inglés, I spotted some attractive laptop bags from an Italian producer, Piquadro, that I had not heard of before. I was interested in the company as a peer (and a potential takeover target) for Samsonite. Looking on the internet later, it transpired that the company was quoted and was about to open a store on Regent Street. I figured it would take little time for London hedge fund managers to encounter the product and move the stock price up, which indeed happened. I didn't pursue it as the liquidity was limited and management seemed reluctant to take the time to meet.

Figure 2.1: Piquadro share price

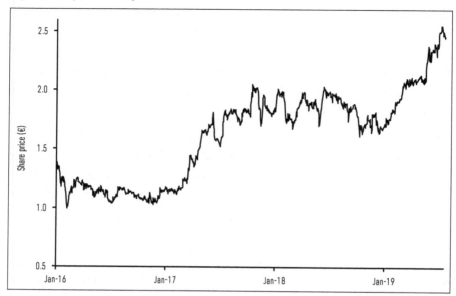

Source: Behind the Balance Sheet (www.behindthebalancesheet.com) from Sentieo Data.

The world is now rather more sophisticated than in Peter Lynch's heyday. I remember a salesman in our New York office flying up to Boston to give Peter Lynch a bottle of champagne when his fund cracked the $1bn mark. In those days, the late 1980s, that would ingratiate you with the fund manager. Probably not today, when he would have to report the gift to someone in compliance, who would probably end up drinking it.

It's surprising how often personal observation can pay off handsomely. In the 1990s, I was following the UK bus companies, three of whom, in the space of a few months, made acquisitions of bus businesses in the US. I flew out to visit some of the new subsidiary companies. Every restaurant I visited had a sign: 'Now hiring'.

Labour was the single largest cost for these businesses – it was obvious that the bus companies faced a significant headwind to growing profitability. And at the time, I could not identify a domestic UK player which had managed to succeed in the US. My note was entitled 'UK Bus Heads West – will it get chopped and sectioned?' The cover had my picture of a 1947 school-bus hot rod, which had been chopped and sectioned (several inches taken out of the roof pillars and the middle of the body to lower it radically). That was my favourite research cover.

Keeping your eyes open is one of the first rules of investment.

OTHER INVESTORS

One of my bosses had a very strict rule about not discussing positions with other investors, a rule which he had no hesitation in breaking himself, but which was rigorously enforced for the rest of us. As a consequence, broker ideas dinners were frowned upon. These are occasions when a broker invites a dozen or so hedge fund managers to a swanky London restaurant (Boulestin in St James has a perfect private room), and all the managers pitch in an idea and a view on the market.

On such (very rare) occasions, I had to resort to presenting the ideas my boss had rejected, or that I knew he would reject. I never learned any great ideas from these dinners (and was not concerned, as I always had plenty of ideas), but they were good fun and you could have a laugh, make some friends among the investor community and check what the prevailing mood was.

Such events have developed and are now considerably more sophisticated. More recently, since I have had access to fewer sources of information, they have become more valuable. Having lunch or a cup of coffee with a fellow investor is usually time well spent, as you can swap ideas and problems, and add to your knowledge of a stock or sector. You might not come away convinced about copying a friend's position – although the best investors present their investment ideas in an irresistible and compelling way – but it can be fertile ground for lateral ideas, and often you can learn something from someone else's approach or point of view.

PERSONAL CONTACTS

I am fortunate to know a lot of people in different industries and from different walks of life. Talking to friends can often illuminate a corner of the market that was otherwise unclear or simply unknown. A friend's comment that their shop could not get enough of a particular product might be traced back to an opportunity for the company that makes the product, or even the machinery supplier further upstream.

Retailers can tell you whether they are doing well or badly to the week, or if a competitor is losing people or gaining share. They can give you an insider's insight into sector trends, or into morale at company HQ. One of the mums at school had a very senior position at one of the top UK retailers. After a couple of glasses of wine, and in response to my prompts, she was complaining about how low morale was; that sort of anecdote is useful support for a fundamental short.

A hedge fund billionaire will be well connected and will doubtless have sources of information unavailable to lesser investors.

FOLLOWING MANAGEMENT

I tend not to pick stocks on the basis that there is an outstanding management team. Usually, this will be recognised by the market and reflected in the share price, and I don't consider this one of my skills. I also think it can be quite an inconsistent strategy.

Look at Sir Martin Franklin, who was staggeringly successful with Jarden, an outstanding stock over many years. His attempt to build several roll-up businesses – the so-called platform companies – was unsuccessful for an extended period, with both Platform Speciality Products (chemicals sector) and Nomad Foods falling from stock-market favour.

This a strategy where you grow by acquisition within an industry vertical. Platform Speciality Products was renamed Element Solutions. Tip: be careful when looking to buy a stock which has recently changed its name – usually it's to mark a break with a troubled past. The stock has still not recovered several years later. Nomad Foods fell by over 50% in 2016, although more recently its price has started to increase.

Occasionally I may look to buy into a stock where an outstanding manager, usually one whom I know, goes into a turnaround situation, but it has to be cheap.

QUALITY IDEAS

Another highly profitable strategy is buying long-term quality or growth at the wrong price – or at a price which undervalues the opportunity. I explore the issue of quality in much more detail in later chapters.

COMPANIES YOU KNOW WELL

One route that some people use is to select a group of companies that they understand well and would like to own at the right price. By staying within this selection of companies, possibly owning the same stocks multiple times, it's possible to stick to what you know. The attraction of public markets is that, if you can be patient, the volatility of the marketplace will give you the chance to own companies you like at your price. Such a strategy requires a lot of discipline.

I sometimes return to a past stock, but usually only if it was a winner. Avoiding stocks where I have lost money in the past is not a firm rule – after so many mistakes over the years, it would limit the universe. I am, however, slightly superstitious – not unlike a number of people in the industry. One manager I know refused to change his lucky cufflinks for a couple of months during a winning streak.

FUNDAMENTAL IDEAS

My largest opportunity set is in straightforward fundamental ideas. These can be sourced from a wide variety of places. Contrary to popular perception, good investment ideas – especially in larger institutions – do not generally originate from the sell-side analyst community. I tend to get ideas from a number of different sources. I discuss these one at a time in the rest of the chapter.

MARKET ACTION

IPOS AND PRIVATISATIONS

I like IPOs, as there is an equal opportunity for all market participants – very few people will have a real advantage in assessing the stock. Privatisations, in particular, can be profitable because management, set free, has the potential to create substantial value for the new owners.

I actually started my investment career working on privatisations as the stockbroker research analyst writing about the imminent flotation. Back then, they were ill-understood by the UK market – there were often no comparators and the government wanted to sell them cheaply. Of that era, only British Airways was a poor long-term investment, as I identified at the time, much to the chagrin of Colin Marshall, then CEO. BAA, in contrast, was an obvious winner, while British Gas proved even more profitable.

Sir Chris Hohn, of the Children's Investment Fund (TCI), one of the most successful hedge funds in the world, has had repeated successes with privatisations where he has seen a good company being sold off cheaply and the management freed of political shackles. He has made fantastic profits with the privatisation of Australian railroad Aurizon, Spanish airport operator Aena, and the reduced role of the state at Airbus.

SPIN-OFFS

Stocks which have recently emerged from bankruptcy, and new spin-offs, can also be fruitful opportunities. The management team has the wherewithal and the freedom to pursue an independent strategy, while the market's understanding of their business may be limited.

Spin-offs are particularly interesting, and come in two forms – a glamour growth stock being spun out of a less glamorous parent (Chipotle spun out of McDonalds) or an untouchable stock being spun out of a more exciting parent (Juniper out of E.ON).

The spin-off generally finds itself in the hands of unnatural owners, especially if the spin-off company is significantly smaller than, or different to, the parent. For example, a spin-off may lead to an ETF or large-cap fund shareholder holding a small-cap within its portfolio, forcing it to sell the shares. That can create an adverse technical position in the shares, which can depress the price. Much has been written about spin-offs, but the attraction to me is similar to IPOs, in that few market participants have an information advantage.

WATCHING THE MARKET

Markets generally overreact to events, so a sharp sell-off can often be a useful point to revisit a past stock, or an idea you previously discarded as being overvalued. Events like threatened litigation, management departures, the loss of a customer or, more recently, the threat of disruption from Amazon, can cause a stock to collapse. More common are execution issues, particularly an earnings miss, which can create an opportunity to revisit a stock.

I tend to look at the impact of such events on *next* year's earnings. Often the stock will be beaten up for missing the current year consensus forecast, but the outer years see a much lower revision, suggesting a potential bargain for the patient investor.

EXTERNAL SOURCES

READING

I have not met any successful investors who did not read a lot. Understanding what is going on in the world, and how that might affect future growth and company prospects, is essential.

First on the list, and highly accessible, are good-quality newspapers and journals. I cannot track the markets without reading the *Financial Times* each day. I read it in hard-copy form, as the physical paper has a particular layout which aids recall. With my memory, I need every bit of help I can get.

But reading a daily newspaper does not really give you stock ideas. Indeed, the chat about what has driven a particular stock up yesterday in the stock-market report is:

- usually wrong

- always a distraction

- unhelpful in forming a view about its future potential.

In truth, I would probably be better off if I avoided the market reports, but it has become something of a habit and I enjoy it.

Specialist financial publications and blogs are more likely to generate ideas on thematic issues, especially short-term trends. However, they can also waste your time covering old, tired, or already well-trodden ground. I believe that even the really smart bloggers and journalists will rarely take you to a brilliant idea. And for every good idea, there will be several more which should be discarded.

Investment geniuses are rare. They are usually managing money, not writing blogs, although there are a few that produce thought-provoking content and occasionally helpful data.

My favourites are: John Hempton's Bronte Capital blog (brontecapital. blogspot.com), an exception as he is a professional manager; Ben Carlson's A Wealth of Common Sense (awealthofcommonsense.com); and the Felder Report (thefelderreport.com/blog), from uber-bear Jesse Felder. Felder posts some interesting material, although I don't necessarily subscribe to his conclusions.

There are many specialist financial publications now. *Barron's* and *Bloomberg Businessweek* are among my favourites, as well as *The Economist* of course. It's not a specialist finance journal but is essential business reading (although the covers are occasional contraindicators, notably, the end of oil cover indicating the bottoming of the oil price).

SELL-SIDE BROKERS

I wonder if private investors assume that professionals simply wait for the latest piece of research to arrive from their favourite analyst at Goldman, or Morgan Stanley, and then everyone jumps on it. Of course this happens, but it's not a great route to outperformance.

Analysts, or at least the best ones, are brilliant at understanding industries, and saving the fund manager or investor time. They are, generally, less good at identifying stock opportunities and timing entry points. But sometimes an analyst's note can lead you elsewhere: to a theme, or an upstream or downstream opportunity.

Equity salespeople are, in my view, a far better source of money-making stock ideas. I would occasionally engage with an equity salesperson's idea, but tended to use brokers in a different way. I might take an idea and look at it laterally. For example, if prices are recovering in the US for a producer, should I be looking at shorting its customers, or should I consider buying the European competitor? I cover lateral ideas later in the chapter.

Generally speaking, the bulge-bracket firms are great at providing waterfront coverage, doing cross-border comparisons, giving feedback on flows (is money going into or out of the market?), and economic analysis. Regional or local brokers are usually better at picking stock opportunities within their market and providing *colour*, which is often simply market gossip.

The most important service of the broking analyst is the production of forecasts and, hence, the creation of consensus forecasts. This is an essential tool in my armoury, as I operate by identifying *where the consensus is wrong*. I explain later how I deconstruct the consensus by drilling down into the forecasts of individual brokers.

INDEPENDENT RESEARCH PROVIDERS

In recent years, a whole industry of specialist research providers has emerged, ranging from one-man strategists or sector analysts, to whole teams of economists and strategists. In the former camp is the brilliant Ed Yardeni, who provides a lengthy daily summary of what's going on in the markets, with a huge amount of statistical back-up. In the latter camp are firms like Strategas, which provide a useful weekly round-up, with technical analysis, and some interesting baskets of stocks with exposure to different themes. Also in this camp, Ned Davis has a massive statistical library and a comprehensive understanding of long-term trends in economics and markets.

Those are all US firms. In the UK, Andy Lees has the Macrostrategy Partnership; Peter Warburton has Economic Perspectives; and I understand that The Analyst provides good investment ideas, although I have never used its service. Many more ideas can be found on platforms like Russell Napier's ERIC (Electronic Research Interchange), where you can buy research in the form of single reports. Russell is a brilliant economist and strategist, and I benefit immensely from his understanding of the world.

SPECIALIST IDEAS EXCHANGES

There are a number of specialist ideas exchanges, where professional and amateur analysts can pitch ideas to the wider public. Some of the users (who are generally obliged to post once or twice a year) can be highly competent analysts, but the quality is highly variable. The best known of these, at the time of writing, is SumZero. I find the ideas less than compelling for me, as research is generally biased to deep-value investing, or to small and illiquid stocks.

THEMATIC INVESTING

Themes, such as energy efficiency or ageing populations, often provide opportunities. The problem here is that they tend to be well flagged and, therefore, the upside is usually limited. I divide them into tactical (opportunistic) themes and structural trends; the latter sometimes linked to demographics.

TACTICAL THEMES

Opportunistic themes vary widely. For example:

- A commodity price fluctuation: when the oil price falls, sell the service companies. The second order effect is usually the most effective one to exploit – similar to the adage, 'in a gold rush, buy the shovel manufacturers'.

- A move in a macro-economic variable, such as a view that labour cost inflation will pick up in the US, leading to a short in the restaurant sector (which has a high labour-cost-to-sales ratio).

- A potential change in geopolitical outlook. For example, after listening to a presentation by Niall Ferguson in 2015, I realised that Obama was inward looking, and that the next US president was perceived as likely to be much more outward looking. The anticipated increase in defence spending might lead me to invest in defence stocks.

- A likely change in policy, such as an increase in infrastructure spending by governments as central banks run out of options on interest rates and QE.

In 2017, developed economies – particularly the USA – were in a traditional late phase of the cycle. Infrastructure spending had been anticipated to pick up, so buying construction companies where the pickup was not already fully reflected in share price, looked a fruitful strategy.

I had previously selected Irish construction conglomerate CRH on this basis, and it performed extremely well. Indeed, it appreciated over 60% in the 18 months after I had first recommended it. Some profit was then banked, and the remaining position cut when the anticipated further upside failed to materialise.

Figure 2.2: CRH late stage price appreciation

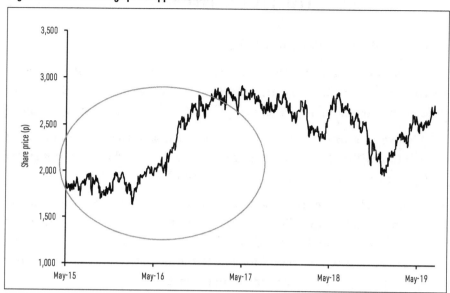

Source: Behind the Balance Sheet from Sentieo Data.

STRUCTURAL THEMES

Structural themes are longer term and can be particularly effective when they relate to a more-or-less unstoppable tide. An example would be Japanese or American ageing. It's highly likely that more hearing aids, false teeth, retirement homes, etc., will be required, and that this segment of the population will drive less, consume less, and generally be a less positive driver of economies and indeed stock markets.

These themes are obvious, however, and stock prices will generally reflect such well-known trends. This is not to say that related stocks will not deliver excellent long-term returns, but they would not have met my outsize return targets.

I prefer to focus on themes which are similarly likely, but where stock prices may have priced with less upside for various reasons. Water is a well-known resource that is becoming scarcer globally – too much is used, much is wasted, and aquifers are running low. It is a fertile field for investment.

Yet, water shares have generally underperformed. Certain water-sensitive stocks which are highly likely to see significant increases in demand for their products over the long term can be bought for a much lower rating than, for example, hearing aid companies, which operate in a technologically sensitive area and a highly competitive industry.

For example, I found one investment in this sector which I believe is highly likely to be acquired by a Chinese player, as its product allows more effective use of scarce water resources in agriculture.

GEOPOLITICAL THEMES

Geopolitical trends can generate a theme. This was highly topical in 2016–2017 with Brexit and Trump. Watching Trump's 2017 inauguration address, my notes have one main point: **protectionism**.

As a result, my enthusiasm for Harley-Davidson was reinforced:

- Harley exported 30% of its products and would benefit from any move to a border tax system.

- If imports were not penalised through taxes, they might face direct tariffs. This would affect Harley's competitors, which are Japanese and European.

- While labour costs might escalate, Harley should benefit from US workers having higher disposable income.

- Similarly, higher small-business optimism might feed into consumer confidence and increased sales.

- If Trump were successful, the US public's appetite for US products would likely increase.

Actually, I never got as far as opening Harley's 10-K. I believed that clear risks, such as electric bikes, Japanese competition, and rising steel costs, were already reflected in the stock's sub-market multiple. It went on my watchlist, but I was fortunate not to investigate further. The stock fell, notably on fears that its European sales would be hit by European tariffs on US auto and related imports – a risk factor I should have given higher weight in my initial analysis.

A HEAVILY THEMATIC APPROACH

Some investors operate a heavily thematic approach, which can be risky as you can end up having to pay for well-advertised themes. But it's a great way of helping to structure a portfolio, introduce diversification and hunt for opportunities. The best example I have found of this is Crescat Capital, who publish the themes they follow in structuring their portfolio. In one report, their themes included:

- Ageing population
- Asian contagion
- Aussie debt crisis
- Broadcast auction
- China currency and credit bubble
- US consumer comeback
- European disunion
- Fed moderation
- US fiscal stimulus
- Global fiat currency debasement
- New oil and gas resources
- Peak deflation
- Rise of the machines
- Security and defence
- Twilight in utilities

By having a large number of themes, and by having such a distinctive mix, they likely produce a highly differentiated and esoteric portfolio, which will have a broad mix of exposures. I suspect they have a limited concentration in each theme, which is the converse of my approach, but it is a very valid one. They are also good at clever titles!

MACRO FACTORS

COMMODITY PRICES AND SIMILAR MOVES

Moves in commodity prices, exchange rates, or other input costs can have a significant impact on the profitability of companies far beyond the direct producers of the commodity. Revenue driver changes – for example, in the case of a hotel group, a change in the number of inbound tourists – can have a similar or even larger effect. It can be difficult to anticipate such moves, or be ahead of the market, but it is often where the greatest opportunity lies.

Oddly, on a few occasions, I have been convinced that we were due an oil price correction or rebound, or a similar move in the price of coal or iron ore. Agricultural commodities are trickier because of the multiple inputs and the effect of the weather, and bulk commodities are particularly difficult.

Investments made on such a flimsy base are really punts, as there is no good way to get ahead of the commodity markets on the oil price, for example. Similarly, FX rate changes can create compelling investment opportunities and are the single largest macro influence on share prices in my view, but are really difficult to get right consistently.

Even so, sometimes it is possible to have conviction that the valuation of an oil services equipment company has become compelling, and that the oil price, or at least drilling activity, is more likely to increase than decrease. Then you can make reasonable bets, knowing that if the oil price or drilling activity does not turn immediately, at least you have some value protection in the stock you have purchased. The potential upside is usually sufficient enough that you are paid for waiting.

RANDOM INPUTS

RANDOM IDEAS ABOUT
WRONG PROFIT FORECASTS

A good piece of analysis can create an information edge over the market. The primary objective is to identify stocks where the market has under- or overestimated the company's medium- to long-term profit opportunity.

Triggers to look for include: changes in a company's demand profile, a change in input costs (e.g., the oil price and airlines), and similar factors. Changes in a relationship with a key supplier or customer can be revealing about potential problems, while the shortage of a key component can cause immense problems further up the supply chain.

In 2016, the CEO of Airbus commented that the A350 was a highly sophisticated aircraft and he had not expected to be held back by a poor supply of toilet doors. They single-sourced this item from Zodiac, which ran into manufacturing problems and undermined the whole delivery schedule. The supplier's issues caused a significant downgrade downstream. While the impact was significant in the short term, the long-term earnings power was likely unimpaired.

Figure 2.3: Zodiac Aerospace showing weakness in 2015

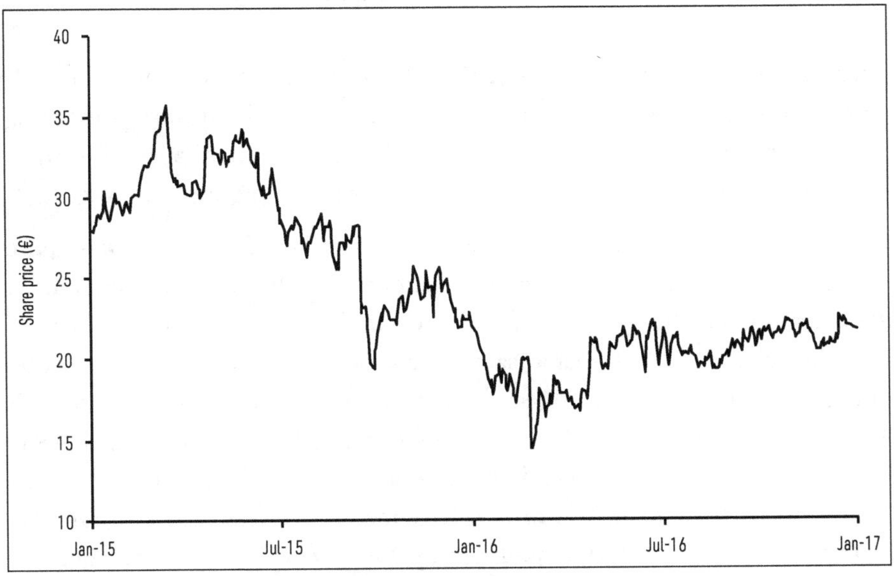

Source: Behind the Balance Sheet from Sentieo Data.

Similarly, single-year effects from an external event (such as a fire in a facility) sometimes create buying opportunities, as the share price falls in response to the short-term earnings setback, but the longer-term earnings potential of the company is unaffected.

Exchange rates are one of the biggest macro drivers of stock moves in international markets. Airbus is sensitive to the euro-dollar relationship as it builds largely in euros and sells in dollars, and its many customers in emerging markets were disadvantaged by depreciation of their home currencies against a strengthening dollar from 2015 to 2017.

Understanding what is happening is the first step. Determining the lateral, the best stock idea, is the real skill.

INSTANT IDEAS

Ideas usually take a lot of time and effort to develop, and even longer to verify, but occasionally they just pop out effortlessly. Somebody says something, you get an idea, and you *know* you are right. It has only happened to me a few times in my buy-side investing career, but it was highly satisfying.

One company was presenting at a big investor conference. It was quite a large company, presenting for the benefit of global investors outside of their region, but the meeting was not well attended. The company's head of investor relations stood up and said, "We have ample liquidity." Not a good thing to say in such a forum, as the market would then worry about their liquidity – especially as their argument (that they had sufficient) was pretty weak. A hedge fund manager I spoke to after the presentation told me he was short of this stock, and one of its competitors which was in an even worse situation, and I had enough for a priority text message to the boss.

Another occasion was somewhat ironic, in that the presenter this time was a fund manager at a group which was about to be floated. He tipped his company's stock at a brokers' ideas dinner; the fact that he saw the need to do this raised my suspicions, and his arguments in favour were so weak that I was convinced the stock was a short. I reported back and, although my colleagues were less convinced, the stock crashed within a year.

Long ideas especially are sometimes very simple and you can identify an undervalued asset situation very quickly. A couple of times this has happened to me when attending an investment conference. All you need to do is to listen!

A Middle Eastern company was presenting at an emerging market conference in a fancy hotel in Knightsbridge. The CFO stood up and explained that he thought the asset value was more than five times the current share price. A quick investigation back at the office suggested that there was external valuation support for a value three times the share price, and a lot more long term if the economic situation in the country panned out. We bought the stock and it doubled, then started to trade out, as the economic situation looked like it might become a concern.

More recently, the CFO of PPHE Hotel Group, a former client of Hardman & Co (where I have been a shareholder and occasional analyst), presented at one of our Investor Forum events for high-net-worth private investors. He explained the share price, the asset value and the programme – it was clear from the development programme that the property was going to be worth twice the share price. Irritatingly, our compliance rules prevented me from investing at the time, but many of our clients made great money. The stock has nearly quadrupled since.

Figure 2.4: PPHE Hotel Group share price

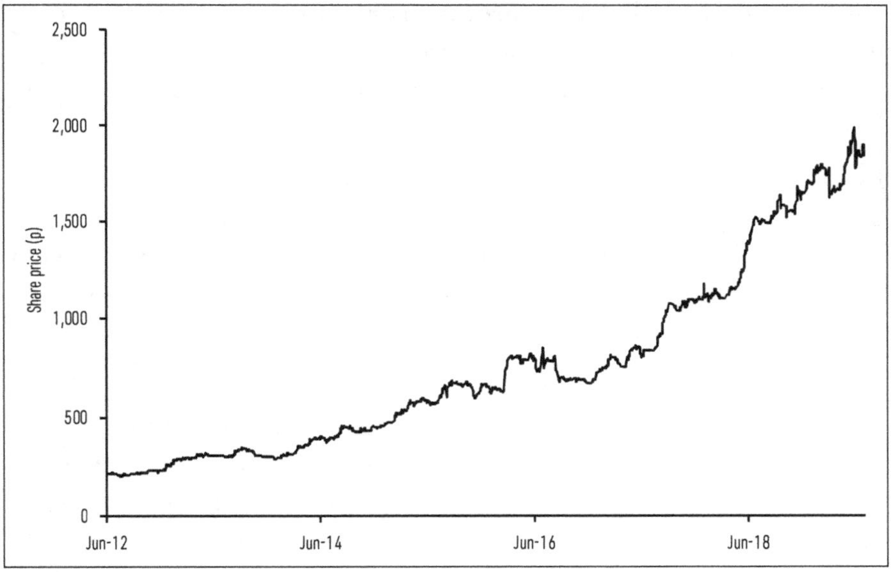

Source: Behind the Balance Sheet from Sentieo Data.

LIGHTBULB MOMENTS

Sometimes, an idea does not come instantaneously, but a germ is planted and there is later a "Eureka!" moment. In September 2016, I attended a series of lunches at a bulge-bracket firm. Their analysts each gave a teach-in on their sector. I was particularly interested in the European media sector, as I had owned WPP and Sky in the past.

The analyst gave an excellent walk through the various industries (and stocks) in his sector and I was intrigued by his explanation of the music-streaming business, which he reckoned would be a positive for Vivendi, the French mass-media conglomerate. Music-streaming apps, like Spotify, charge their customer $10 or £10 per month, of which they immediately pay 60% to the record company and a further 10% to the publisher. The remaining 30% is their gross margin, out of which they have to advertise, acquire customers and develop the service.

The analyst explained that music was $10bn in his sum-of-the-parts calculation for Vivendi, which made it quite cheap. Vivendi's subsidiary, Universal Music, had a global market share of over 30%. The attraction of music, in contrast to film, is that customers listen to it over and over again, and Spotify and its peers pay the record companies on the basis of total listening time.

I was mulling this over on the way back to the office. I knew a little about Spotify, having helped review a placing of stock by a wealth manager. When I sat down at my desk, the first thing I did was to look at Spotify's valuation, which had been $8.5bn in July 2015, at the time of the placing. But since then, the number of paying subscribers had increased dramatically, as shown in the chart below.

On the same basis, Spotify should have been worth well over $10bn, even allowing for a cooling off in unicorn (unquoted tech companies valued at more than $1bn) valuations generally and allowing for a bit of a raciness in the Spotify multiple. Of course, I didn't know then to what extent the valuation had been levered up by the use of fancy conditions; this has been an increasingly common practice in Silicon Valley and is used to protect the new investor in the event that an IPO is later conducted at a lower price. I suspected that may have been a factor in the Spotify valuation.

Albeit with those reservations, my rough valuation of Spotify was similar to the sell-side analysts' valuation of Vivendi's music business. Yet from streaming alone, Vivendi had 20% of Spotify's revenues (one-third of the 60% paid to the record companies) versus Spotify's 30% gross margin – and it had no incremental costs. Spotify was actually making a loss at the time, since its costs were over 30% of sales.

Vivendi would not only collect from Spotify, but also from Deezer, Apple Music, and all the other streaming services – some 400 in number. If the Spotify valuation, ascribed by hard-nosed and well-informed venture capitalists, was anything near accurate, then Vivendi's music division, which must be much more valuable than Spotify (which has to compete with Amazon, Apple and everyone else), must be worth much more than the analysts and the market had ascribed.

Figure 2.5: Spotify paid subscriptions

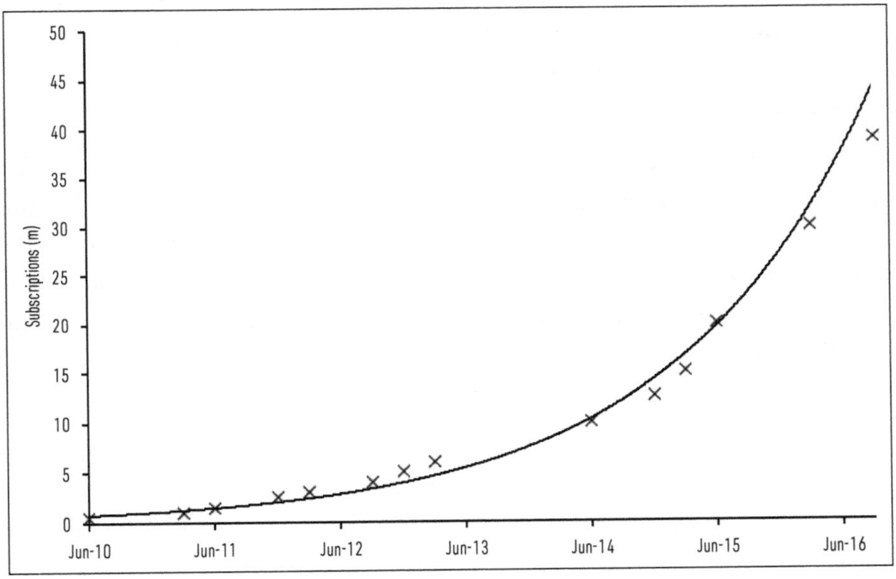

Source: Billboard.

A discounted cash-flow analysis using a figure of 500m users in 20 years' time, and for 25 years thereafter, confirmed that the value of that cash flow to Vivendi was some $20bn today, before paying the artist's share. That was twice the analyst's estimate. It transpired that Vivendi was an incredibly complex situation, and the stock market resisted the Universal Music valuation story, although a stake was eventually sold to Tencent. Spotify's market capitalisation peaked at over $35bn, but had fallen to $25bn by early 2020.

Such simple ideas are usually the best investments. The rationale is clear and the valuation premise simple. Clearly a lot can go wrong with any investment but, where the market has misunderstood the basis of pricing, you have the greatest upside and, hence, the best protection.

CONCLUSIONS

As a special situation investor, I am drawn to areas where there are unusual rewards. This usually involves a higher element of risk. The trick is to find companies which have asymmetric pay-offs. In these cases, there is an element of downside risk, but the upside is significantly higher and you have a good reason to believe in the positive pay-off, because of a change in a fundamental driver.

There are many routes to a successful equity idea. The best ideas are always the simplest and the quickest ones are usually the most profitable (although they still require due diligence). In my experience, a different view of the consensus profit outlook is almost always better than a valuation anomaly – stocks are usually dear or cheap for a reason. Once the idea has been identified, the next step is to test the hypothesis.

3

TESTING THE HYPOTHESIS

B Y FOLLOWING the approaches in the previous chapter, I figure out new investing ideas. The next step is to research these further. In this chapter, I talk through my process under the following headings:

- Prioritising ideas

- Initial checks – the first hour

- Putting the idea into context

- Tailoring the work to the opportunity

- Understanding the counterargument

- External confirmation

- Minding the gap

- Going forward – stick or twist?

A detailed review of a stock can take 100, or even several hundred, hours, so it's essential to invest the time looking at fruitful ideas. Therefore I put the idea into context, try to get some external confirmation that it's worthy of pursuit, and then plan the work (which depends on the nature of the idea). A key part of my process is to understand the alternative view.

Testing the hypothesis is an iterative process. I conduct the research in several waves, checking and re-checking, drilling down deeper and deeper, until the risks have been properly evaluated and I am satisfied that this is a sensible investment proposition.

I often initiate a position during this stage of research, adding to it as knowledge and comfort is increased, or exiting if I fail to convince myself of the merits of the opportunity.

PRIORITISING IDEAS

Prioritising ideas is the prelude to testing them. This is a very subjective process, where rules are hard to apply. Factors I consider are:

- Does the stock have a good fit in the portfolio? For example, if the portfolio is already short, or has a lower than index weighting in the US market, a US long is more likely to be attractive than a US short.

- Do I have a non-consensual view? Such ideas are more likely to be successful and, if so, generally more profitable.

- How much time is the analysis likely to take? This is a critical question, but one that is hard to estimate. It might be better to avoid really complex situations which are going to require extensive research in the middle of results season.

- What is the potential gain? Again, hard to predict, but I used to aim for big winners, so if something only looked 20–30% mispriced, I would not consider it a special situation opportunity.

Prioritising ideas is difficult as, at this stage, you don't have enough information to make the decision. This is why a one-hour quick review is so helpful, as it gives enough information to make an initial assessment of priorities. As a professional analyst, I would be constantly juggling a long watchlist of interesting stocks. Of course, the key factor in determining priorities was the share price action – stocks become more interesting longs as they fall.

INITIAL CHECKS – THE FIRST HOUR

Before I do any research, I check one critical factor: liquidity. I look at the stock's market capitalisation and the daily average volume traded. The best idea in the world is useless if the stock is too small or too illiquid.

Clearly this is a more significant issue for professional investors, as funds will have different thresholds for the size of company in which they can invest. But it's also a significant factor for the private investor. If you buy very illiquid small companies, you may find it difficult to exit if you discover that you have made a mistake. I am surprised by how many new investors fail to consider this factor.

When I started on the buy-side, I was warned not to make this mistake. I remember talking to one of the partners at Sir Chris Hohn's hedge fund, TCI, in 2010. He happened to be working on Sotheby's (which became my largest personal holding at one point – more on this stock later) and explained that Chris would not invest because it was too illiquid. Even the most successful firms make mistakes!

Having reassured myself on the liquidity front, I run through the following checklist:

- Share price chart – what has the stock done lately and over the longer term? Is this a fallen angel or a consistent performer – there is a message about the stock in the price trend, and it informs me about market sentiment towards the share, which is critical to understanding why it may be cheap.

- Valuation screen – what do the forward multiples look like? If the starting valuation is high, does this fall over time as profits increase? A stock which may not be cheap today can become cheap in two years' time if it's growing quickly enough or generating sufficient cash. This informs where I need to focus when I conduct the research.

- Earnings estimates – I like to look at the trends in profit forecasts to see if they are rising or falling. I like to buy stocks with rising estimates. If they are falling, I need to be comfortable that the trend is about to reverse (if I am thinking of a long position). Share prices tend to follow the estimate revisions, so if a share price has been rising and the estimates have been falling, that would be an unusual signal and worth an investigation.

- Historical valuation – I look to get a quick sense of where the stock has been rated in the past and where it is rated now. Am I paying a premium or discount to the stock's historical valuation? Sometimes a premium to past valuation is justified if the stock's prospects have improved. The historical context is a useful shortcut to understanding what has changed.

- I usually try to get a flavour of what type of company it is (e.g., high or low quality) by looking at returns on equity and returns on capital employed, checking if any of the divisions are loss-making, or at depressed or peak margins.

- I am trying to ascertain if this is a high quality business – I explore my criteria in chapter 5. If it is not high-quality, it's important to understand where we are in the cycle. I like to have a quick look at sales growth over a longer time period. Has the sales trend been volatile, as with most cyclical businesses, or has it been more consistent? Are sales growing fast?

- Holders – who owns the stock is often a critical component as to whether the idea is worth pursuing. Are the top holders *smart money* (sophisticated investors, often large hedge funds), and are they increasing or decreasing exposure? It's nice to be in good company, but if they have owned the stock for years and are now decreasing exposure, they know the stock better than you so perhaps it's better to pursue the next idea. The shareholder base is an underestimated factor, in my view.

- Analyst recommendations – are the analysts all bullish, or is there a mix of views about the business? If the analysts are all bullish but one, I would be interested in the outlier's rationale – why he is negative – and would focus on the short side.

- I then look at the broker research, printing off six to ten notes on the company. Ideally, I look to have at least one buy note, one sell, and one hold. I shall also look for a sector note, which places the company in context, and an in-depth note, preferably 40+ pages. If possible, I try to have a cross section of research from bulge-bracket banks, regional brokers, sector specialists and, if available, independent research. This is, of course, easier if you are at a large institution and have access to a wide range of research. Although this is harder to do for the private investor, there is a lot of research freely available on the internet and so I search for commentary – both bull and bear. Perhaps unsurprisingly, there is more bear commentary available freely on the internet than I ever saw in professional research from the big banks.

- I think it's vital to read at least one note which is taking a contrary view. This can be more difficult for a long, as sell notes are scarce. When I was a sell-side analyst, I always used to get much more interest in a sell idea. If I can't find any recent sell notes, I read even an 18-month-old report, just so that I understand the counterargument.

I read through this material to decide whether further work is warranted. I usually look at the company's website, its investor relations page, and recently I have started to check the Twitter feed, to see if there is any particular angle. I may print the accounts or the 10-K, or I may focus in on something of particular interest, depending on what has drawn me to the stock.

This process is clearly more difficult for a private investor without access to a Bloomberg screen or a similar system. It's still possible to look at the charts, to assess the valuation, to look at the historical sales and margin trends on any number of free internet sites, and to review positive and negative commentary on sites like Seeking Alpha. It may also be possible to dig up commentary from a fund manager's investor letter or blog, which can often be really helpful at this stage.

For US stocks, there are various sites which give information about shareholders (funds have to file holdings with the SEC) and the company's Twitter feed may occasionally give an insight. The company's investor relations site will often have a recent presentation which gives the investment case.

You do not have to, and should not, do a full, *drains-up* intensive research straight off when you get an idea. The research can be an iterative process, increasing the holding as knowledge and comfort is increased.

PUTTING THE IDEA INTO CONTEXT

Once an investment idea has passed my initial checks, I think through the upside/downside relationship and try to put the stock into some sort of context. To do so, I consider the following factors:

- macro environment
- market psychology
- micro environment
- right type of stock
- time horizon
- information edge

MACRO ENVIRONMENT

Does the stock have the correct economic characteristics and is this a defensive or a cyclical company? This is not to say that you cannot buy a cyclical company when we are at an advanced stage in the economic cycle, but the valuation has to be lower to compensate for the risk.

MARKET PSYCHOLOGY

Where are we in the cycle and does this stock fit with the current view of the world? This is not necessarily an economic perspective. For example, if this is an acquisitive company, and a similarly acquisitive company has just gone bust, it may be better to put the stock on the watchlist rather than spending time investigating it now.

Stock-market fashions, however spurious they may seem to the real world, can affect stock price performance for an extended period. Some may see this as short term, but the investor must be realistic – in public markets, you need to be aware of how the next potential buyer will view the situation. Of course, fundamentals will always eventually assert themselves, but there has to be a new buyer for a stock to go up, and it simply takes longer and is harder to make money if going against the trend.

MICRO ENVIRONMENT

Is the sector attractive currently and is it likely to remain so? Buying out-of-favour sectors can be a better strategy, as long as you have reason to assume that the sector will not remain out of favour indefinitely.

RIGHT TYPE OF STOCK

Is this a founder-led company, which is likely to be a more reliable long-term investment? Or is it a concept stock, which doesn't make a profit? Or is it an acquisitive platform/roll-up company?

Such stock characteristics may well dictate the time horizon and the extent of work required (a subject which I cover later).

TIME HORIZON

Is there a catalyst which dictates that research must be completed quickly, or a lot of interest which similarly increases pressure to complete the process fast? Perhaps you should take a small position initially, then top up as you do more work.

If this is a short idea, and a trade (a short-term investment), rather than a structural short (a short position used to exploit a long-term theme, which may be held for years rather than months), then it warrants less research time.

INFORMATION EDGE

This can come in various forms, although the best edge is from a detailed piece of analysis.

There are other ways to think about this, notably, how you would classify the idea. For example, independent research provider, Ahead of the Curve™, classifies its reports as falling into one of three scenarios:

1. Non-consensus idea – "Most investors think one way, but we think differently."

2. An investment controversy – "Investors are split on a controversial topic, there is no consensus and we wish to take a stand."

3. When there is a topic investors need to focus on in more depth, that they have not fully understood to date, that will be a key driver of the stocks in a particular sector.

Phil Huber, a well-known US wealth manager and blogger, believes that there are three edges in markets: informational, analytical, and time horizon. He suggests that the first two are near impossible for most investors and that private investors in particular should focus on the third. Professional investors tend to be short term in horizon, which gives the longer-term investor an advantage.

Sheelah Kolhatkar's book about SAC Capital describes three types of information edge, as defined by an SAC insider. White indicates legitimate expert insight, grey is where a company executive drops hints ahead of results and black is inside information. Internally, they apparently used a scale of 1–10 to define conviction level.

I think it's rare to have an information edge, as I will not trade in grey or black areas and, if I have a genuine information edge, I tend to act quickly and research later.

A good example of an information edge was the case of a mining company which floated on the London market. It owned a coal mine and a power generation business in Eastern Europe, making it a vertically integrated producer of ferrochrome, a product much in demand in China at the time of its float. Ferrochrome production is a highly energy-intensive process, with the majority of global production located in South Africa.

Eskom, the state-owned South African power utility, had arranged a call for its debt investors, on which the CFO revealed that to fund a major capital investment programme to expand capacity, the government had approved a 35% increase in the price of power. This translated into a significant increase in the cost of South African ferrochrome, and hence its market price, which would drive a more than doubling of the Eastern European miner's profitability.

Yet the miner's share price barely moved in the days following that call, indicating that there was a real information edge. Other investors had not picked up the now public information about the increased cost of ferrochrome production. Subsequently, it quadrupled from its flotation price before later collapsing.

If I don't know what my information edge is, I probably don't have one. I find it helpful to ask myself if I have a non-consensual view on some aspect of the business and its stock-market rating. Where am I thinking differently from the market? This can then form the focus of my research, as I don't need to spend as much time on issues which are accepted by the consensus.

TAILORING THE WORK TO THE OPPORTUNITY

The objective of this preparatory stage is to form an impression of whether the ducks are sufficiently aligned to make this a high-priority idea. Evaluation is not a one-size-fits-all process – work should be focused according to the type and size of investment, and also to the likely time horizon. It's no good doing a full, in-depth study or investigation of French stocks that will benefit from Macron's election, unless the work can be completed before he is elected.

If this is a long-term quality company which is likely to be a multi-year position, then I would do a lot more work on the business model, and the long-term outlook for sales and margins. If this is a distress situation, I would do a lot more work on the debt, its maturity and the value of the assets.

The nature of the investment dictates the focus of the research – you don't need to do everything in every case. There are, of course, a few things that you cannot omit, or do so at your peril, the cash-flow forecasts, for example.

UNDERSTANDING THE COUNTERARGUMENT

This is the stage at which it's really important to have a good understanding of the counterargument. If you are buying a stock, you almost need to understand the bear case better than the bull case.

I worked with one fund manager who had invited an analyst from Goldman Sachs to present the bull case on a stock we already owned. I didn't see the point in the meeting and proposed that we would be better off listening to one of the bears. The fund manager didn't get it, but it was perfectly obvious to me that you would learn much more from the bear than from the bull.

US hedge fund investor, David Einhorn, made a great comment on this subject: when you buy a new stock, you don't know who is on the other side of that trade. The probability is that it will be someone who is more familiar with the stock than you are (perhaps excess humility on Einhorn's part) and therefore you need to have an edge in the analysis. You may be buying the stock from an insider or someone who has owned it for years and knows it much better than you do. Hence, understanding the opposite argument is essential.

You can do this by discussing the idea with colleagues and fellow investors. This dialogue is beneficial as other investors may spot an omission from the thesis or have some peripheral knowledge which is helpful – they may have encountered the CEO or CFO in a different role and may have a positive or negative view which will reinforce or invalidate the idea.

Many private investors I know are involved with investment groups or clubs, where they share ideas and similarly debate the merits of a stock with their fellow investors. It's a great way of checking a thesis.

EXTERNAL CONFIRMATION

Testing the hypothesis also requires external confirmation. This will likely start at an early stage, but may continue through the research process, even after initiation of the position. I like to use several avenues of research:

- Competitors, especially unquoted companies

- Trade suppliers

- Customers

- Suppliers of capital equipment

- Landlords, especially airports and factory outlet malls for retailers

- Industry consultants and other experts, who can be sourced through expert networks like Gerson Lehrman and Coleman Research.

COMPETITORS

Competitors are an obvious source of information. Senior management of quoted companies tend to be quite circumspect in their comments on competitors, but those lower down the hierarchy are usually more open. One of the best sources is sales teams, as they have intimate knowledge of competitive products and customer attitudes. Another is the R&D facility, as they tend to have some ideas about the quality of competitors' technology. Best of all, I find, are private company competition; they have no axe to grind, and can give you an open and honest assessment of quoted competitors.

TRADE SUPPLIERS

Suppliers are another useful source – this can be a supplier of parts to a finished product or a supplier of services. They can give early warning of inventory problems, of fast- or slow-selling lines, and generally have a good understanding of their customers. Some companies are feared for the ferocity of their purchasing departments (UK supermarket Tesco in the old days), others for their technical excellence and rigorous standards (many of the oil companies), and the supplier can give you a good impression of the quality of management.

I learned of the importance of service suppliers in a Virgin Atlantic limo to the airport. The driver told me how he, and the company he worked for, were in difficulty because one of their principal customers, an airline, had delayed paying its bill. An airline which couldn't afford to pay the limo company was clearly in trouble and, indeed, the news became public a few weeks later. Fortunately, I was ahead of that event.

CUSTOMERS

Customers clearly have a very good understanding of the quality of products and their own price elasticity. Asking why they favour one company's products over another can be very illuminating. This is particularly helpful in the B2B environments where I have focused and where the product specifics may be beyond my technical competence.

SUPPLIERS OF CAPITAL EQUIPMENT

Suppliers of capital equipment can often offer a different insight into the target company. Good companies are rigorous about the control of capital spending and obsessive about returns; saving money on the capital cost is just as effective at improving returns as taking costs out of the production process or bill of material. Running a plant inefficiently, or failing to upgrade equipment, can be the sign of a company under pressure, or one which could see quick wins if there is a change of management.

I saw the reverse of this in August 2016 on a trip round the European capitals to visit transport companies. We were proudly shown the Aeroport de Paris (AdP) baggage system and, when I found out how much it cost, I nearly fell over – it had cost five times my estimate.

The manufacturer was Siemens but, when I got back to the office, it transpired that Siemens had sold the business – no opportunity for a short on the basis that guided vehicles and AI could be adapted instead of the fixed conveyors.

LANDLORDS

I have often found landlords to be a great source of gossip. A friend in the property business might mention a preference for Whitbread's Premier Inn over Travelodge as a lessee, as they have a stronger balance sheet. Landlords of airport retailers and factory outlet malls have an especially useful insight, as they see their tenants' revenue figures, and have a very good idea who is running an effective operation. This can give a helpful perspective. Luckily, I have friends and contacts at both. At that same Paris visit, the AdP retail staff (inadvertently) gave me some interesting perspectives on Hugo Boss, a stock we were then investigating as a potential long – this helped us decide against it.

EXPERT NETWORKS

A number of funds use expert networks, like Gerson Lehrman, to source gossip from former employees and industry consultants. This can be a great source of information for an activist investor. Rishi Sunak – now UK chancellor of the exchequer, then a member of Sir Chris Hohn's team – told me that they discovered from such a source that US rail operator CSX owned a country club. This was the sort of embarrassing titbit that could be used as leverage to force management into action.

In Philip Fisher's book, *Common Stocks and Uncommon Profits*, he reveals that he used this type of research extensively in finding quality growth companies – he described it as "scuttlebutt". I thought I had been quite smart in thinking this way, but he published the book in 1958, before I was born. It's probably less effective now, too, as it has become established practice.

MINDING THE GAP

At this stage, before moving forward to do further work, and perhaps taking an initial stake, I like to double-check that:

- there is a gap between the share price and my initial impression of intrinsic value

- I understand the reason for the gap.

For example, I was reviewing Bolloré, a French holding company which was trading at, roughly, a 50% discount to its real value. If I did not know why the gap existed, I would be reluctant to pursue it further. However, I knew the following:

1. The apparent discount is much smaller, equivalent to a normal holding company discount to a sum-of-the-parts valuation. But in Bolloré's case, the holding company has subsidiaries which, in turn, have stakes in the holding company; therefore, the economic value of one share is much higher, as the real number of shares in issue is much lower than the headline, and hence the discount is understated unless one adjusts for the cross-holdings.

2. The business gives very poor disclosure, which looks suspicious and makes it harder to ascribe valuation.

3. The group owns ports and logistics businesses in Africa – good businesses as they are essential infrastructure – but the market generally has a limited understanding of the economies there, and consequently applies a discount.

4. The shares are quite illiquid because of the concentrated ownership.

5. The business was indebted.

6. Mr Bolloré, the billionaire founder, has been undertaking a number of long-term transactions which look odd – his strategy is unclear to the market – although he does have an excellent record of creating value.

In addition, because of the Florange law, a French rule which gives long-term holders double voting rights, I expect some of the cross-holding structures to be eliminated and value to be realised for shareholders. Bolloré can achieve control with a lower direct shareholding, as he retains a voting majority.

Bolloré is a complex situation. I decided that there was an opportunity for a long-term investment, but the research required was extensive, and the visibility of return was quite low. It might be cheap but it could also stay cheap for a long time. I did not pursue it although it would have been a decent investment, as can be seen from the chart.

Figure 3.1: Bolloré share price

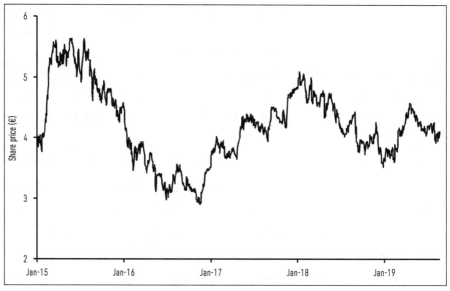

Source: Behind the Balance Sheet from Sentieo Data.

Investing is often about exploiting a gap between perception and reality. My process involves understanding the stock-market perception first, before checking the reality, which is a longer and more involved process. To do this more effectively, I have developed checklists that facilitate the process, which I cover in the following chapters.

GOING FORWARD
– STICK OR TWIST?

At this point, an idea is often rejected, not because it's a bad idea necessarily, but because of wrong timing, or because it's not a positive and diversifying addition to the portfolio, or the idea is simply not strong enough and not worth the additional work. But if it passes this first hurdle, there is a lot more work to do.

I might take an initial, say, 1% position – possibly after further due diligence on management and their reward structure, business quality or valuation – and then plan to do more detailed work, with a view to taking the position to 2% or 5%, depending on my conviction level.

This means a comprehensive research process, conducted using a checklist which I explain in the following chapters. It's important to recognise that, at any point, the research process may be abandoned for any of the following reasons:

- The share price moves significantly, diminishing the potential opportunity.

- Something happens which changes the fundamentals significantly, reducing or improving the company's earnings power.

- A competitor to a potential short is bid for, indicating interest in the industry.

- The research process uncovers something fundamentally unattractive, which prevents the inclusion of a long in the portfolio.

- Changes to the portfolio mean this stock's inclusion would cause a concentration issue.

The ability to abandon work and write off hours of effort is an important discipline. It often happens to me when I feel that the subject is just too difficult, or that the prediction of an outcome is too imprecise. It is difficult, emotionally, to write off the time invested. It may be easier for the professional or institutional investor, for whom it is part of the job. Private investors need to be careful not to justify the energy and time expended by seeking evidence that a bad idea is instead a good idea (confirmation bias). The time spent on an idea is sunk cost and irrecoverable; you'll only make things worse by investing in a dud stock.

In one case, I spent weeks researching a stock, including a visit to one of its facilities, but received an initial rejection from my boss on the grounds of insufficient knowledge. I then went on a one-week international trip to visit a competitor's facilities and meet management, returned and re-presented the idea, and still failed to persuade him of the stock's merits. You just have to accept this, or understand that perhaps you have not done a good enough job in presenting the investment idea (I show you how to do a good job in chapter 9).

In this particular case, the stock doubled in the next 18 months and continued to outperform hugely, before finally being bid for by a Chinese competitor at a multiple of my original recommendation price. That was a bad miss, but part of the job. Best to buy the stock for your personal account and smile at each set of results.

PLANNING

Before I started in the City, I used to be a management consultant. With a huge array of tasks requiring completion each week, I spent one day per week planning. This is quite normal in that role but, in stockbroking and fund management, it seems to be quite normal to spend no time at all planning; perhaps this is a function of the unpredictability of markets. You are certainly a more effective analyst if you plan your time.

Of course, you don't know how long it will take to complete the research, but having a plan tells you when you are spending too long on an idea.

I believe there is too little emphasis on effective use of time by analysts, because the job is hard to define and it's done differently by each person. I liked this Twitter poll on 16 August 2017 by *FT* journalist Katie Martin (@ katiemartin_fx), where 283 people voted on what has been the single biggest waste of time in the last two years:

- 28% Fed watching

- 9% OPEC watching

- 32% reading Zerohedge

- 31% arguing about Brexit

In fund management, too much time is wasted on events which don't affect the portfolio or whose impact is hard to assess. Macro-economics is a common time trap.

I determine my priorities on the basis of return on time invested. It's not a popular concept, but it's an effective one. By now, you have an idea of the potential return stock, as well as an estimate of how long it will take to evaluate a position based on your experience in the sector, the geography, the complexity of the situation, etc.

Although it can sometimes be highly profitable to spend several weeks investigating a really complex position, it can end up being totally wasted time. Unless you think there is something major the market has missed, it can be better to go for smaller wins.

CIRCLE OF COMPETENCE

It's important in investment to stick to what you know. I had colleagues who were former prop traders who believed that you had to learn each stock, understand what makes the price move, and how market participants and the stock react to news flow.

I will not, therefore, research or invest in pharmaceutical stocks – I don't understand the business. I generally avoid banks for the same reason, albeit I have occasionally used a bank as a proxy for an emerging market economy. This might have been where I wanted to get exposure to, say, India, and the simplest and most direct route of doing so was through a bank. It's complicated for the private investor to buy individual stocks in India, so one option would be an exchange-traded fund (ETF), while another is ICICI Bank, which can be accessed via an American Depositary Receipt (ADR) in the US.

I tend to avoid retail longs, as the fickleness of the consumer is something I find hard to gauge. Although I have on occasion done shorts or pair trades.

I tend not to invest in Australia, as the local pensions have an undue weighting in the market, and prices are usually stretched. For the same reason, I tend not to short there; the other problem being that there are a lot of smart locals in front of me in the queue. A disproportionate number of billionaires seem to have emerged in Australia, often using the stock market. The Packers and Murdochs are well known, but the Loewe and Holmes à Court families are also very talented investors. Having said that, I have in recent years looked at opportunities in Treasury Wines on the long side and Wesfarmers on the short side.

I tend to be less comfortable in Korea, China and Japan, where local customs and language barriers sometimes obscure accounting, and heavy involvement by private clients (notably in China) make the art of fundamental analysis much trickier. I have a higher return requirement threshold when looking at these sorts of markets.

As Ha-Joon Chang explains very effectively in his book, *23 Things They Don't Tell You About Capitalism*, "The free market doesn't exist. Every market has some rules and boundaries that restrict freedom of choice." Hence, investing in markets where there are cultural and language barriers is inherently much more difficult.

Another good example is Russia, where I believe you not only have to have a bargain valuation (even a bargain by Russian standards), but you also need a local and native language speaker onside in order to navigate the political landscape. It's not good to find, one morning, that your favoured stock has just been nationalised, or a law has just been passed which makes its activities much less profitable. These things can come without any warning, which makes investment in such areas inherently riskier.

Dealing with Russian oligarchs can be another headache – one such individual was selling some of his own stock as the company raised money in a rights issue. My Russian colleague asked him why he needed the money, and he explained that he wanted to build a new stadium for his local football team. My colleague joked, "What, like Chelsea, you mean?" The oligarch jumped out of his seat and started shouting, upset at being compared with Abramovich, much to my consternation and to my colleague's amusement.

My professional focus has tended to be industrials – stocks offering a B2B (business to business) service. Although many investors prefer to focus on tech and consumer staple names, I have found industrials to offer significant mispricing opportunities.

CONCLUSIONS

Not all investment ideas turn out to be good ones. As in-depth research of an idea will likely take at least a week, potentially even longer, it is essential that you first perform a series of initial checks to test your hypothesis. One of the most important aspects of this initial research is to understand the counterargument to your thesis. No matter how long you spend on this research, if you can't make a convincing case for the investment, you should abandon the idea.

Once an investment idea has passed your test, you are ready to perform in-depth research on the company. This requires planning.

In chapters 4 to 8, I describe this research process in detail, providing checklists to help you in the task.

4

UNDERSTANDING THE INDUSTRY

WHEN I begin researching a new investment target, I prefer to start with an understanding of its industry – competitors, customers, suppliers, and trends in supply and demand. A comprehensive understanding of the industry is the first step in properly evaluating the investment opportunity.

In this short chapter, I outline a few checklist questions which help in gaining this understanding. I first discuss why checklists are important.

HISTORY OF CHECKLISTS

In the airline industry, mistakes cost lives. Consequently, the industry uses checklists extensively, notably at the start of a flight. Their introduction is an interesting story dating back to 1935.

The US army was in the latter stages of an aircraft evaluation to assess the relative merits of three bombers: Martin Model 146; the Douglas DB-1; and Boeing's Model 299, which was in the lead. Major Ployer P. Hill (his first time flying the aircraft) was captain of the Model 299 that day, while Lieutenant Donald Putt (the primary army pilot for the previous evaluation flights) was the co-pilot. With them was Leslie Tower, Boeing's chief test pilot, with many hours at the helm of the 299.

The aircraft is reported to have made a normal taxi and take-off, and begun a smooth climb, before suddenly stalling and crashing. Hill and Tower died in the accident. The investigation found 'pilot error' to be the cause. Hill, unfamiliar with the aircraft, had forgotten to release the elevator lock (a mechanism that locks control surfaces while the aircraft is parked on the ground and non-operational) prior to take off. Once airborne, Tower would have tried to reach the lock handle, but it was probably too late.

Although the Model 299 programme could have collapsed, Boeing was given a chance to continue with the project and 12 aircraft were delivered to the 2nd Bombardment Group at Langley Field, Virginia, for further testing. The pilots there realised that for this new and much more complex aircraft, they needed a method to ensure that all steps were carried out and that nothing was overlooked. What resulted was a pilot's checklist. Four checklists were actually developed – take-off, flight, before landing and after landing.

With the checklists and rigorous training, those 12 aircraft flew 1.8m miles without a serious accident. The US army accepted the Model 299, and eventually ordered 12,731 of what became the B-17 Flying Fortress. The pilot's checklist has been a standard feature in the industry ever since.

Some years later, this experience was repeated in the medical field. Peter Pronovost is an intensive care physician and professor at the Johns Hopkins School of Medicine, but is best known for his investigation into central venous catheters (inserted into a vein to administer drugs and take blood samples). Related infections cause 31,000 deaths in the US each year.[1] Pronovost's simple five-point checklist is estimated to have saved 1,500 lives. In an 18-month trial in Michigan from 2003, checklists reduced the incidence of catheter-related infections from 0.27% per 1,000 days to zero.[2]

And the real reason why bands like the Rolling Stones demanded that there be a bowl of M&Ms with all the brown (or yellow) ones removed in dressing rooms backstage? It's not that the artists hated brown (or yellow) M&Ms,

---

[1] 'An Intervention to Decrease Catheter-Related Bloodstream Infections in the ICU', *New England Journal of Medicine* (December 2006).
[2] L. Landro, 'The Secret to Fighting Infections', *The Wall Street Journal* (28 March 2011).

or were demonstrating their credentials as first-class prima donnas, but to ensure that the show organisers had read all the safety requirements in the contract.

Checklists should be an essential part of the investment process, ensuring that no stone is left unturned in the pursuit of effective analysis. It puzzles me that relatively few professionals use them.

AN INDUSTRY CHECKLIST

There are a few reasons why I start with the industry:

- One of the main influences on a stock's performance is the performance of its sector – understanding what drives market sentiment towards the sector is therefore critical.

- Pricing is a key driver of revenue, particularly profit margin. This is often a factor driven at a sector level and so sector history is significant.

- The supply-demand balance is critical to pricing and this is a sectoral factor.

- It's critical to understand the *competitive dynamics* of the industry from the outset. Sometimes a large part of the industry is quoted and that facilitates comparisons. Conversely, shareholders in the UK food retail sector were surprised by the emergence of new low-cost German private competition, because their focus was on the quoted retailers.

Some investors focus extensively on competition and see this as a neglected area of research. For example, Phoenix Asset Management in the UK had holdings in easyJet. Every six months they reviewed 2,500 city pairs serviced by the airline and checked the competitive landscape – a good example of the level of detailed understanding that is possible if the data is available. It is impractical for the private investor to do this, it's unusual even for professionals to undertake this depth of analysis, but it's illustrative of a trend in research.

Understanding the competition helps with an understanding of the industry, which is the first step towards understanding the company and investment.

Listed below are a series of questions which form a framework for approaching a new, or indeed an existing, investment. My process begins with understanding the industry context and then looks at the company's position in the industry – only after that would I examine its financials in detail.

It is worth emphasising that some aspects are more appropriate than others, depending on circumstances. If you are buying a stock at a really depressed valuation, it's highly unlikely to be a quality investment, while buying at a discount to book, for example, requires an emphasis on risk and survival. I would spend a lot of time on the downside case and expend relatively little effort worrying about the business model or moat. This would include a focus on the valuation of the company's debt, as the debt markets are more attuned than equity markets to survival risks.

A stock trading at a high valuation, in contrast, implies a greater requirement to understand the business model and the sustainability of returns. The nature of the work is thus dependent on the type of investment. I therefore think of the questions and factors below as a menu.

- How does the industry work; who are the main players, the customers, and the suppliers? The fragmentation of each group usually gives an initial indication of where the balance of power lies. Often, my initial examination of the industry has led me to discard the original stock and pursue the opportunity by an investment in a customer or supplier, as I have learned that this is where the highest upside lies.

- What has been the growth in the market over the last several years, and what growth is projected? An industry may have grown steadily for several years and its growth is often simply extrapolated. It's particularly helpful in such cases to go back further in time to check how consistent growth has been over an extended time frame and to understand why.

- What are the demand drivers? Are they strengthening or deteriorating? This is often a complex question to answer, but a clear understanding is essential. The status must be closely monitored if and when the position is established.

- What are the competitive dynamics of the industry? How is the industry structured and what is the level of consolidation? Does the sector have any pricing power and who controls industry pricing? Looking at the stability of the market share of the major operators over time is generally a good indicator of the real barriers to entry in the business.

- Is capacity entering or leaving the industry? This is actually one of the most important questions to ascertain, because if capacity is entering the industry, you need to be absolutely sure that demand growth will be ahead of supply. If demand growth is lower than the growth in supply, this is a *red flag*. Conversely, any sign of capacity leaving the industry is likely to be highly positive for future returns. It is interesting that this element attracts much less commentary than the demand side of the equation, but it's often a simpler and more reliable route to success. It is one of the main differentiators of UK fund management firms Marathon Asset Management and Hosking & Co.

- If the industry is global, where are the main players based and what features or what historical events caused them to be the winners? Often the largest firms are based in the US and are the most highly valued; a European alternative may appear more attractive, but it's important to understand the reasons for the past relative success – the US firm may be the main player in the larger US domestic market, for example.

- What are the key success factors to superior performance in this industry? How (and by how much) can a good company differentiate itself from a bad one? Thinking through why companies have been successful in this industry is really helpful.

- To what extent is the industry regulated and who are the regulators? A change in regulation can affect a company's share price instantly. When a company is regulated, it's essential to understand the motives and attitudes of the regulatory body.

- Does the industry rely on any government subsidies? Note that it need not be the company which is the potential target investment receiving the subsidy; if a competitor is receiving subsidies, that can be a threat or an opportunity as the subsidies can be increased or decreased without warning. Subsidies may also affect the supply chain, both suppliers and customers, which can have a knock-on impact for the business.

- A good illustration is Spain after the Global Financial Crisis (GFC). For 19 years, Spain was the largest buyer and installer of solar panels. After the crisis, the Spanish government reversed the policy and retroactively changed their legislation. The solar panel manufacturers, as well as the owners of the Spanish assets, were wiped out.

- What technical aspects of the industry distinguish it, and do you understand them in outline? This is actually a good question to address early on. At one fund, I was looking at semiconductors. I was confident that this would be a lucrative opportunity, but I found the technology difficult to understand. To get a position in the fund, I would have had to explain the rationale to my colleagues. I decided, instead, to focus my energies elsewhere.

- What are the barriers to entry in this industry? If barriers to entry are weak, or are reducing, then it's more important to understand the nature of competition. Is there a history of firms co-existing peacefully with each other, making the industry profitable as a whole, for example, where there is an oligopoly? If not, then it's important to assess operational efficiency and management quality in greater depth, and to assume that margins may not remain at current levels for an extended period.

- Finally, I ask myself if this is a good business, and do I understand it? If the answer to either of these two questions is no, then perhaps you should move on.

One of the most important industry factors to assess is *quality*. Many investors are obsessive about it, notably, Warren Buffett and Charlie Munger of Berkshire Hathaway. I have therefore devoted the next chapter to it.

CONCLUSIONS

Understanding the characteristics of an industry is the first step towards building a view of a company. The competitive framework in which the business operates is a critical input to its future revenue growth and margin trends. This initial research is an essential foundation for the analysis of an individual company.

In this short chapter, I have outlined some of the key issues relating to industry context that investors should address when approaching an investment for the first time. Expending time at this stage can result in a potential investment being discarded or substituted for another company in the same sector. More often, my initial examination of the industry has led me to discard the stock and pursue the opportunity through an investment in a customer or supplier. In the next chapter, I drill down into greater detail on quality.

5
QUALITY

E VALUATING A company and its industry helps me to understand the quality of the business; to evaluate what Warren Buffett described as the "moat", a measure of how enduring above-average returns are likely to prove.

In this chapter, I set out some of the criteria I use in assessing quality and I discuss different aspects of moats. This is a subject that has been covered exhaustively by many commentators, but which is an essential element of the analytical process – particularly for the private investor.

I focus here on the qualitative aspects. There are two quantitative elements to bear in mind: the critical parameter to evaluate is the level and volatility of returns on capital, while the other is financial leverage. Quality stocks tend to have low, if any, debt leverage. I have also omitted here quality of accounting, which I cover when discussing the accounts.

SEARCHING FOR QUALITY

As a sell-side analyst, I never worried much about quality. It was perfectly obvious to me that my sector – transport – could be divided into high-quality companies, low-quality companies, and those in-between:

- **High quality:** AB Ports and BAA were examples of high-quality businesses. They had asset backing, effective local monopolies, little chance of sales or profits falling, and intermittently decent management (their management was generally quite weak, but they were such strong businesses that they only needed competent people to run them).

- **In-between:** bus companies which had fairly consistent revenue streams, limited competition and were sometimes indebted. They had management of variable quality and their rail subsidiaries were franchises with limited lives.

- **Low quality:** airlines like British Airways, which had little control over its revenue, low margins, and highly volatile profit streams. Trucking companies were similarly low quality.

It was clear to me, then, that a fund manager should hold quality companies in size for the long term, perhaps occasionally trimming holdings when ratings got too high or they did a stupid deal. You could then juice your returns, partly by buying the middle-quality companies when they looked cheap, but especially by adding the likes of British Airways when it was strongly out of favour.

When I moved to the buy-side, as a special situations investor, I tended to look for stocks with good potential for extremely high returns. When I started to advise a UK wealth manager investing for private individuals, whose tolerance for loss is much lower than professional investors – quality became a much more significant factor. Quality, in this context, means companies which are much less likely to experience a significant downturn in performance or share price.

For the wealth manager, we developed a screening system to pick reliable high-quality stocks. I was actually amazed at the results. Not only did the high-quality stocks outperform in year one, year two, and year three, but their outperformance continued. Eventually, we optimised the holding period at seven years. As part of our back-testing – over 70 annual observations – the selected group only underperformed three times, and then only by under 2%. I consider this an astonishing result.

The question, then, is how to identify high-quality companies. The current vogue is to use return on invested capital (RoIC). Companies with consistently high RoIC should outperform in the long term. Many investors are happy to own high RoIC stocks, almost irrespective of valuation. Some professionals I respect, notably John Hempton of Bronte Capital and Terry Smith of Fundsmith, believe that valuation is virtually irrelevant. They focus on holding quality companies for long periods, so are much more concerned with the quality of the business.

Figure 5.1: Coca-Cola performance relative to S&P 500

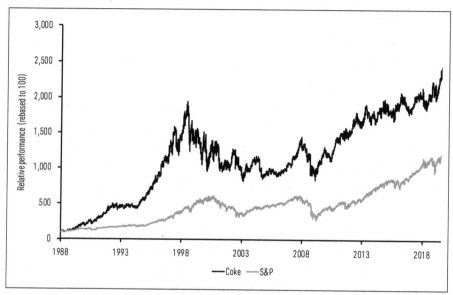

Source: Behind the Balance Sheet. Data from various sources, including Macrotrends and Sentieo.

Smith cites Buffett's acquisition of Coca-Cola, which was done at a very opportune time, as an example of investing in quality. But with the power of its compounding returns – the true engine of portfolio growth – he could have paid twice the price and still beaten the market.

This is fine with hindsight. But how many of us, like Buffett, can predict the value of these compounders in 20 years' time? And Coca-Cola in that period proved a truly exceptional business. You could also argue that this would be much more difficult today:

- The internet has accelerated the pace of change and led to much more disintermediation, making it much harder to predict the long-term quality of particular business models.

- The power of compounding returns is much better understood, and RoIC is much more closely scrutinised, hence less likely to be undervalued by the stock market.

- Similarly, long-term secular trends of population growth, increasing GDP in emerging markets, and the development of wealthier middle classes, are all well understood and priced into stocks. Of course, these too are subject to the vagaries of currency, local competition and many other factors.

A factor often overlooked when considering high RoIC stock is *reinvestment rate* (how much the company can reinvest in its business to grow). This can be done by looking at past investment, although, as ever, the past may not be indicative of the future. A company which makes a high RoIC, but has limited reinvestment opportunity is likely less valuable than one that can reinvest surplus cash at similar rates of return. The former is forced to find something else to do with the money or return it to shareholders. This is why many investors pay such close attention to management's capital-allocation skills. Hopefully, if they cannot reinvest wisely, they will return the cash to shareholders.

Imagine two companies. One can reinvest all of its surplus cash at its present group RoIC of 10% – this should compound at 10%. The second, in the same industry, can reinvest half its cash flow at 20% and return the other 50% to shareholders. The latter should be a better investment.

Quality is clearly one route to outperformance, but it's not straightforward. The calculations of future returns are fraught with uncertainty, a factor which many people overlook in their zeal for academic answers. Certainly, a focus on value can lead you to underestimate the contribution that quality can make. For most private client portfolios, a quality base is essential. But I recall one outstanding fund manager who had on a sign on his desk: 'Never be afraid to sell quality.'

ECONOMIC MOATS

Another way of thinking about quality is to look at it, not in quantitative terms as with RoIC, but in qualitative terms. Warren Buffett coined the term "economic moats", a concept which is clearly fundamental to his investment process. An economic moat is a structural impediment which obstructs competitors from entering a company's markets and reducing its returns on capital; the effect is a sustainable, high RoIC.

True economic moats are hard to duplicate and, therefore, longer lasting.

Technology (perhaps with a few outstanding exceptions such as some of the FAANG stocks) has not generally been a source of an enduring moat, because it can usually be duplicated and is often short-lived. A tech advantage or innovation may not last longer than a catchy advertising campaign or a hot fashion trend. Like a strong management team, technology can produce advantages in the short and medium term, but in the long term, it tends to be copied (or in the case of management, poached) by competitors.

A sustainable economic moat is, in my opinion, something more structural. One example, cited in the US, is Southwest Airlines in the 1990s. The culture was deeply ingrained in every employee and other airlines could not copy it. Although it was clear what Southwest was doing, competitors faced hostile labour forces and found it impossible to replicate.

Moats can be created by any of the following advantages.

MOAT ADVANTAGES

ECONOMIES OF SCALE

These generally have to be substantial, at least relative to competitors. Walmart is an example of this, as is Cintas in the uniform rental business, or Amazon. It can be derived from a process, such as the direct-to-consumer offer pioneered by Dell Computers, or from size. For example, Ryanair had a much lower cost base than even its low-cost rivals for many years, partly because it was larger.

Coke has had economies of scale because its brand was built on TV advertising. As it was much larger than all but one competitor, it could afford to outspend its rivals, creating a virtuous circle. That relative advantage is now diminishing, as the internet and social media allow new entrants to reach consumers in different ways. Economies of scale are relative, not absolute.

NETWORK EFFECTS

Networks benefit from having more participants, so the moat strengthens with size – the network's value lies in its coverage or participation. Represented by companies like eBay, the credit card businesses (Mastercard, Visa and American Express), and Western Union. The latter, however, is a good illustration of the subjectivity of a moat, because mobile payment technology is effectively leapfrogging its business in many developing countries – an example of how technology can be disruptive to moats, without creating a real moat itself. Another example of a network with weaknesses is Uber – it is effectively a series of local networks. Although it is often the largest player in a city, by grading drivers it has lowered barriers to entry for potential competitors.

INTELLECTUAL PROPERTY RIGHTS

These are generally thought of as patents, trademarks, or regulatory approvals, but they can also apply to brands where customer loyalty is high. Drug companies are good examples. For a company like Qualcomm, whose chips power mobile phones, its principal value lies in its intellectual property.

CUSTOMER LOYALTY

Disney is a good example, although customer loyalty is a more transitory moat as it requires companies to maintain the quality and essence of their products. Brands can reduce customer time, as in the case of buying Tide detergent consistently; they can create a positive halo, for example Rolex; or they can confer legitimacy, for example Moody's, the credit rating agency.

CUSTOMER CAPTIVITY

Habits are the investor's friend, and they create captive customers in consumer products like cigarettes, cola and toothpaste. If you smoke Marlboro Lights, you will stop smoking that brand when you stop smoking, or when financial circumstances dictate a cheaper brand. There is enormous inertia in these products. Contrast this with beer: you might drink Budweiser at home, but when you go for a Mexican meal, you might drink Corona or, for a Thai meal, a Singha. People usually do not switch cola brands, however.

HIGH CUSTOMER-SWITCHING COSTS (ALSO SEARCH COSTS OR RISK OF DISAPPOINTMENT)

Microsoft is a good example of a company which benefits from high customer-switching costs, owing to the learning process required to adopt a different platform. In other industries – like banking and mobile phone manufacturers – this may come in the form of customer inertia, where the process of switching is considered too onerous. Businesses may enjoy *some* benefit from this inertia, but it's not, on its own, sufficient to afford them a high return on capital (notably the banks!), which is the key distinction of a moat.

Search costs are another version of switching costs – it may be hard to define, or find, a reliable alternative, and there is a high risk of disappointment, for example in professional services.

COMPANIES WITH A PURPOSE

Researching impact investing – investments made with the intention of generating a beneficial social or environmental impact alongside a financial return – led me to believe that sustainability is an essential part of a quality investment and of a moat. Companies which do not factor in sustainability will be at a disadvantage. This goes beyond a simple ESG score; it is part of the culture and business model for a great company, and must be factored into the research process.

DIGITAL MOATS

Technological developments have fundamentally altered the characteristics of moats. Many tech markets are characterised by a winner-takes-all structure, and some of these have moats which would not exist, or be very unusual, in the physical world. Some are obvious, such as Google's dominant share of search or Facebook's ubiquity as a social network, making it obligatory for many. The following two, less obvious, factors are critical to digital success.

TALENT ATTRACTION

In IP businesses, talent is absolutely mission-critical and therefore the ability to attract talent is a key differentiator. Tech giants have massive brand equity, which not only attracts potential customers, but also prospective employees. In industries where the quality of ideas often dictates success, this ability to attract talent should not be underestimated as a moat factor. This also creates a hurdle for conventional companies seeking to develop their digital capabilities – the CEO of Electrolux complained to me that they were finding it incredibly difficult to attract software engineers, an increasingly vital part of their product development.

R&D SCALE

Tech giants have an ability to invest in R&D at far greater scale than most conventional businesses. In 2018, they were among the largest R&D spenders in the S&P 500. I suspect that this spend is actually overstated, that the companies involved are being overly generous in their allocation of overhead to R&D.

Nevertheless, the amounts involved are breathtaking. In automated vehicles (AV), the original equipment manufacturers (OEMs) spend more on R&D overall, but few older industries can compare. This is significant as R&D can be a key driver of future margin – Lawrence Cunningham's book, *Quality Investing*, and the team at AKO Capital cite dominance in R&D spending as a key factor in maintaining outsize returns.

Figure 5.2: R&D spend by tech stocks in automated vehicles versus top 25 quoted auto OEMs

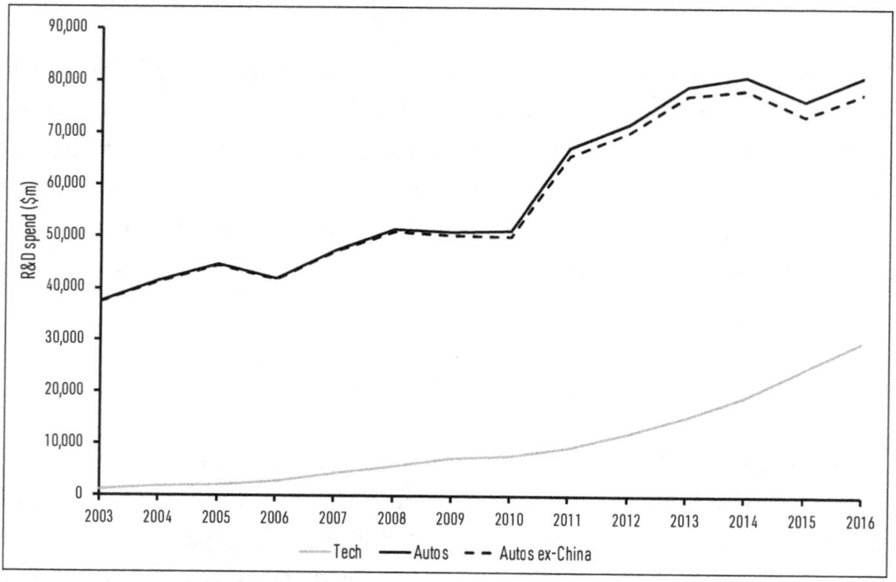

Source: Behind the Balance Sheet. The tech stocks included are those involved in AV development in 2017.

Both these factors, investment in people and R&D, are likely to increase in significance as sources of moat as the share of the knowledge economy increases.

PRICING POWER

This is a feature of quality businesses that enjoy moats. Apple has pricing power and, until 2018, appeared never to discount its products – only when new versions of the iPhone or iPad were released would the old model be discounted. This practice has receded recently, as the brand has pushed up the price of new phones.

At the bottom end, discounters like Aldi have an enduring cost advantage which they invest in continuous low prices; at the other extreme, Ferrari constrains its output in order to maintain a waiting list, which underpins the residual price. Indeed, one friend of mine enjoyed several brand-new Ferraris at almost no cost. Once his brand-new model was ready, he would sell his one-year-old car to the dealer at the price he paid for it. The dealer could sell the used car at a premium to the price of a new car – to customers unwilling to wait.

Monitoring the pricing activity of brands is a helpful part of the analysis, for example retailers without overdue emphasis on repeated promotional sales are likely to be more consistent performers. Brands which rely on repeated heavy price promotion are conditioning their customers to wait for the next discount. Hence the biggest-ever sale has to be followed by another biggest-ever sale, each time reducing customer trust in the brand.

It can, however, be difficult to ascertain the underlying like-for-like price trend over a long period. You can however monitor the number and duration of cut-price sales for retailing stocks; an increase in the number of sales, or days of sales, is usually an important warning signal.

MOAT LONGEVITY

The internet is reducing the strength of some moats. For example, in consumer-packaged goods, the fragmentation of media has reduced the cost of reaching the mass market, as has the use of social media – I shall try that new craft beer because of its popularity with my peers. The best example is Dollar Shave Club and its impact on Gillette.

Network effects tend to be more prevalent in internet businesses. Think Auto Trader in the UK, which is the dominant portal for advertising used cars; similarly, Rightmove in the case of homes. Network effects can be enhanced by subsidy (e.g., Uber, which uses price to stimulate demand, especially in a new market) and by engagement (e.g., Facebook). Note that moats do not arise because you have a high market share, a technological advantage, or a great new product – all of these advantages tend to fade over time.

A simple way of calculating the likely strength of a company's economic moat is to list the competitors in the sector by market share for each of the company's business segments. In particular, look at the stability of market share over time, which indicates the real barrier to entry in the business.

Another way of thinking about quality is to think longer term – try to identify companies with characteristics which are likely to deliver a high

RoIC a long way in the future. The company may or may not have a high RoIC today, but high returns can be fairly reliably predicted in the long term. Dan Abrahams at Alfreton Capital, a young but brilliant hedge fund manager, introduced me to this concept.

An example of a high RoIC company today, which Dan sees enduring, is Hargreaves Lansdown (HL) – the premier UK personal investment platform. HL has a massive economy of scale relative to its competition, which enables it to pressure investment managers to offer reduced fees in order to benefit from Hargreaves' scale. This, in turn, is passed on to customers in the form of institutional-style reduced fees. It's a great business, with very limited capital requirements and a very loyal customer base.

My problem with the company is that in addition to the fund charges, its investors pay HL a 0.45% platform fee, plus additional hidden charges for foreign currency transactions, contract notes, etc. In my view, the company is over-earning and is, thus, highly vulnerable to a tech-savvy competitor entering its market. Its valuation – consistently above 30 times earnings, and a double-digit EV/EBITDA multiple – gives a limited margin of safety.

Dan's judgement on this has proved very successful, although the loyalty of the customer base is now in question following the Woodford fund debacle. This may significantly affect Hargreaves' perception, as they continued to recommend the funds despite performance faltering and redemptions undermining liquidity. Investors ended up nursing significant losses, which were readily avoidable.

Another way of thinking about quality is Charlie Munger's trick of inversion – what does a bad industry look like? The automotive industry is a classic example and worth a brief discussion.

Automotive Original Equipment Manufacturers (OEMs) are highly cyclical, with sales contracting and margins collapsing when the economy is weak. The industry is characterised by significant over-capacity and a high degree of government intervention. Although fewer manufacturers are directly owned by the state (Renault being a notable exception), these are big employers and the state will act to protect jobs. The UK's Conservative government's assurance to Nissan that it would not suffer as a result of Brexit is a good example. It's harder for efficient companies to make extra profit if their competitors are receiving indirect or direct subsidies.

The product cycle is short, and getting shorter, which means that margins are dependent on the position of models through the product cycle relative to competitors. A new product will generate additional demand which will decay with age. This need to constantly invest in new products means that these companies don't make great margins, even though they are highly efficient.

The companies also have cash demands that are exaggerated by the down cycle. In good times, companies tend to have a positive cash flow as sales are rising, dealers pay on delivery, and suppliers extend credit. When sales contract, this cycle reverses, which is why OEMs in the auto industry generally carry up to 10% of sales in cash.

Today, OEMs face multiple challenges – a move to mobility, the need to develop electric vehicles creating a huge additional R&D investment, and the long-term move to autonomous vehicles creating an existential threat, and hence even greater R&D spending requirements.

It is possible for an investor to make gains in this highly cyclical sector but, in my view, the automotive industry (including Tesla) shows few characteristics of a quality investment.

It's important to assess not just whether the company has a long-term, sustainable competitive advantage, but also if it is building and enhancing that advantage. The ability to maintain or widen a moat is as important as its width. Understanding this, and assessing a company's willingness and ability to innovate, are critical. One way of doing this is to study competitors and to watch for tech companies making forays into adjacent or similar areas.

Jeff Bezos talks about focusing not on what is going to be different in ten years' time, but what is going to be the same: "I very frequently get the question: 'What's going to change in the next ten years?' And that is a very interesting question; it's a very common one. I almost never get the question: 'What's not going to change in the next ten years?' And I submit to you that that second question is actually the more important of the two – because you can build a business strategy around the things that are stable in time … in our retail business, we know that customers want low prices and I know that's going to be true ten years from now. They want fast delivery, they want vast selection. It's impossible to imagine a future, ten years from now, where a customer comes up and says, 'Jeff, I love Amazon, I just wish the prices were a little higher [or] I love Amazon, I just wish you'd deliver a little more slowly.'" This comment, from a recent annual report, is a useful insight into Jeff Bezos' assessment of his ability to maintain and widen a moat.

MOAT CHECKLIST

Barriers to entry are a key feature of a moat and are likely to exist for a company if:

- It is possible to identify them.

- RoICs are stable, or growing, and high.

- Gross profit to assets (or tangible assets) is high relative to peers, and is stable or growing.

- The company has a stable or growing market share.

- There is a consolidated industry structure (geographical or product/service).

- There is an element of customer captivity (e.g., tobacco or Coke/Pepsi), inertia (financial services), high switching costs (technology), or high risks of switching (flavours and fragrances).

- There is a deep entrenchment with customers, or the product is mission-critical and has a relatively low cost to the customer (e.g., Spirax Sarco steam traps in a refinery).

- There is a network effect, e.g., Microsoft Windows, Office, iPhone apps.

- It is a complicated or difficult to replicate service which cannot be objectively measured, and its cost is minor to its customers – a low-cost service where reliability is mission-critical can often have substantial pricing power. Facilities management is one example, although it is a sector where a number of construction companies have been disasters (for example, Amey and Mitie in the UK).

- Access to resources like raw materials is a differentiating factor (e.g., limestone for cement or aggregate quarries).

- Product patents, process patents, or trademarks are significant factors.

- Other intellectual barriers exist, such as technological know-how, a complicated process, or a long/steep learning curve

- Regulation is relevant – a regulator often prefers the status quo.

- Economies of scale apply where there is a marked difference in the market share of the incumbent versus its nearest rival, or where fixed costs are spread across a much larger number of units, e.g., marketing costs. A good example is contract catering company, Compass, which is the size of its two largest rivals in the US combined and has additional economies of scale – it has a food purchasing arm which buys on behalf of third parties, giving it major economies of scale in the purchase of the main input.

CONCLUSIONS

Quality comes in different forms, but you know it when you see it. There is plenty of evidence from highly successful investors like Nick Train and Terry Smith in the UK, that quality is a very reliable factor in investment. High returns on capital are a primary feature and are the result of one or more types of economic moat. It's important to invest in companies which are widening their moats and which have a focus on sustainability.

6

ANALYSIS OF COMPANY QUALITY

A s WE saw in the previous chapters, the detailed examination of a company overlaps with the evaluation of its industry and can be conducted concurrently.

Company analysis requires both *qualitative* and *quantitative* approaches. The latter approach is concerned with picking apart the company's accounts to understand its financial performance and accounting policies. I cover this in chapter 7.

In this chapter, I look more closely at how to analyse the qualitative, or conceptual, characteristics of a company. I expand on the previous discussion about moats, explain why I think a company's history is important, and explore sustainability.

To understand the business, however, is not enough. It's also necessary to put the stock in context – I discuss the importance of the shareholder base and share price trends, both long term and short term. I then explain how to test that you have a reasonable understanding of this, before drawing some conclusions on the qualitative aspect of the research.

Most public companies are not single-activity businesses, so it is necessary to conduct this exercise for each of the component businesses, spending the greatest amount of time where the exposure (primarily profits but also revenue, assets, and employees) is greatest.

A low single-digit percentage of my personal portfolio is in venture capital and private equity – generally early-stage investments. In order to form a view on a business, and to understand the likelihood of success, it's necessary to understand the product and the market, and it's important to assess the team, the execution risk, and the incentives.

But it is also vital to understand the competition – what constraints create the opportunity for this business, and how likely are they to persist? Are the constraints different for existing competitors than for new entrants, and how expensive are they to remove?

It's the same approach for quoted stocks and these are all key questions examined below.

THE BUSINESS

Understanding what a company does is the foundation of the research process. In his famous book, *Common Stocks and Uncommon Profits*, Philip Fisher highlights 15 points to look for in a high-quality growth company. Only one of these concerns valuation and they are all company-specific rather than related to the sector. While today, few public companies would disclose much of this information, his characteristics of an attractive investment include: the ability to grow sales; management which develops new products; effective R&D; above-average sales distribution; adequate margins; and, importantly, strong labour relations.

I find that writing down what the company does is a useful first step, but it needs to be a clear exposition of the business. For example, to say that a company is in the software business is not much help; it would be much more useful to say that it provides accounting departments with critical software for reconciling bank balances, on a subscription basis, paid annually in advance, with a 3% cancellation rate. The act of putting pen to paper (or finger to keyboard) helps me frame the questions I should be asking, which would include some of the following checklist:

BUSINESS

What does the company do? What are its major business segments, and what is its industry rank in each? Does the company have any loss-making businesses? This can be a vital question when it comes to considering valuation parameters, as well as being a major potential risk factor. For each of these segments, it is useful to list the competitors by market share. I may create a table which lists:

- each activity
- its significance (% revenue, % EBIT, etc.)
- revenue growth over the last few years
- market growth
- position in industry
- principal industry drivers.

Do you understand the industry structure? Where do the company's activities fit in the value chain? Is consolidation occurring – of suppliers, distributors, customers? What is the relative power of customers, suppliers, competitors, and regulators?

Are there any overseas operations in countries which you are unfamiliar with or uncomfortable about? It may be better to delay the purchase of a stock with 30% of revenues in Turkey, if you are concerned about the region – assuming it's not yet priced in.

ECONOMICS

What are the economics of the business and how does that compare with competitors? Who controls industry pricing? Does the company/sector have any pricing power? In today's lower-growth world, this is an increasingly rare quality and usually confers a significant valuation premium.

Can you distil the business down to a single unit of capacity (e.g., one hotel, one cruise ship, one shop)? Do you understand the economics of that unit? How much would it cost to lease a single shop, fit it out and stock it? How long would the payback be? Using unit economics is an invaluable tool in the assessment of businesses.

DEMAND/GROWTH

What is the market opportunity and how do competitive products address this opportunity?

If this company is growing by acquisition, is it sustainable? At what point will the company need to move overseas or into a different industry line because it runs out of opportunity? How will its growth rate be impacted as it becomes larger, and how will the risk profile increase, if it changes industry or moves into overseas markets? The issue of headroom for growth is critical, because venturing into new markets usually increases risk significantly.

What is the selling model: multi-year recurring revenues, one-off big-ticket sales, or small-ticket consumables? Terry Smith at Fundsmith prefers companies that sell small-ticket items which their customers purchase on a daily or weekly basis. These are recurring revenues, in contrast to the sale of major capital equipment.

Are there any cross-border sales or purchases which mean the company is highly exposed to foreign exchange movements? Are these likely to be in your favour? Understand the sales process – from order to delivery.

What is the backlog, or order book, and how does this compare with history?

SUPPLY

What is the company's rate of capacity addition versus those of the industry as a whole? Is it gaining or losing share, is the industry growing or consolidating? I am attracted to industries whose capacity is growing more slowly than demand, as I explain further below.

QUALITY

Why is the company good (or bad) at what they do, and is this sustainable? Compare this company to a weak competitor in the same industry – what is the difference and why?

What are the barriers to entry (moats)? If you had access to capital, what are your chances of successfully competing against this company? This is an example of Charlie Munger's technique of inversion, which can be a really helpful technique when analysing a new company.

Is this a good or a great company? When was it founded? How many leaders has it had? Will it look the same in ten years' time?

INDUSTRY STRUCTURE

Clearly, there is no 'right' number of customers. But if there are only a few customers, say for a supplier to the major OEMs, the product will have to be outstanding and mission-critical for the customer not to have the upper hand in pricing negotiations. At the other extreme, if you are selling a product to every dry cleaner and drugstore in the US, then customer acquisition and servicing costs can destroy margins.

Some distribution companies operate in the *hourglass* sweet spot, between a plethora of suppliers and a multitude of customers. Such distributors can enjoy strong relationships with both suppliers and customers allowing them enhanced margins – although, even here, digitisation allows a competing bridge. Notably, Amazon looks to be making inroads into some of the traditional industry-vertical distribution niches.

In contrast, consider the creative tension between large consumer product companies, like Unilever and Kraft Heinz, in their relationship with large supermarket chains like Carrefour and Tesco. To date, neither side has had an enduring competitive advantage, although the momentum will swing from supplier to customer for a period, depending on the external environment.

ASSESSMENT VS PERFORMANCE

Do these qualitative assessments marry with the financial results and, specifically, the historical revenue and margin trends? If you have identified a steady growth industry, and this company has had a blip in its revenue or margin pattern, it's important to understand the reasons for that blip and assess the likelihood of a recurrence. I like to spend a significant amount of research effort reviewing the long-term, organic, revenue trends, as well as the margin trends. More on this in later chapters.

SUPPLY

The relationship between capacity and demand is a critical variable for most companies.

I am wary of industries where everyone is expanding – it can be good for a while, as the public companies may steal share from smaller rivals, but generally what happens is industry unit costs fall and prices eventually follow. Buffett likens this to everyone standing on tiptoe at a parade – self-defeating.

A key factor in this analysis is therefore a review of industry capacity. Although theoretically simpler than the often highly complex demand picture, this is an area which does not always attract the analytical time it warrants. The exception is the transport sector, whose profits are acutely sensitive to even small variations in capacity growth.

A sure sign of a losing stock is one operating in an industry where capacity is increasing at a faster rate than demand. In contrast, an industry which is unprofitable, but where capacity is being shut down, is often a highly attractive investment opportunity. Such sectors are usually out of favour and often reviled, the selling pressure tends to be exhausted and the market pays little attention. If capacity is exiting, and profits start to improve, a turnaround can occur.

HISTORY

I find it really helpful to understand the history of a business and I think that it's a factor often overlooked by investors. It confers an advantage on the long-term holder of a stock, and on the older analyst and investor. Just because a company has been around for 100 years does not guarantee its endurance for the next century. Conversely, a company that has been around for under 25 years can be highly successful. Kodak and Amazon are notable examples, respectively.

Nevertheless, longevity and consistency are unusual traits that should not be overlooked – I was amazed when Nick Train (of Lindsell Train) put up a slide of Unilever's dividend history from 1962 to 2016 at the 2017 Value Investor Conference in London. Unilever had grown dividends at 8% *per annum* over that period.

I had never looked at Unilever in any detail, but a 50+ year record of dividend growth is clearly exceptional. In a recent article on brands, Lindsell Train highlighted the importance of Unilever's history, which effectively made it a local brand in many emerging markets:

> "… the really valuable aspect of this company's emerging market exposure is its long history of selling into certain regions. The forerunner of many of today's brands, Sunlight soap was launched in India in 1888, followed by the still popular Lifebuoy in 1895, Pears in 1902, Lipton Red Label (as Brooke Bond) in 1903, Pond's in 1947, and Surf in 1959. Lever Brothers India was incorporated as early as 1933, with a soap factory built in Mumbai the following year. Compare this lengthy history with Procter & Gamble, which only entered India in 1964. We think that Unilever's years of operation in India and other regions makes its brands uniquely resonant with, and deeply ingrained in, the daily lives of consumers in these markets…"[3]

An article published by 13D Research highlights how soap companies and many other brands prospered in the US in the 1880s, as railway track mileage quintupled and wages grew by 60%.[4] A middle class emerged and

---

3   Lindsell Train, 'The Growing Appetite for Brands' (March 2017).
4   13D Research, 'Will the great packaged goods brands offer a safe haven or are they poised

the railway provided a distribution system to satisfy that demand nationally. Consumers who could not afford the high-quality soaps sold by pharmacies, gravitated from local shops' offerings (often of dubious quality) to good-quality, national brands, offered by the likes of Procter & Gamble, who ran national advertising campaigns promoting quality-branded products. Local brands could not compete on quality or reputation. Today, 130 years later, social media, digital shopping, and consumer reviews have enabled local brands to re-engage in that competition. Hence, longevity may be less valuable than hitherto.

A good illustration of how the history of a business can help the analyst is the example of Adidas, as described by John Hempton of Bronte Capital, who has one of the most analytical minds I have encountered. He bought Adidas before it had its massive run in 2016, and this is how he described it:

> "Herzogenaurach in Germany is a funny (and small) town quite close to Nuremberg – and a couple of hours drive north of Munich. Once upon a time, two brothers started a sports shoe company (and it was successful). The brothers split up and one brother started another sports shoe company. Those companies are Adidas and Puma. And for a long time they considered each other the enemy. Then along came Nike, especially the Michael Jordan partnership and basketball shoes, and exposed Herzo for what it was – an out-of-touch German backwater."

Out of touch, because the Germans hadn't recognised the trend in sports shoes as fashion items. Trainers as streetwear originated, mainly, with African-Americans. In time, the trend attracted middle-class, white Americans, and then made the leap to China. As Hempton puts it: "Basketball shoes were the path to cool … I went to Herzo to visit these companies because they were super-cheap (and for no other reason)."

I had not seen the history of Adidas delineated like this before, and it underwrote for me that to understand where a company has come from is an excellent discipline for the analyst. A historical perspective can truly offer added insight. It's something I have observed of several accomplished investors, of which Nick Train and John Hempton are two of the best.

---

for disruption on a scale not imagined?' (3 May 2017).

I like to check whether there have been any books written about the company or about its founder – reading these often reveals unusual insights. Generally, I am a fan of reading biographies of business leaders, as there is usually a snippet about a technique or methodology that provides some insight into one of your stocks.

SUSTAINABILITY

This is a factor which is gaining interest and will only grow in importance. In recent years, I realised that sustainability is an issue fundamental to quality investing. I learned that mining companies file in their accounts the number of accidents and fatal incidents that occur each year. I thought this was a very sensible policy, and I wondered why I had not spotted it before.

The reason I had not realised this was that I had never considered a mining company as a serious, long-term, fundamental investment. These were always stocks to be rented, not owned. And if you are not going to own it forever, do you need to know everything about it? You certainly need to understand the outlook for the commodity price, which is the dominant driver of profitability over the next couple of years, but that's about it.

This encouraged me to think about ESG more broadly. ESG stands for Environment, Social and Governance. I had always rather dismissed this as secondary; potatoes to the investment meat of earnings, cash flow, and valuation. But I then wondered if, perhaps, companies which had good governance might be safer investments, and those which cared about the environment and sustainability were likely to be better companies, managed by more thoughtful leaders, and, hence, more likely to constitute an attractive fundamental investment. This was the way I was leaning, at least for my wealth manager's private clients, until the Volkswagen scandal broke.

In September 2015, Volkswagen (VW), under pressure from US regulatory agencies, admitted to using *defeat software* to beat emissions tests illegally. I had always thought of VW as an excellent company: great products, good management, a pillar of fortress German manufacturing. Yet here they were engaged in what appeared to be scamming and cheating.

VW was a pillar of the ESG establishment; the stock was even a member of the Dow Jones Sustainability Index. But if VW's competitors were unaware that it was scamming US EPA, how could an index provider be aware? Clearly, it could not.

VW's chairman, recently outed, had previously appointed his wife to the board. He married the nanny and appointed her to the board of a €200bn company. I simply do not understand how this could have gone unnoticed, not just by the legion of analysts following Volkswagen (that's bad enough), but also by the ESG experts.

How can the chairman appointing his wife to the board be considered good governance? Certainly, a number of VW customers must be young mums and some input from the wife/nanny might have been helpful round the breakfast table. But I am amazed that her presence around the board table could be thought of as a positive.

Generally, I think that investors should pay attention to ESG as part of the investment process, but I am less sure that consultants, indices, and scores will give you the right answer. Perhaps better to use your own common sense, until such time that ESG criteria are the subject of serious fundamental analysis.

I worry less about governance, but if you are going to own a stock long term, the wife on the board surely has to be a no-no – except perhaps in a founder-led, family business. One of my sales colleagues in the 1990s had a rule: no beards or brokers on the board. Beards are now too fashionable and ubiquitous, while brokers are too scarce, but the principle that board members should be appropriate applies.

Three simple ESG-related questions can tell you quite a lot:

- Does the company have a purpose?

- Will it improve people's lives?

- Will it improve its customers' lives?

Such companies have a better prospect of being more enduring and meeting the quality threshold.

TESTING MY UNDERSTANDING

When researching high-quality, long-term investments, I like to test myself to make sure I have understood the business. I ask myself a series of questions which summarise the issues I raised at the beginning of this chapter, looking at competitive advantages and returns, and market growth expectations. This element of the process is intended to ensure that I have not missed any steps and that I understand the risks.

TECHNICAL ISSUES

In my research notes, I have a technical section which looks at the share price history, insider transactions, and the shareholder base. This information can tell you a lot about a company and warrants more attention than is usually dedicated. I am not sure why this is commonly overlooked, perhaps owing to some snobbery about technical analysis being less intellectually rigorous.

Indeed, David Dreman devoted a chapter of one of his books to denigrating the practice of charting. I believe the history of a stock price can be incredibly informative. Looking at this early in the process is more likely to influence a go-ahead/abandon decision than some other facets of my research.

SHARE PRICE HISTORY

A five-year chart of price and price relative to the index, together with an explanation of the reason behind the major moves, is essential, because it ensures that you understand what are (or at least, have been) the key factors driving the stock price. It's a mistake beginners often make, and it was a rule at my former employer, Credit Lyonnais Laing, that the inside front cover of every note had to have that chart with the analyst's explanation of each major move. Interestingly, this is one of the few checklist items that I believe applies to all investments, as do most of the technical issues in this section.

Here is a great quote on this subject, from legendary investor, Stanley Druckenmiller:

"When I first started out, I did very thorough papers covering every aspect of a stock or industry. Before I could make the presentation to the stock selection committee, I first had to submit the paper to the research director. I particularly remember the time I gave him my paper on the banking industry. I felt very proud of my work. However, he read through it and said, 'This is useless. What makes the stock go up and down?' That comment acted as a spur. Thereafter, I focused my analysis on seeking to identify the factors that were strongly correlated to a stock's price movement, as opposed to looking at all the fundamentals. Frankly, even today, many analysts still don't know what makes their particular stocks go up and down."

I am not sure that I would go as far as Druckenmiller, but it's an aspect which is possibly underplayed, at least on the sell-side.

Figure 6.1: Facebook share price relative to the S&P 500

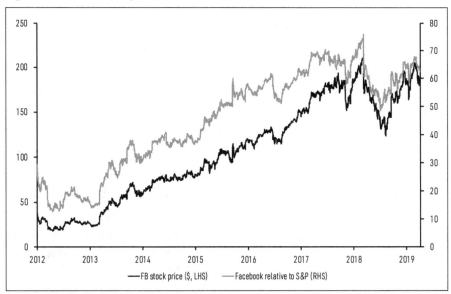

Source: Behind the Balance Sheet from Sentieo Data.

The chart illustrates the process – Facebook underperformed the S&P 500 for the first year, and then started to gain ground as the mobile opportunity became apparent. Then, in mid-2018, there was the fallout from the privacy scandal, with Zuckerberg subsequently being called to the Senate. The stock fell until the end of November 2018 – a dire period for the stock market. Facebook actually bottomed a month before the market bottom, as investors thought it had already fallen and would be less affected by US economic problems than the market as whole.

INSIDER TRANSACTIONS

I explore the question of management and its incentives in the next section, but the act of buying or selling shares with their personal wealth is the most informative action management can take.

Insider buying is likely to be more meaningful if the shares are depressed, especially if there have been problems with the company. Given that most directors focus on operational performance, if they are buying a stock when it's depressed, it can indicate that a recovery is likely. Such signals give me greater conviction in my idea and it will be more likely that I initiate a position before all the in-depth work has been completed.

You should take particular interest in share sales after a long period during which sales have been scarce. And you should almost never listen to the explanation. I recall, in the 1990s, one CEO suggesting that he had sold shares because he needed a new dining table.

More recently, management has become more inventive. Mark Dixon, the founder of Regus (since renamed IWG), told me in 2017 that he regretted a recent share sale and wished he had kept the stock, which had subsequently risen significantly. Later on, the company issued a profit warning and the shares collapsed. I am sure that Dixon had not expected the profits warning, but management usually know what their shares are worth. This is particularly true of founders like Dixon or Mike Ashley at Sports Direct, who has profited handsomely from selling his stock and buying it back more cheaply.

SHAREHOLDERS

Reviewing the shareholder base is one of my first checks and I take comfort if certain holders are already on the share register. A key factor is whether the major shareholders have recently been buyers or sellers.

I occasionally go against some of the gifted people in the industry by buying something they are selling, or shorting something they own, but I always think carefully before doing so. If you buy a stock where, say, top hedge funds with outstanding research like TCI or Lansdown have a big position, and have built that up quite recently, the chances are that they have almost certainly done even more and better homework than you have.

Such shareholder analysis is straightforward using Bloomberg. In the US, stocks have disclosure requirements, so it's easy to see who owns what. There are a number of websites dedicated to this, or you can use the SEC EDGAR search tool.[5] Similarly, many developed-market stock exchanges require disclosure when an investor owns more than a specific amount; in the UK this is 3% and the breach of every additional 1% threshold must be declared.

The concentration of the shareholder base is another important factor. I look carefully for a shareholder base which has an element of exhaustion: the stock has fallen, the big owners have stopped averaging down, and the fundamentals have changed for the negative. This can be a good short candidate, as it requires new investors.

Conversely, the presence of 'fast money' on the register (or particularly if the short interest is too high) is a major concern for me. Although you might enjoy the ride up, they can all decide to exit at once for reasons totally unrelated to the stock and that can be a real problem.

A good example is that of AA, which was an idea I submitted to the 2017 Sohn London Investment Idea Contest (I was one of four finalists). This is a competition where anyone can submit a piece of research to a panel of judges and the winner gets to present their idea at the conference – all in aid of a worthwhile charity. AA had a very concentrated shareholder base, as shown in the table below:

---

5   www.sec.gov/edgar/searchedgar/companysearch.html

Table 6.1: AA major shareholders (Q4 2017)

Name of shareholder	% held	Announced	Cumulative
Parvus Asset Management Europe Ltd	24%	09-10-17	24%
The Capital Group Companies, Inc.	16%	31-01-17	40%
Woodford Investment Management	14%	27-09-17	54%
Citigroup Global Markets Limited	8%	11-10-17	62%
Blackrock	6%	29-09-17	68%
Standard Life Investment	5%	12-04-17	73%
Goldman Sachs	4%	31-01-17	77%
Aviva plc	4%	31-01-17	81%

Source: AA 2017 accounts and subsequent 2017 RNS filing (economic interests).

I discounted the Citigroup and Goldman Sachs holdings, as they were likely to be held on behalf of Parvus, but that still left 69% of the shares in the hands of six institutions. To be short of the stock, you would need to understand the intentions of Parvus. Backed by Sir Chris Hohn, the fund was likely to be smart, aggressive, and with a game plan.

The bulk of the other shareholdings had bought in on or around the float, and were, therefore, invested on the premise that the management team would deliver on a cost-saving plan and significant cash-flow improvements.

The management team, however, had changed, and the new CEO had backpedalled on the savings. This suggested that there was an element of exhaustion about the stock, and the large holders would find it difficult to get out. Moreover, the concentration of holdings affected the liquidity of the stock, putting off potential purchasers.

This is a good example of the information content in the shareholder list – it can be one of the more critical areas affecting the investment decision. My fundamental research suggested that the shares were headed down and the shareholding concentration was an important supporting factor.

CONCLUSIONS

At this stage, I now have a good understanding of the nature of the business, the quality of the company, and the key factors which drive profitability. This has required extensive research into the business and industry. I have studied demand and the nature of supply, studied the moat, and made some assessment of sustainability. I have also looked at the stock-market-related factors, such as the shareholder base, which can weigh on a share for an extended period. This analysis does not complete the qualitative aspects, however.

Before looking at the financial accounts, I discuss management – an area of analysis where there are a wide range of views.

7
MANAGEMENT

MANAGEMENT IS a vital factor in determining company outcomes and I find it one of the most difficult areas to assess. There are several issues to consider, both quantitative and qualitative. I review in this chapter the quantitative issues such as salary and incentives, as well as the more subjective issue of evaluation, including whether investors should meet management. I also discuss the virtues of founder-led businesses, and why it can make sense to invest with billionaires and even crooks.

QUESTIONS TO ADDRESS

A key aspect of understanding the company is to make an assessment of management and governance. Importantly, some objective analysis can be conducted without even meeting the people involved, as we explore here, with further discussion of the softer factors in the following section.

What is the background of the CEO (and CFO), and what do their former colleagues, investors, and anyone else say about them? What is their experience and track record? Have they been successful in the past in an industry with similar characteristics or where the transfer of skills is a reasonable assumption?

Is this a company with a stable management base or have several people been in and out of the CEO's seat; if the latter, what gives confidence that this CEO will last?

Have management been good at allocating capital? This is one of the critical questions, but it is relatively easy to assess from both the tone of their statements to the investment community, and track record in buybacks, special dividends, and acquisitions and disposals.

Are insiders buying or selling stock? How much, as a percentage of their holdings, and why?

If this is a family-run business, have the family shown a willingness to delegate to professional managers, and how long till the next generation takes control?

Is the company a good employer? What is the employee turnover rate and is the company an employer of choice in its industry?

Is the culture stable and are management processes strong?

- Does the company usually find its CEO from inside the firm?

- Are employees shareholders? Do employees feel invested in the company's success and do employees believe they are treated well?

- Does the management team take an entrepreneurial approach to the business? For regulated businesses, do they have a constructive relationship with regulators?

Is the board using the right language? Studying 10-Ks, call transcripts and similar investor communications can tell you a great deal about the mindset of management without a physical meeting.

- Do they talk about capital allocation and is this accorded a high priority in the discussion?

- Do they talk about per share results, an indicator of management who understand capital allocation?

- Do they discuss free cash-flow generation?

- Do they talk about cash returns and cash generation?

- Or do they talk more about empire building, flags on maps, and company size, which should be a red flag?

The significance of such metrics in management's communication with investors gives a real insight into their mindset. Warren Buffett's letters to shareholders are the best example of how to communicate, and others vary in the degree of promotion.

Generally, good letters will address both what went right and what went wrong for the company, review relevant KPIs vs the company's strategy and goals, help the readers understand management's decision-making process, and address the critical issue of capital allocation. Good letters include Next, where Lord Wolfson is clearly the best communicator of a shareholder-friendly attitude in the UK (and probably Europe), and Constellation Software.

It's important to look at board composition. Is governance adequate?

- Check board composition – there should be no relatives on the board.

- Separation of chairman and CEO roles is preferable.

- Non-executive directors (NEDs) should be fully independent and should not have worked together on other boards, or as executive managers, in the same company in the past (harder to find than you would think).

- The board should not be so large as to be unwieldy – Bank OZK, formerly Bank of the Ozarks, for example, has 18 directors. Its executive committee has seven members. It's obvious which will be more effective.

The board should be representative of its key stakeholders and should be diverse enough to offer a range of opinion on relevant matters. The best way of demonstrating what I mean is to use an illustration of a board – Ralph Lauren – which I perceive as not being sufficiently diverse (see table below).

It's not just that there are only two women on the board. I would guess (and I admit to having no real insight into this) that the typical Ralph Lauren customer is a man in his forties. It's notable that the board contains only two men under 55, one of whom is the CEO, the other being the founder's son. Both were recent appointments, bringing the average age down by five years. I would wager that were it not for the connection, neither would be shopping in the store.

Table 7.1: Ralph Lauren board (July 2018)

	Age	Years on board
Ralph Lauren	78	21
John R. Alchin	70	11
Arnold H. Aronson	83	16
Frank A. Bennack, Jr.	85	20
Dr Joyce F. Brown	70	17
Joel L. Fleishman	84	19
Hubert Joly	58	8
David Lauren	46	1
Patrice Louvet	53	1
Judith McHale	71	14
Robert C. Wright	75	11
Average	70	13

Source: Company filings.

While the board is clearly very experienced, it's hard to see why it would be particularly well suited to oversight of this company's strategy, a company which is being disrupted by online retailers, social media and newer tech developments in online clothing. One such example is Zozo, a new Japanese bodysuit which captures all your measurements and creates a 3D map of your body, in order to allow made-to-measure suits to be sold online. It's hard for me to imagine such an initiative being proposed and discussed by the Ralph Lauren board.

INCENTIVE SCHEMES

The qualitative aspects of assessing managers is a difficult art, but a certain level of comfort on alignment can be gained without leaving the desk. The objective is to determine whether management are 'onside' with investors and that their objectives and their incentives are appropriately aligned. In practice, it's surprising that there are not more senior management incentivised beyond earnings per share (EPS) and share price performance.

ARE MANAGERS' AND SHAREHOLDERS' INTERESTS ALIGNED?

Look in detail at their compensation plans – are their interests aligned with shareholders? What targets do they have to meet and does this include some form of return criteria or is it solely based on EPS and total shareholder return? There is an increasing body of evidence that where management compensation includes return criteria, stocks are more likely to perform. Beware of EPS growth criteria where there is no organic element – this encourages managers to make acquisitions (almost automatically EPS-enhancing these days).

- Sensible levels of compensation which are high enough to make the aspiration of achieving the target highly desirable but not ridiculous – i.e., tens or even hundreds of millions of dollars where people may be induced to resort to cheating to achieve targets.

- Equitable sharing between the CEO, CFO and the divisional management tasked with its achievement, and incentives for team working.

- A good company, especially in the consumer space, will have some form of sustainability measures built in to the top management packages, and resource companies should have some safety measures included. Absence of such factors should sound warning bells.

- How much stock does management own and have they been sellers or buyers recently? Plot the insider activity on a share price chart or use the Bloomberg function. I have no problem with CEOs selling some of their shares in the business, it's really only prudent for them to do so. Some CEOs demonstrate a shrewd appreciation of the value of their stock and can be worth following. For example, Mike Ashley, the much-hated founder of Sports Direct, is reviled by the investment community, but has made more money through his personal dealings in the company than any professional investor and is worth following.

- Has the company paid a special dividend? Such payments are often an indicator of an 'outsider' mindset (after the book, *Outsiders*, by William Thorndike) and a management team dedicated to delivering shareholder value.

The quantitative aspect of incentives attracts a great deal of investor interest. Ideally, the team should be incentivised primarily on returns on capital invested. This is rarer than you would think, given the amount of investment writing devoted to the subject. If not on returns, then incentives should at least be based on EPS growth, share price performance or total shareholder return, and preferably some form of relative measure compared to an appropriate peer group.

Research done by various banks has shown that stocks whose management have incentives based on return on capital measures perform much better than those whose managers are incentivised on measures such as growth in EPS, revenue growth, total shareholder return, or cash flow. Every study I have seen has drawn the same conclusion: incentivise managers to maintain or improve return on capital.

The choice of peer group can tell you a lot about how the board perceives the business; for example, Darden, the largest casual dining restaurant chain in the US, includes a number of retailers in its peer group, highlighting that the board understands its reliance on consumer spending. The names included should not frighten or surprise you. If one of the names stands out, ask yourself why it has been included. If you cannot answer, email the Investor Relations (IR) representative, as this can tell you more about how a board perceives a business and may give you some surprising insight.

EPS growth targets are extremely popular with US CEOs as well as with some in the UK – Sir Martin Sorrell at WPP used to be the loudest example. For people like Sorrell, it is an excellent way of explaining their financial model and how they will deliver growth. I have mixed views on the practice. Targets based on EPS growth encourage acquisitions and aggressive accounting, and such targets generally bear no reference to the capital employed to achieve the EPS growth, which is a more critical factor.

The good news is that, as an investor, you at least understand the objective; this is particularly helpful when you feel that the target has become too challenging – a downward revision of such targets usually results in disaster for the share price. Return on capital incentives are generally recognised by investors to be more effective than EPS targets, and this is borne out by the academic (as well as sell-side) research.

I always try to bear in mind that the industry is usually a more powerful driver than the CEO. Capital allocation takes time and is largely a function of the new CEO's predecessor. Where companies have low dividend payouts, the proportion of capital employed that the new CEO is responsible for grows relatively faster.

The chart shows that after ten years a company with a 50% payout ratio and at a 10% post-tax return will still have 60% of its capital dictated by the former CEO. Companies with a lower payout, e.g., 10%, will see the present CEO responsible for 60% of the capital. But even with such a low payout, the former CEO is responsible for 40% of the capital allocation after ten years, which is more than the average CEO's life in a major company. Therefore, for a CEO to effect real change may require either acquisitions or disposals, which are inherently risky, or a major change in employee attitude or product marketing, both of which are extremely difficult to achieve.

Figure 7.1: Percentage of capital attributable to new CEO at 10% return and different dividend payouts

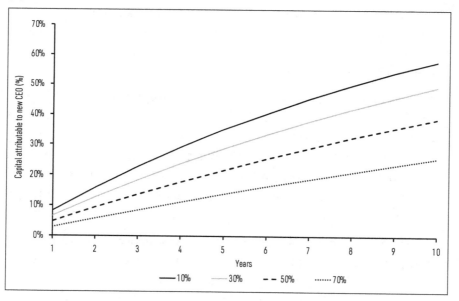

Source: Behind the Balance Sheet estimates.

CONNECTED BOARDS

Management's track record is significant (although generally reflected in share prices). I like to record how long the CEO, CFO and key managers have been in their roles and how long their predecessors lasted. Since the Volkswagen scandal, when I learned that the CEO's wife was on the board (as mentioned earlier, something I had missed and certainly had never seen mentioned in an analyst's report), I pay much closer attention to the board composition.

Outside of a founder shareholder environment (and even then), I don't like to see family members on the board. Chris 'Jock' Miller, then CEO of Wassall, successfully persuaded me that having his father as chairman was not a risk, since his father would never hesitate to tell him what to do; that is quite sensible, but Jock is an unusually gifted manager who has made shareholders a huge amount in Wassall and successor company Melrose.

The old boy network is a similarly insidious aspect of a board – and it's not confined to the UK. The website, Visual Capitalist, has produced a chart of interconnected boards in the top 100 companies in the US. It looks like a spider's web, so frequently do executive and non-executive directors sit on each others' boards.

Identifying who is good and who is bad on boards is a whole different matter and I am actually extremely wary of some of the captains of industry who have gone on to chair numerous FTSE 100 boards as, in my experience, they are often clueless. For obvious reasons, I don't like to name names, but an hour spent with a very famous knighted City grandee and chairman of three FTSE companies persuaded me not to invest in any of them. In fact, ten minutes was enough.

On the other hand, I have a number of chairmen whom I follow and have respect for – people like John Allan, currently chairman of Tesco and Barratt Developments – but this is a very personal issue. In general, I think it's better not to hope management will pull something out of a hat because a bad industry will usually get the better of a talented management team.

MANAGEMENT CHANGES

Where possible, it is extremely helpful to monitor changes in the middle and senior management ranks. An extensive level of senior changes is generally an indication of a problem – Tesla is a first-class example. Sometimes this can be the product of a new CEO coming in and having a clearout, otherwise it may reflect anxiety in the ranks. Regardless, it always warrants further enquiry.

This can be hard to spot, although sophisticated data analysis can help. Short sellers are often good at identifying middle management changes in troubled companies; it's possible to monitor this, but it can be extremely time-consuming. Large investors can scrape LinkedIn and the company's own website to monitor such changes. This is one of those areas where the encroachment of big data is a potential opportunity, but which will advantage a small group of professional investors. It's difficult for private investors to do, although Google Alerts may help identify an unusual level of management moves.

SHOULD YOU MEET MANAGEMENT?

As is often the case with equities, there are two schools of thought on this subject of dealing with management.

ARGUMENTS AGAINST MEETING MANAGEMENT

In one camp is the group who, like Terry Smith (the highly successful founder of Fundsmith), believe that the answers are all in the numbers and that there is no point meeting management. Either they don't know what is going to happen or they will lie – they rarely give you bad news. Similarly, value manager Nick Kirrage, of Schroders, believes that his investee management's time is better spent running the business than meeting shareholders.

I understand this sentiment – CEOs have got to the top of large organisations by being persuasive and are often highly personable individuals. Institutional investors are probably unlikely to be sufficiently good judges of management that they can create *consistent* alpha as a result. Some highly respected fund managers, with outstanding track records, have admitted to me privately that they don't think they are good judges of management.

Once a company CEO is accepted as a star – and once they have the track record – it will usually be reflected in the stock's rating or multiple, so there is then usually limited scope to create alpha.

Probably the best argument against listening to management is one founded in behavioural finance. James Montier, now with GMO and one of the brightest thinkers in our industry, explained it best. He cited five reasons not to meet with management:

1. It drowns you with information, which does not lead to better decisions and just wastes time and creates noise.

2. Management are likely to suffer from over-optimistic views about their own business – they don't usually tell you to sell their shares. Generally true, although a few, such as Martin Gilbert when CEO of Aberdeen Asset Management, are not scared of saying the stock is ahead of events.

3. Confirmation bias: you listen for what you want to hear and are imbued with a false confidence. I know one fund manager who refuses to meet management of his holdings after a profit warning, in order that he can make a dispassionate judgement about the stock.

4. Montier believes we have an innate tendency to obey figures of authority, so analysts can be over-awed by senior management. This can be especially true of young analysts when facing major figures – people get excited to meet industry titans and believe what they say.

5. We aren't very good at detecting deception. We like to think we are, but the facts apparently don't support this.

ARGUMENTS IN FAVOUR OF MEETING MANAGEMENT

In the other camp, obsessives pore over every last remark by management and try to create some form of information advantage by studying every last detail about the business. This too is a waste of time.

I believe that you should meet management before you make a big investment in a stock for one simple reason – to get some comfort that they seem honest.

Speaking to a company's management should better your understanding of how their business operates and how they view industry trends – they know their business better than anybody else.

They can also give an extremely valuable insight into customers (although they may be reticent about being critical), suppliers, and competitors. They are much more likely to be open and truthful about related companies than about their own.

Once you own the stock, a regular dialogue with the management team is useful as it can give you an early signal of trouble ahead – after an extended period of dialogue, management may well be relaxed with you and their body language can give away that a problem is brewing.

Some portfolio managers profess that their ability to identify outstanding managers is a core skill. Bill Ackman is a notable example, but backing Mike Pearson at Valeant was a huge and costly mistake for him.

Assessing the quality of management is one of the most difficult things for an investor to do, but meeting management is helpful to assess whether you think they are trustworthy stewards of your investment and to watch for early warning signs of strategy drift or problems – that is the limit of my competence.

LISTEN CAREFULLY AND CRITICALLY

The view that one should not listen to management is wrong in my view. I believe that you should listen carefully, just don't feel obliged to *believe*. Let me give you some examples of management lying to me – if I am charitable, not necessarily with intent to deceive, perhaps more through naivety or stupidity – and an example of management telling the truth but my leaving with a false impression.

1. The divisional head of a very large Fortune 500 company who told me his returns were 20% pa and his boss was always asking for an improvement. He was lying on the first count – I subsequently established that his returns were far higher which attracted a flood of capital into the industry, destroying returns – and the second should have been enough to make a sane person run a mile.

2. Never underestimate the importance of the stock price trend and the ability of a persuasive management team to sway the market in the short term. I had the CEO and CFO of one European company come in to see me after they had made a huge acquisition. They had bet the ranch and subsequently came close to going bust. When they came in, it was obvious they had no idea what they bought; in fact, I thought that I knew the company better than they did, yet they had spent over $10bn on the deal. They would have been very convincing, had I not studied the acquired business in very close detail, and indeed they managed to ramp their shares on the story of the supposed potential benefits. Our short eventually came good, but it was badly timed.

3. Early in the quoted life of the European low-cost carriers, Ryanair and easyJet, I persuaded my clients to short Ryanair, as market capacity that winter was growing much faster than demand. We made out brilliantly on the Ryanair short, up 40% in a couple of months, after the company warned on profits. The CEO of the principal competitor, easyJet, claimed they had no such issues. My top client agreed to switch their Ryanair short into easyJet, which had only fallen a few percent after the Ryanair warning and easyJet denial. It took another few months for us to make 70% on the easyJet short. When I later asked the then CEO of easyJet, Ray Webster, what had happened, he privately admitted that he had misjudged the advance bookings curve. He probably wasn't the most brilliant CEO and should have spotted this as Ryanair had, but he was sincere in his denial – he genuinely believed that easyJet would be fine.

4. I went on an engineering and construction company visit overseas to a new refinery project. I had a long drive with the manager of this multi-billion-pound project and he told me that he was tired and ready to retire to a new house he had purchased with a sale of shares. At dinner that night, the head of the division told me that he too was exhausted and ready to retire. I came away seriously worried that the senior talent in this division, which was reliant on a dozen senior people capable of managing these major construction projects, were no longer committed and were now rich enough, post the recent IPO, to not have to work. I recommended selling the stock, as there was an unquantifiable risk, only to watch it double in the following 12 months.

The moral of the first three examples is that management are just people. They can be naïve, stupid, or have their own agenda – often to support a share price which is critical to their own wealth. My conclusion is to listen to management but then make up your own mind and try not to allow yourself to be unduly influenced. This is quite hard to do, but it makes no sense to me to ignore their comments, as they are almost invariably best placed to tell you what is going on.

The fourth example was entirely my own mistake, although I am not sure that I would form a different conclusion today – the risk was significant, even though it did not crystallise in practice, a good example of Nassim Taleb's alternative versions of history.

All this makes a technique for being able to extract information from management – on that overseas visit, I persuaded senior managers to trust and confide in me by developing a personal relationship. That is more difficult to do in a company-meeting environment; building a rapport and asking open questions is not going to work with seasoned Fortune 500 CEOs – they are far too smart for that. But it's amazing how body language can give people away and how even the most guarded executive can reveal his concerns in the *way* he answers questions, rather than in the content of his answers.

- Sometimes the fact that the CEO has not asked himself a question and that nobody else has asked it, can be very revealing. I asked Bob Ayling, then CEO of British Airways, what percentage of revenue would stem from Business Class after they introduced the then-new flat beds in the mid-1990s – he did not know; none of the management team had asked themselves this simple question. He did not last much longer.

- We grilled the head of IR for a major Asian company at fashionable night club until 4am; he was so drunk that he would tell us anything we wanted to know.

- At dinner with the CEO of a major Fortune 500 company at the Four Seasons in New York, we flattered him so much that his ego took over – helped by a bottle of very fine wine.

- Sometimes CEOs simply lie – the attractive female CEO of a private company in which my boss was invested was more interested in flirting than explaining the recent performance; it was subsequently revealed that the company was a fraud.

The departure of a super-talented CEO requires careful assessment. Tesco's Terry Leahy is a great example – he got out at the right time, before his strategy started to crack. The departure of Richard Cousins at Compass in 2017 was thought to be safe, as the company has such a strong market position, but it clearly represents a risk. An overly dominant CEO's departure – a Jack Welch or perhaps now Dave Cote at Honeywell – can leave a black hole in perception and in cash flow.

I doubt that there are any simple rules for judging management. But your investment process can control the risks from evaluating management incorrectly. My only tip is to watch and listen very carefully, especially in meetings, and where you feel there may be a risk, cut your position. You may miss out if, say, Jack Welch's successor turns out to build an even higher perception in the market, but what are the odds of that happening? And you can always go back in, if the business proves to be more enduring than the manager.

WHAT PRIVATE INVESTORS CAN DO

Although meeting management, especially at major FTSE 100 or S&P 500 companies, is mainly a matter for professional investors to consider, there are many opportunities for private investors to engage with companies:

- Earnings call transcripts are freely available.

- Many large companies webcast investor events, e.g., Capital Market Days – this allows the private investor to observe management presenting and answering questions.

- Some organisations, like ShareSoc in the UK, organise events where private investors can meet IR professionals. This may not be the same as meeting the CEO, but a good IR director will give an excellent exposition of the business and its strategy.

- AGMs are another opportunity to engage with management, but they tend to be closely controlled, and there is generally limited opportunity for the type of dialogue which will add real value to the analytical process.

Things may have changed, but I have tended to avoid AGMs – both when I was on the sell-side and particularly on the buy-side.

- An email to the IR team may elicit a response, although not always.

GREAT MANAGEMENT

It's possible to get some positive signs of what to look for, rather than what to avoid, by observing great companies and great management in action. Unfortunately, they aren't too many of these and usually it's the application, rather than the methodology, or software rather than hardware, which makes the difference, making replication impossible. But a meeting with a former senior Amazon executive revealed some interesting facets of their unique management style.

Amazon is distinguished by having a very intense and highly focused environment, although managers have a lot of latitude to experiment, and have time to see these experiments come to fruition. There are a lot of tools available, for example, internal APIs (application programming interfaces or automated integration tools), which are freely available. A key factor in my view is that there is an intense operational discipline, and every business has a weekly internal dashboard. A country head will literally have 10,000 metrics per week, and all he has time to do is scan to look for red figures.

Amazon's decision process is interesting – they talk internally of one-way doors (a decision which cannot be reversed) and two-way doors, where the decision can be reversed. They will take a lot longer to decide on the former, as it is much more difficult and expensive to abandon an experiment. Amazon has low margins, but its business economics and returns are driven by its negative working capital and extremely high stock turn (better than Walmart's monthly turn).

Amazon is clearly a superbly managed business and investors can learn from this, especially if ex-Amazon people go on to run other businesses, or a company talks of adopting Amazon philosophies or practices. The outcomes are, however, rarely as transferable as the management processes.

FOUNDER-LED BUSINESSES

Founder-led businesses tend to outperform. That's the conclusion of a considerable amount of research and is a generally accepted principle. Management consultants Bain & Co have published research on this, which indicates that total shareholder returns at founder-led companies beat others by over 2 times over a 25-year period from 1990.

Credit Suisse have produced similar research, indicating a more than 50% outperformance over a 10+ year period from 2006. Their work suggests that family-owned companies outperformed in every region, from 3.1% pa in Asia ex-Japan to 5.1% pa in Europe, a trend that occurred in every sector. Of course, some of this effect was down to fantastic performance generated by a few very large businesses, notably Amazon in the US and LVMH in Europe.

When trawling for ideas from the 2017 London Value Investor Conference, I came across a fund that I had not heard of. Quaero Capital adopts a deep-value approach in its European small-cap fund; it too suggested that family-owned businesses outperform others – they estimated that between 2002 and 2016 family-run listed businesses on the Dax returned 397% vs 149% for the Dax index. They define a family-owned business as one that controls at least 20% of the supervisory board. The family are stewards of the company but often outsource management.

All of this makes perfect sense, although I have not seen any of the detailed research. Reasons why family businesses outperform include:

- longer-term thinking, as opposed to financial quarters
- risk aversion and conservatism
- strong balance sheets and aversion to debt
- avoidance of dilution – reluctant to issue shares
- cautious acquisition policies
- generous dividend policies ensure strong element of income return.

Some investors believe that the second generation tends to be more of a liability than an asset. Think of Ralph Lauren struggling in the mid 2010s; Vincent Bolloré handing over to his son Yannick; or Richemont founder

Johann Rupert appointing his 29-year-old son to the board in 2017. Almost certainly, not all of these are the best candidates for the role, and that certainly represents a risk.

When Disney was rumoured to be buying some Fox assets, talk was of James Murdoch going to Disney and being a possible contender for the next Disney CEO. This illustrates one of the problems of investing in founder-led businesses – the price Disney pays for the assets might be affected by the commitment to provide a role for a family member. Hence, my general rule is first generation founders are acceptable and likely to be a positive; second generation inheritors are more likely to be a risk and, although the hope is that they will be careful stewards and should not do anything daft, there is a risk that the minority may be disadvantaged.

This is not an isolated issue, especially in Asian markets. Hong-Kong based Ronald Chan, of Chartwell Capital, believes that of 2,075 stocks then listed on the H share market in Hong Kong in 2017, some 968 were family owned. Many of these, including some of the largest local stocks, mainly Hong Kong property-based conglomerates, are currently undergoing this transition from founder to second generation. These risks must be factored in when looking at such businesses. Similarly, there is always the risk with family-controlled businesses that they may not always act in the best interest of the minority shareholders.

INVESTING WITH BILLIONAIRES

This is an attractive subset of founder-led companies. The chances are that someone who has built up a billion-dollar fortune on his own account (rather than inheriting it) will continue to be successful. Although sometimes the journey can be fraught and far from smooth, most billionaires are worth backing.

Often, the strategy is unclear and it involves taking a lot on trust. Sometimes there is the risk of being disadvantaged as a minority shareholder; this is more common in developing markets, such as Korea. In developed markets, corporate governance is usually better and offers an element of protection.

There are many examples in the US and around the world. Backing tycoons like John Malone, Rupert Murdoch or François Pinault has been a highly successful strategy, and it's not been necessary to get in on the ground floor. Backing these people after they have become highly successful has generally been a winning strategy.

A notable exception is the Vivendi acquisition of a controlling stake in Havas from its own controlling shareholder in mid-2017. I could not see the logic of the deal – I did not like the price – but was powerless to do anything other than to send an email to the CEO asking questions about the strategy and its communication to shareholders.

The Vivendi CEO, Arnaud de Puyfontaine, not two months earlier, had told a breakfast organised by one of the bulge bracket firms that that there was no imminent intention to effect a combination with Havas. He said that there was a long-term intention to do *something*, but nothing was on the cards at that stage. I asked what had changed and how the board assessed the relative merits of a buyback of €4bn of Vivendi shares vs the acquisition of Havas, given management's contention (with which I strongly agreed) that Universal Music Group was clearly undervalued by Vivendi shareholders?

There were serious questions as to how they evaluated the Havas transaction value, as they paid a premium relative to WPP, the leading global media agency, which had grown earnings per share at 15% compound over the previous 23 years. To acquire Havas, they paid a near 40% premium on P/E and a small premium on EV/EBITDA. A premium for control was understandable, but the market had derated agencies and there appeared to be little justification for their valuation. They professed synergies but offered no concrete examples of co-operation between the two companies and how that would be increased, enhanced or cemented, by common ownership. They were also reluctant to offer any estimates of cost or revenue synergies.

Management apparently were reluctant to respond to investor queries of this nature. This is a good illustration of the risks of investing with billionaires who may have a different strategic vision and may be prepared to play a much longer game than a professional investor can afford. They may also have another agenda, for example, to derive an advantage from a transaction, e.g., a transfer of assets, to the detriment of external shareholders.

Less easy to identify is to avoid investing with losers. There is a long list of people who have been highly successful in other areas, but have failed to capitalise on their strengths when operating in the stock market. A good example is Sainsbury, which cost both Robert Tchenguiz and the Qatari Sovereign wealth fund a significant amount of money. Tchenguiz made a number of ill-fated stock-market investments in the mid-late 2000s and was worth watching – he provided some great short ideas.

From 2015 to 2018, Bill Ackman, the formerly highly successful hedge fund manager at Pershing Square Capital, made a number of costly investment blunders – he famously lost $2bn+ on Valeant Pharmaceuticals. But, less well known, is that he also made significant losses in two so-called platform companies which specialised in roll-ups (buying several smaller companies and merging them). Again, his run of bad luck provided opportunities to short sell, particularly because such a performance in the public eye invokes fund redemptions which, coupled with the short sellers (circling like vultures), can create a strong selling pressure in the portfolio's stocks.

INVESTING WITH CROOKS

Investing with crooks, real or perceived, can be highly profitable. For example, Teddy Sagi, the billionaire Israeli entrepreneur behind Playtech and onetime owner of Camden Market, was sentenced to nine months in prison after being convicted of fraud and bribery in 1996.

Playtech was a phenomenal growth story from its IPO. It came to the market in 2006 at 273p, and traded up to 850p, although it subsequently fell from favour. Sagi still owned one third of the company, which was valued at £2.75bn. His conviction clearly has not held him back, as he has numerous business interests and apparently once stated that sex and betting are the most profitable businesses on the internet; moreover, his lavish lifestyle has included a number of famous girlfriends, including supermodel Bar Refaeli.

A number of highly successful businessmen have been to prison. Duncan Bannatyne, the *Dragon's Den* TV star on the UK's BBC, spent time in Glasgow's notorious Barlinnie prison (the Bar-L), while Gerald Ronson was sentenced to prison for his role in the 1980s Guinness scandal. Today,

Ronson owns three major businesses, most notably a property business which developed the Heron Tower in the City of London.

In the stock market, the opportunity to invest profitably with crooks arises because the majority of institutional investors will shun stocks associated with people of doubtful reputation, let alone former criminals. Hence such companies often trade at a discount, but that discount will generally dissipate over time with cash flow and performance delivery. Also, as the offence becomes more distant in history, greater weight is given to the more recent record and people come to accept that the individual has successfully rehabilitated.

Investing in a company founded by an ex-convict might be highly profitable, but leaves the professional investor with no defence if it turns out to be a fraud, or underperforms significantly; their superiors or their investors will have little sympathy if they incur losses in a company which has such an obvious black mark, so why take the risk?

And the offender need not be a criminal. The same thing happens to people who let themselves down with a silly remark, as when Gerald Ratner likened Signet's jewellery to a prawn sandwich; or to issues of corporate governance where a dominant founder continues to run the business his way, in defiance of City or Wall St etiquette. A good example has been Sports Direct in the UK, where the founder Mike Ashley has had a love/hate affair with the market; after falling to 30p post IPO, the shares rebounded to 800p, before collapsing again amid poor trading and a spate of controversy.

My simple reaction in most of these cases is to ask how likely is it that someone who has built a huge business and created such immense wealth, will have gone off the rails and won't make it back. Of course, entrepreneurs sometimes get it wrong and don't bounce back and each case must be evaluated on its merits. But the strategy of investing with crooks or those out of favour, or indeed investing with billionaires can, I believe, be a sound strategy – albeit not one favoured by professional investors.

EMPLOYEES

The Parnassus funds follow simple investment principles: invest in companies with exceptional long-term profitability during periods of temporary adversity, or when the market is negative on the prospects of an entire sector, and that are socially responsible. In particular, invest in companies that are good places to work and that treat their employees well.

Investing in companies with good employee relations is smart. Wherever possible, I try to find alternative sources of information, whether that is the trade press, an *Economist* article, specialist bloggers or even social media. I have found that a review of Twitter and LinkedIn (and, on one occasion, Medium) for people who work at the company may offer some unusual insights.

I have not found Glassdoor (a website where employees can review their employers) a particularly useful resource for this, but I have not done any detailed work on it. Glassdoor reviews tend to be negative, but overall scores versus industry peers may be indicative. I use Glassdoor as a negative check, rather than a confirmation of any positive aspects, as it's quite easy for a company to game the results.

Many hedge funds today use expert networks to gain insight into the business from former employees and industry consultants. I think employee relations will become a more fruitful area of exploration, especially as there is greater competition for young talent.

Looking at average salaries, employee shareholdings and bonus plans can also give a sense of how involved employees are. It's particularly important to conduct this sort of assessment when looking at professional service companies and similar.

CONCLUSIONS

Management is critical to investment outcomes, but assessment is difficult and hard to define in a checklist. Meeting management before you buy and regularly afterwards is essential. Founder-led companies are often attractive opportunities, sometimes even more so if the market distrusts the founder.

8
COMPANY FINANCIALS

THE QUESTIONS discussed until now relate primarily to the conceptual quality of the business. I would normally also initially look closely at a number of financial parameters, but for the purposes of clarity in this book, I have considered the qualitative and financial aspects separately.

Obviously, in order to evaluate an investment properly, a solid understanding of the financials and the accounting policies is necessary. For my initial assessment, I focus on some key parameters, such as the revenue growth record, the gross margin, operating margin, the returns on invested capital, and cash generation. I also briefly look at capex and working capital requirements.

For my more detailed review, I generally start with an understanding of the accounting policies, although one of my first checks is whether the accounts can be trusted, by checking the audit report, the contingencies note, and the related parties note. These are quite a good guide as to whether it's worth bothering with a long position (as opposed to shorting a stock, often attractive if the accounts are misleading) – I explain why below. I then work through the financial statements.

First, though, I explain why the accounts are important and how this might be a source of an information edge. I know the general assumption is that everyone reads the accounts in detail and therefore there is no information edge to be gleaned, but my personal, as well as academic, experience of the topic suggests otherwise.

READING THE ACCOUNTS IN DETAIL

One of my advantages as an analyst is that I have two accounting qualifications and this, coupled with lots of practice over many years, has enabled me to become quite expert at reading balance sheets. I have long believed that relatively few investors are adept at this aspect of analysis, and that some of the best investors are distinguished by this skill. A notable example is John Armitage, the principal of Egerton Capital (one of the most successful and longest standing hedge funds globally); he is known for reading company accounts, including the detail in the notes.

My scepticism was confirmed by an academic study conducted by two professors at the University of Notre Dame. They examined downloads of accounts from SEC EDGAR and concluded that very few investors bother to look at the accounts:

> "The average publicly traded firm has their annual reports requested from the EDGAR site only 28.4 total times by investors on the day of the filing and the following day. On its filing date, the median publicly traded firm has only nine 10-K requests."[6]

This could make reading the accounts even more important to the serious analyst, as it suggests that there could be undiscovered information. Honestly, while I am sceptical about investors spending enough time on the accounts, I doubt the conclusions of the academic study – most investors access the accounts via the investor relations sections of company websites, or through Bloomberg and similar terminals.

---

6 'The Use of EDGAR Filings by Investors' by Tim Loughran and Bill McDonald, University of Notre Dame.

Yet, General Electric's then CFO claimed in an article in *The Wall Street Journal* that their 2013 annual report was only downloaded 800 times from the GE website in the whole year. This for a company with millions of shareholders. It's possible that accounts have simply become too large and unwieldy – the average 10-K in 2013 was 42,000 words, 10,000 more than ten years prior. HSBC's group accounts, for example, peaked at over 520 pages, and they also publish accounts for several subsidiary companies. To wade through all of those documents would probably take half a man-year. GE's 2014 report (over 100,000 words/257 pages) was downloaded 3,400 times – I was one of those.

I have found over the years that many investors pay scant attention to the annual report. I reviewed one client's internal note on a stock and every number had been pasted in from Bloomberg or a similar terminal. There was no reference to the accounting policies, because the analyst (at a highly successful institution) admitted to not having opened the financial statements.

My scepticism is confirmed by my experience of sell-side analysts. I was trying better to understand the returns enjoyed in a particular division of a $75bn US conglomerate. None of the sell-side could calculate or estimate the returns for this particular segment. Yet, when I re-read the 10-K, the number was actually disclosed – not one of the sell-side I surveyed (and I asked a dozen) had bothered to read the accounts! I still find this staggering, even though I know the constraints on the US sell-side, particularly the shortage of time and the focus on the quarterly EPS number.

WHY SEC FILINGS ARE BETTER

Although SEC annual filings actually seem to be rather unpopular with sell-side analysts – there are too many of them, they take too long to read and there isn't enough time – they can contain a massive amount of valuable information, generally much more than in European, Asian or other financial statements.

For the serious analyst, this makes US companies a better proposition in some respects, as the information is readily accessible, particularly in terms of the qualitative description of the business (what it does, who it sells to, etc.); the risk factors that are spelled out in excruciating detail by the lawyers (we sell overseas, changes in the dollar can affect our results); and the MD&A (management discussion and analysis), which spells out the reasons why results have fluctuated. This saves the new analyst a tremendous amount of time.

Foreign companies with US listings have to file Form 20-F; I always used to read these when available, as they are much more informative than the conventional annual report. Yet few analysts bother.

In my first meeting with Ryanair, I met then COO and O'Leary deputy, Michael Cawley, a terribly nice man – some would say in contrast to his boss, although I always found O'Leary highly professional and usually amusing. I surprised Cawley with a question about the loss of market share on an established and critical route. He asked me how I knew the information and in a stupid attempt to impress him with my diligence, I explained that I had read the last two 20-Fs and had calculated the difference in volumes; he responded that he would delete this data from future editions. He had never previously been asked about this disclosure.

The SEC also requires a myriad of other filings from US quoted companies, and both the content and timing of such regulatory statements can contain useful information. Indeed, there are research firms which do nothing but scan company filings for unusual disclosures – a useful service to identify shorts. They talk about filings late on a Friday evening (between 4pm, when the market closes, and 5.30pm, when the SEC filing window closes) or on the night before Thanksgiving, as being particularly fruitful areas for exploration.

UNDERSTAND THE ACCOUNTING

It's essential to understand the accounting policies followed – some big mistakes are otherwise possible. And if you don't do this upfront, you will never do it, in my experience.

Of course, by the time I start my detailed review of the accounts, I have already had a decent look at the company qualitatively and at some of the key financial parameters. At this point, I am now more or less committed to doing an in-depth review and will cover almost every number in the accounts and most of the text. But I have a slightly unorthodox approach – I don't start at the front.

In his book, *Accounting for Growth*, Terry Smith suggests reading the report and accounts backward – start with the contingencies and commitments note, if memory serves me right. I don't actually ignore the first 100 glossy pages of the accounts, I just never start there.

This did get me into trouble when looking at Thomas Cook, whose statutory cash flow made no sense – some of the answers were in the financial review at the front. And clearly you do need to look at the unaudited front section of the annual report, as it can contain useful information. But it's the last thing I look at, I start with the most technical parts of the accounts.

FOUR TECHNICAL AREAS IN THE ACCOUNTS

1. THE AUDIT REPORT

One of the first things I look at is the audit report. This contains some important information, particularly today, given improvements in recent years.

- Audit report – are there any qualifications and, if so, is it worth continuing? Are there matters for attention, particularly any disagreements over accounting policies or bases of estimation? These are red flags requiring close scrutiny and potentially abandonment of the project.

- Size of auditor – which firm is involved and have you heard of them?

- Auditor changes – if the auditor has changed, it's important to find out why and how long the previous auditor was in office for; if it was a short period, that is another major red flag.

- Audit committee – is there one and are the directors independent?

As part of my profit and loss (P&L) review, I look at the size of the audit fee in relation to the size of the company and its turnover base, as well as relative to competitors of similar size. I am looking to see if the audit fee is reasonable and if it has risen over the years in line with inflation and the size of the business. If it has not, that could indicate an issue.

I would also be concerned if the audit fee was dwarfed by non-audit fees paid to the auditor for tax and consultancy services. A client who is paying heavy fees to its auditor for non-audit work is more likely to be able to pressure the auditor to accept accounting decisions at the limit of tolerances and beyond.

Figure 8.1: Ontex audit fee vs revenue

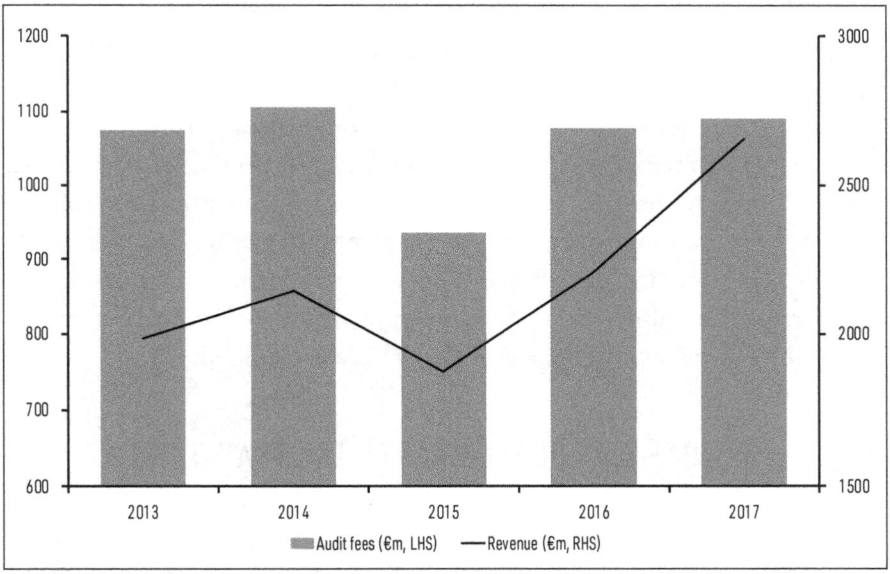

Source: Behind the Balance Sheet from Ontex annual reports.

In this example, Ontex had made two significant acquisitions, in Mexico in 2016 and in Brazil in 2017. It was inconceivable that the auditor would not have incurred significant additional expense with each of these deals. That the audit fee was static was a major red flag to me.

2. CONTINGENCIES AND COMMITMENTS NOTE

I then turn to the contingencies and commitments note – if there is a fundamental, major uncertainty disclosed, that alone may be serious enough to cause me to shelve the analysis and await a resolution, unless the price is so attractive that it's an irresistible proposition anyway. Litigation issues can be particularly difficult to evaluate – estimates of losses and probabilities of success or failure are really tricky to evaluate, and occasionally create a bargain, but more usually a headache, for the investor.

A good example of the sort of headache was Amec in the mid-2000s. Its contingencies note ran to over two pages and included issues like a lawsuit because a bridge had not been erected satisfactorily. Now this was a big bridge and conceivably the cost of rectification could have been the entire market capitalisation. And this was but one of many such litigation contingencies.

The problem with this type of situation is that it creates a very wide possible range of outcomes for the valuation. Such risks are also extremely hard to quantify – there could easily be a range of £100m (as much as 10% of Amec's then market capitalisation) or more in the likely settlement of that dispute over the bridge construction. Generally, in such situations I would be inclined to move to the next stock, as the chance of gaining an information edge or being able to quantify the value is slim. Sometimes, a stock can be cheap regardless, although I would venture that the share price may not reflect the full value until the contingencies are crystallised.

3. NOTE ON RELATED PARTY TRANSACTIONS

I next like to look at the note in the accounts concerning related party transactions. This is best looked at upfront – if there are questions about honesty of management or controlling shareholders, then, again, it's best to move on. As a general rule, it's probably best to avoid companies with large, frequent, or unusual transactions with related parties, particularly if the party is related to the CEO, as you are leaving yourself more exposed to the risk of fraud than otherwise.

4. RESIGNATION OF DIRECTORS

The other issue which I cover at the start, in case it causes a change of heart, is resignation of directors – this can be innocuous, but it's also a potential warning signal and may warrant a question to management as to the reason for the departure. If, say, a respected non-executive director has resigned and there appears to be some major disagreement on the board, I may put the stock on the backburner and await developments.

If there are major question marks as a result of the review of these four areas, I may abandon the quest. Or sometimes I may decide that it's probably not a long but a short and worth examining further anyway. I then move on to the accounting policies.

ACCOUNTING POLICY REVIEW

Analysis requires quite a lot of dull, old-fashioned desk research, and reading the 10-Ks or annual accounts in detail is, in my view, a basic requirement of thorough analysis. The way facts are disclosed in the accounts and the precise wording can tell you a lot, especially when that wording changes.

It's possible to review the differences in accounting policy statements from year to year by comparing this year's accounts with those of last year. This can be done by copying sections into Word and using the 'review versions' function. Bloomberg and similar tools offer this functionality at the click of a mouse, as do some specialist websites for SEC filings (they are filed electronically and can be interrogated by a computer). I used to do this manually for all the companies I covered on the sell-side, every year.

It's important to read between the lines of the filings and ask why they have expressed something in a particular way – is there anything that I expected and which is missing? This can be particularly significant when reading the description of the accounting policies.

This review has the objective of understanding whether the company's accounting policies are conservative and in line with its peers. Sometimes a quantitative assessment is required, but an initial review of the accounting policies notes should flag up areas of potential concern. My main steps are listed below.

ACCOUNTING POLICIES NOTES

CHANGES IN POLICIES

I review the accounting policies note for this year and last and check for changes in policies, bases of estimation, and in estimates, such as depreciation lives. I will later calculate this for myself, but sometimes the range of lives quoted will change, e.g., 'plant and machinery is depreciated over 5–10 years' changes to '5–15 years'; that type of change usually indicates a relaxation of standards and diminution in earnings quality.

I check for anything that I have not come across before, or anything that sounds unusual, odd or out of keeping with the business. This is particularly sensitive in the case of revenue recognition policies, which is one of the most critical areas for massaging numbers – at what point is revenue recognised, at the point of shipment or before, are there any deferred revenues? I check for consistency and quantum against the balance sheet.

LONG-TERM CONTRACTS

Where long-term contracts are involved, this review generally requires contact and detailed discussion with management, preferably face-to-face. This is such a subjective area, and impossible for the auditors to value correctly, so it requires extra due diligence. Companies which account for revenues in this way tend to be much higher risk because of the subjectivity of revenue calculations and the difficulties auditors have in verification.

DEPRECIATION POLICY

I assess the depreciation policy (accelerated vs straight line), estimated useful lives, and average life – this is calculated by taking the cost or gross book value of the asset divided by depreciation or amortisation charge. This includes not just conventional fixed assets but also software and other intangibles. The software depreciation life can be a good indicator of a company which is not of the highest quality – if the software is written off over ten or more years, either the CFO is pushing the envelope or the company is probably not keeping up with technological trends.

Darden Restaurants is a good example – perhaps not obvious, but the company is exposed to some major disruptive trends, e.g., food delivery. Yet the software is being written off over what appears to be around ten years in recent accounts. In the odd case, for example, the banks, this may indicate that there are old legacy systems which they cannot replace – again, hardly a bullish signal.

INVENTORY VALUATION

I always review the basis of inventory valuation (LIFO vs FIFO etc.) and am on the lookout for any unusual language. I may check the inventory note for further clarification and occasionally have come across some simply puzzling statements. For example, Samsonite in 2016 and 2017 had indicated a very small write-down on a very large proportion of its stock, but the write-down made little sense in the context of its margins. At this stage, it's important to make a note and follow up later with the IR. In the absence of a satisfactory explanation, it is sensible to be cautious.

GOODWILL IMPAIRMENT AND INTANGIBLES AMORTISATION

I look at goodwill and related intangibles – the amortisation period and particularly impairment criteria. The latter is more often quoted in the actual goodwill note, but this is part of my initial review of policies. The length of period for the amortisation of intangible assets, such as customer lists, is not mission-critical to the valuation of the business, but it is indicative of the mindset of management.

GROWTH RATES AND DISCOUNT RATES

In the goodwill note, the assumptions a company uses on growth rates, and the discount rates which apply, can also be indicative of a cheating mindset. What is often particularly illuminating is when a company changes these assumptions. For example, in 2015, DIA increased their assumed growth rates in their Portuguese business, but significantly reduced their expectations in the larger Spanish business for the next five years.

This is revealing of management's mindset – they had accepted that the next five years were going to be much harder than they had previously forecast. And, obviously, the immediate five-year outlook is critical to the valuation, as it sets the base of the residual value calculation in a discounted cash flow (DCF), and the next five years have a much higher weight because of the discounting mechanism. I also review discount rates to ensure they make sense.

CONSERVATIVE ACCOUNTING

When looking at accounting policies, I may check to ensure that the company is sufficiently conservative in its accounting, particularly if warranty provisions or doubtful debtors are significant. I look at the rate of provisioning for doubtful debts and the warranty provision (the P&L charge) vs the cash spend.

RESEARCH AND DEVELOPMENT

Treatment of research and development and any capitalisation is another sensitive area. There are some simply daft accounting polices being applied here, and the car industry has some great examples. Think about what has been happening in the 2018–2020 period – Tesla has been joined by a slew of new all-electric models. Car manufacturers are nevertheless still amortising their R&D too slowly. The worst culprit is Aston Martin, which charged £11.5m to its P&L in 2018 out of a £214m cash spend; in addition, there was amortisation of the R&D asset, but it was low relative to the asset.

Aston's balance sheet carrying value for R&D at end–2018 was £653m vs revenue of £1.1bn. In 2017, the R&D asset was £511m vs revenue of only £876m that year! Over what time period is that to be amortised? How confident can the directors be that the R&D investment, presumably largely for the new electric Lagondas (date uncertain) and the 2020 SUV, will pay off? It's pretty uncertain in my view.

The accounting policies should make sense. If I don't understand them or their application, given that I have at this point invested a significant amount of time understanding the business, there is likely something wrong. Or perhaps I have not done enough work to understand the business, and need to go back and check my knowledge of what the company does. Or in the case of the automobile industry, participants may be in denial.

ACQUISITIONS

Although not an accounting policy, I will generally look quite closely at this point at how the company has treated any acquisitions. Acquisition treatment, particularly the size of provisioning, and adjustments made to the target's balance sheets can be quite revealing as to the conservatism of the management of both companies. I like to compare what is coming into these accounts with the acquirees' last filed accounts – any significant differences usually indicate a management team that is pushing the envelope on conservatism. I cover acquisitions in greater detail later, when I look at maintenance, and I discuss how to assess them.

BALANCE SHEET

Once I have completed the review of the accounting policies, I turn to the balance sheet. I review this line by line, looking at two or three balance sheets so that I can get a scale both today and against previous years, often taking a past balance sheet, say five or seven years previous, as a starting point – the movements over a five year+ period gives a good feeling of the growth in the business and how that has been achieved.

Looking at how book value per share has grown in the last several years is usually a reasonable starting point for extrapolation. And understanding where the growth has been achieved – whether from retained earnings, share buybacks or appreciation of overseas assets when translated to home currency – gives me a very good feel of how value has been generated, and how repeatable that might be; those three routes to growth in book value have very different associated valuation multiples.

The purpose of my balance sheet analysis is to understand what assets are required today to generate a pound or dollar of sales – how much in fixed assets; how much in stocks, debtors or other current assets; and what other assets does the business hold? These other assets may have a hidden value to the investor, or they may represent past largesse in the form of goodwill (not necessarily a big problem, unless the same management team are going to repeat the same mistakes).

The liabilities side of the balance sheet is perhaps even more interesting and often contains more clues – provisions, deferred revenue, debt and pension liabilities all warrant close examination. I will generally read and check every line in the balance sheet and read every note to the accounts. Of course, this takes some considerable time.

An exercise I use in my training courses illustrates why all this is important. I give students a snapshot of four companies – an outline common size balance sheet (all lines by percentage of assets) and a dozen critical ratios – and ask them to guess which industry. At first, the class is usually pretty intimidated, as they are naturally accustomed to knowing the company before they look at the numbers, but the numbers tell their own story. We usually are drawn to a stock because of some narrative about why it's very cheap or how it's going to improve profitability. These narratives are clearly important, but so are the numbers, hence my course's strapline: numbers before narrative.

A few of the main items I cover and the issues I look to identify are discussed below. This is a very extensive subject in its own right, however, and easily sufficient for a stand-alone book. So, the list below is really simply a taster, and those seeking the full recipes should do some further reading.

FIXED ASSETS

I like to look at the breakdown of the asset base, how much is property, plant and assets under construction. This is not always disclosed, especially in US accounts, although the 10-K gives a list of major properties which can be reviewed for values. Google Maps is a useful resource for having a look at major properties; it's obviously not as good as a personal visit, but it can give you a good feel for the location/size/opulence of the HQ, for example.

PROPERTY

This is rarely overlooked now, in sharp contrast to the 1960s and 1970s, when Geoffrey (later Lord) Sterling used to buy whole businesses for the real value of the land and buildings. Where property is disclosed, it usually has a reasonably recent valuation. Even so, there are stocks where the property values have been significant relative to the market capitalisation.

I bought Sotheby's, an incredible brand in a sector with effectively inflation-linked revenues, and the valuation was outstandingly cheap after taking account of its properties in New York and London. The London premises in Bond Street would attract some of the highest per-square-foot rents in the city. Another example, where I didn't invest, was a company which owned a cinema in Union Square in New York – the valuation of the whole business was only at a small premium to the alternative use value of their principal asset.

I am interested in the freehold land and buildings as a source of value and downside protection, and potentially also for planning gains etc. I also like to look at the lease costs and off-balance-sheet assets, and to understand how much space the business needs operationally – this gives an insight into the operational costs of the business.

PLANT AND MACHINERY

I am interested in the value of the assets required to operate the business, and how much of this is on and how much off the balance sheet. (The new accounting standard, IFRS16 and its US equivalent, require that all assets should now come on to balance sheets, whether 'rented' under operating leases or owned outright.) The standards have their own shortcomings and are overly theoretical in my view.

What are the depreciation rates and what is the average age of the assets? I like to look quite closely at depreciation lives to determine if these are reasonable, and if they are rising or falling. This applies to both fixed assets and intangible assets. Using too long a depreciation life is indicative of a less conservative CFO who is prepared to push the envelope. I operate on the iceberg principle – if I see something I don't like in the accounts, I assume there may be a lot worse hiding 'underneath'.

What proportion of the assets are sold or scrapped each year and does that create a regular cash outflow for replacement? What is the level and consistency of capex? I may go back several years to understand this. Is this required for growth or to stand still? Is there disclosure of the split between fixed plant and vehicles? Vehicles often tend to require more regular replacement.

ASSETS UNDER CONSTRUCTION

What is the level of Capital WIP and does it change significantly from year to year? Is this required for growth or maintenance? If it's significant, what would the returns on capital look like without this element, and is it realistic to expect the company to achieve that, for example, because a major expansion is coming to an end and the returns will pick up once the new plant comes into production? How much could that move the profitability of the business?

GOODWILL

With the increasing prevalence of intangible assets, and with increasingly high valuations, goodwill has become a larger component of total asset value. I generally rely on a scrutiny of past deals as a more reliable indicator of management's capital allocation talents than the goodwill on the balance sheet. Disclosures on growth assumptions and discount rates are potentially illuminating, and I always check these from year to year, as changes inform the reader of developments in management's own perception of its business – as with the DIA example illustrated earlier.

OTHER INTANGIBLES (E.G., SOFTWARE, R&D)

I look particularly closely at the life chosen for amortisation. When a company writes off its software over ten years or more, I generally assume that the CFO is prepared to push the envelope to inflate his earnings. Sometimes this can be justified if there is a large software project under way, but I would then expect the asset life to fall dramatically when the software is brought into service. Software lives which consistently run at ten years are unrealistic in almost any industry today.

INVESTMENTS

The balance sheet value carries only half the story, of course, and it's necessary to check both what has been invested and what the investments may be worth today. Sometimes the cost is a poor guide because the asset has been held for many years and has significantly appreciated or become a tech unicorn in short order. The reverse is also true, particularly with tech investments – more and more companies are resorting to venture capital speculation and often the carrying values are unrealistic.

The Diageo CFO told an audience at a broker lunch (in response to my question) that he personally supervised the company's portfolio of venture investments. I have no strong view about whether Diageo might be good or bad at investing in craft breweries or gin producers, but I would wager that its finance director's time could be more gainfully employed elsewhere and that there would be other people in its organisation who would be more appropriate stewards of such investments.

WORKING CAPITAL

I study working capital and other current assets and liabilities in terms of sales. I look to see if there is upward drift in debtor or inventory days, both danger signals. As well as trade debtors, I look at other current assets, unbilled revenues and long-term receivables, to ensure I have a total picture. Increases in these balances relative to sales is generally a sign of a potential problem – if your customers cannot or will not pay you, or if you cannot shift your finished product stock, that generally indicates that something may be wrong.

Similarly, a fall in payables relative to sales can mean that purchases of raw materials are slowing, generally a reflection of slowing finished product sales, or that provisions or accruals are being released to prop up earnings. Increase in payables also worry me, as it can suggest that there are liquidity issues.

DEBT

I look at all the usual measures of liquidity and interest coverage, including lease cover and fixed charges cover – I also think about the ratio of fixed to variable costs, another measure of leverage. If debt is quoted and trading at a discount, it is often a critical indicator of failing financial health.

DEFERRED TAX

I generally spend a considerable amount of time trying to reconcile the various tax balances in the accounts, especially if the company is charging or paying below normal corporate levels of tax, as it generally indicates a lower quality earnings stream, although deferred tax can be a distortion. Deferred tax often confuses analysts, but it's quite simple in principle – for example, where this arises on the unrealised gain on an investment (which has been marked to market), this can be thought of as an interest-free loan from the tax authorities, until the owner decides to sell the asset.

PENSIONS

The assumed rate of return is often overly ambitious and disguises the real extent of the liability. Even municipal pension funds often assume unrealistic (often around 8%) long-term rates of return. I like to look at the asset mix, the percentage of bonds vs equities vs other – the required return from equities can be estimated by assuming today's bond yields and assessing whether it's realistic.

Assumptions on the liabilities side often indicate the character of the CFO or FD – aggressive assumptions here are often accompanied by similarly less conservative assumptions elsewhere. I look at mortality assumptions, discount rates, inflation projections and other details. It can be hard to adjust these in order to compare this company with peers, while sensitivities of the liabilities are generally high. Many companies have a website for their pension fund which can help with additional insight.

DEFERRED INCOME

Where deferred income balances are declining, this may be the result of revenue being brought forward or artificially boosted. The level of deferred income is also important. The AA in the UK, for example, has a business where:

- the members pay largely in advance

- cars break down most in the winter

- the year-end is January

- individual members are much more significant in revenue than corporate members.

It would therefore be expected that deferred revenue would be significantly over six months' revenue, and possibly as much as nine months; yet it looks to have averaged around four months. Part of this is corporate memberships, but it's likely that there has been aggressive accounting to bring forward revenue into the current year. The corporate and personal revenue split is not disclosed, but the balance sheet implies that the average membership was purchased at the start of June.

OTHER BALANCE SHEET ITEMS

Each line in the balance sheet can be relevant, depending on the company and the circumstances, but it's too long a list to detail here. I do, however, look at each line to check:

1. if there is a significant value, I aim to understand the rationale behind that and any movements from year to year

2. if it is not significant, and from the industry I expect it to be – say an oil E&P company which had no provision for decommissioning

3. unusual swings from year to year; if it has moved from having a value to a zero value or vice versa, there is usually something unusual behind this.

After looking at the accounting policies and balance sheet, I have a pretty good understanding of how conservative the accounts are and a reasonable picture of the financial health of the business. I then look at the P&L and cash flow, which I cover in the next chapter. Interestingly, this is the opposite sequence from most analysts, who in my view do not place nearly enough emphasis on the quality of the accounting and on the balance sheet.

PROFIT AND LOSS

I really only start to look at the P&L in detail once I have finished the balance sheet, although I have already spent quite a bit of time understanding both sales and margins.

UNDERSTANDING SALES TRENDS AND MARGINS

The sales line is my first port of call, and it forms the foundation of my analysis. The sales line generally does not lie, or at least is less prone to fudging than the EPS line. Some CFOs accelerate the recognition of revenue (right through to outright fraud). Generally, though, turnover is one of the most reliable numbers in the accounts.

As I explained earlier, one of the first things I like to do when looking at a new company is to review the long-term revenue and margin trends. I look back at the 10–15-year revenue history to determine how sensitive the business is to changes in its environment and the macro backdrop. (I used to use a five-to-ten-year window, but the slow and steady economic expansion since the GFC requires a longer history to identify companies' performances during an economic dip.) Is the company a steady revenue producer or is revenue (and growth in revenue) lumpy and volatile?

It's important to understand why there has been a big jump, or a big fall in revenue, in a particular year – often this is the impact of a major acquisition or disposal which, in turn, means that the record going forward is likely to be slightly different to the past.

In conjunction with this is a review of the company's margins. I generally look at EBIT margins as I believe that longer term, in a steady state environment, depreciation and capex should come into line. This is a shorthand for cash flow excluding working capital – a better measure to use than EBITDA margins. Here I am particularly looking for the long-term normalised margin, as this is the most critical component of valuation.

For the majority of companies, there will be some element of a cycle in the margin trends – for example, capital-intensive cyclical industries tend to see really major swings in margins. But even for less volatile industries, a cycle can emerge because of an intensification of competition, for example.

Part of this process is understanding the sequence from gross margins, down through EBITDA to EBIT margins, and looking at each aspect of the cost base. At one point, I built a dashboard which represented all this information graphically over a 10+ year period, all as a percentage of sales – I found this a great way of understanding the evolution of margins over time. The input was a standardised database, which meant that I could do the analysis extremely quickly. I now use spreadsheets downloaded from a system, but generally check the accuracy of the data, at least on a sample basis.

GROSS MARGIN TRENDS

Investors have become much more aware of the significance of gross margins since the Novy-Marx 2013 academic paper, 'The Quality Dimension of Value Investing', which persuasively argued that gross profitability outperforms return on equity and similar factors as an indicator of quality.

The rationale is that gross profitability is defined as gross margin multiplied by asset turnover. Asset turnover is a useful measure of capital efficiency, while gross profit should be a good indicator of economic performance – as accounting rules expense economic investment like R&D, brand advertising, etc., gross profit should be a better guide to economic performance. It is also a better measure of quality, as high gross profits can only be sustainable if there is an adequate moat.

While the performance data for gross profitability has subsequently been very good, a paper by Rob Arnott of Research Affiliates[7] is contradictory. It

---

7   R. Arnott et al, 'How Can Smart Beta Go Horribly Wrong', Research Affiliates (2015).

suggested that 90% of the performance differential generated by stocks with high gross profit, since the Novy-Marx paper, has been from rerating – hence, gross profitability may only have worked because it has become fashionable.

Figure 8.2: Rerating of High Gross Profitability Stocks

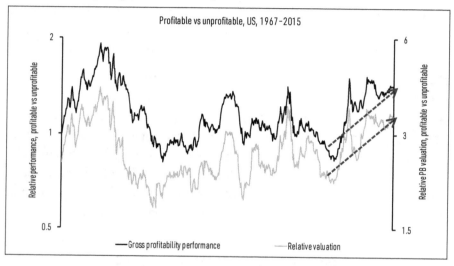

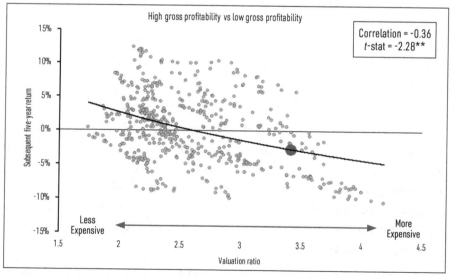

Even so, long-term trends in gross margin are incredibly useful in understanding a company's ability to maintain pricing power. Sometimes the margin can be in decline because of a change in business model, for example, Microsoft's move from a sale to a subscription model. In spite of much lower intrinsic profitability, the latter attracts a much higher valuation because the lifetime value of the customer is higher.

Care is required because many companies have different ways of defining cost of sales. For example, the intensely competitive UK supermarkets are adept at disguising their product mark-up, with only Ocado ever giving an indication of the 'true' gross margin (i.e., the mark-up on cost of the products). The other supermarkets all include an element of distribution costs and similar in cost of sales, making comparisons extremely difficult.

Because there are no accounting standards for cost of sales, companies have a great deal of flexibility in where they book distribution and similar costs – some book this as part of cost of sales, some include this in overheads. It is sometimes possible to normalise these, depending on the level of disclosure and assumptions required.

DEPRECIATION AND AMORTISATION

I have already checked the asset life, but the trend relative to sales is an important element of understanding margin trends.

SELLING, GENERAL AND ADMINISTRATIVE EXPENSES

Different companies have different ways of disclosing this, and the historical trend is often more informative than the cross-sector comparison. I also look quite closely at per-employee ratios – what is happening to sales per employee and to costs per employee?

R&D

Again, I have already covered the asset life and the realism of the balance sheet carrying value, but the trend of R&D relative to sales is informative of the margin trends.

FIXED VS VARIABLE COSTS

I generally spend some time thinking about the relationship of fixed to variable costs and have rules of thumb for some industries. A backward review of margins informs this analysis, which is a critical parameter when looking at cyclical businesses. US analysts often use incremental and decremental margin analysis, which is another helpful insight, although I tend to use this at the segmental level.

SEGMENTS

I also always split the revenue and margin data, where available, down into a segmental analysis and review the history for each of the company's divisions, in order to understand the main drivers for each part of the business. This can get a little more complicated as, while external data is generally fairly reliable at the sales line, there are differences at the EBIT margin level. These differences can be exaggerated at the individual segment level – hence, this process takes quite a lot of time as it requires the review of multiple years of accounts.

Segmental analysis is often useful in identifying 'dog' segments – a business which is lower quality than the rest of the group, which drags margins down, pushes capital intensity up, and which, if sold, will see a significant increase in the multiple accorded by the market. I like to ask myself: what would the rating be if they closed or sold the worst division.

Table 8.1: Alphabet and its loss-making other bets

	Q4	Q4	Year	Year
	2017	2018	2017	2018
Revenues:				
Google	32,192	39,122	110,378	136,224
Other bets	131	154	477	595
Total revenues	32,323	39,276	110,855	136,819
Operating income (loss):				
Google	8,595	9,700	32,287	36,517
Other bets	−748	−1,328	−2,734	−3,358
Reconciling items	−183	−169	−3,407	−6,838
Total income from operations	7,664	8,203	26,146	26,321
Margin:				
Google	26.7%	24.8%	29.3%	26.8%
Total	23.7%	20.9%	23.6%	19.2%

Source: Behind the Balance Sheet from Alphabet 10-K filing.

A good illustration of how the overall picture can be distorted by a loss-making division is Alphabet, as shown in the table. Its 'other bets' include self-driving operation, Waymo, which I believe to have a significant value. Yet, it's loss-making today and will continue to be for some time. The correct way to value Alphabet is to value Google first, and then to value Waymo and the 'other bets' separately.

Note that the difference between Google and total profit also comprises 'reconciling items', the most significant of which was the European Commission fines. While these were probably higher than normal in 2018, in my view these are a recurring part of Google's business, so I would treat it as an ongoing expense when doing the valuation.

QUARTERLIES

I do the same analysis for the quarterly numbers in order to identify the seasonality of the business and to get a sense of the trailing 12-month margin trends – usually the swings are greater than simply using an annual cut-off and this is really important.

What I am trying to do, particularly for the more cyclical businesses I look at, is to understand where the business today is in its margin cycle. Hence, understanding more precisely both the bottoms and tops in annualised margins is really helpful. I usually look at annualised (or trailing four quarter) numbers, since quarterly data is too volatile and too noisy for me to get a clear picture.

This involves a lot of data manipulation and a detailed spreadsheet. I prefer to enter all the data myself as, despite being a really inaccurate transcriber, I find the process oddly therapeutic. But, more importantly, I get a recognition of the numbers that I don't have if someone else has prepared the data for me.

If I am in a rush, I often take the shortcut of using brokers' data – a useful shortcut available to the institutional investor is to ask two or three brokers for their analysts' models and then compare them to the historical record. If all three agree, it should be OK and it's only then necessary to investigate the differences; unfortunately, the instances of three in absolute agreement are less frequent than is ideal. Obviously, this is not an issue for the private investor.

RETURNS

Coupled with this examination of the margin trends (both overall and at a segment level) is the RoCE (return on the industrial capital employed in the business, excluding goodwill). Has sales growth required a major investment in capital equipment and how has this affected the returns being generated? Where assets are given on a segmental or geographic basis, I also look at the returns in these breakdowns as the additional insight is almost always useful information on the quality of the businesses.

INTEREST

I look at the average rate on the debt, which can indicate window dressing at year-end. The balance sheet maturities inform the likely duration of current average rates, and I pay close attention to all the coverage ratios (interest cover, cash-interest cover, interest and lease cover, etc.).

ASSOCIATES

I should by now have already looked at the investments in the balance sheet. This will have included a review of the past performance of associates and joint ventures.

TAX RATE

This is a critical component of the detailed P&L analysis and has a number of elements:

- What is the P&L tax rate and is the company properly providing for deferred tax?

- What is the cash tax rate and does this raise any additional questions? My old friend, Dougie Ferrans, the former CIO of Scottish Amicable, then one of the largest equity investors in the UK, once told me that there are two people who know how much profit a company is *really* making: the finance director and the taxman. If the company is paying very low cash taxes, the analyst needs to understand why.

- If a company is paying very low taxes and there are quasi legitimate reasons – for example, the large tech stocks washing their earnings through Luxembourg and Ireland – then you have to ask how sustainable this is. In the case of tech hardware companies like Apple, the intellectual property is deemed to reside in Luxembourg in a special IP vehicle and is subject to a deeply discounted tax rate; costs recharged to that subsidiary are then also washed through a low-tax unit in Ireland. In the case of software companies like Facebook, Google and Amazon, it's the Irish subsidiary which supplies the service and books the profit. Such practices are fine in theory, but when governments are being denied a legitimate claim on the profits earned from their citizens, and when those profits become large enough, the tax dodges could become outlawed. This could become a serious issue for a company with a single-digit group tax rate.

MINORITIES

I look closely at minority earnings and, as with associates, look at balance sheet values; if possible, I try to assess the total value, as this can move the enterprise value (EV) calculation. Complications can arise with companies with large quoted minorities, especially if they are in high-growth emerging markets. This used to be true of ABB, whose Indian subsidiary was not that large, but which was rated at an earnings multiple of 2.5 times the parent group.

In these extreme cases (Unilever enjoys a similar position), it's essential to include the minority in the EV calculation at market value; I also find it helpful to compare the group valuation, including 100% of the minority, with the valuation excluding the minority. In the case of ABB, this often used to give very different results, which is very important to understand. As such, situations can attract activist investors who may try to persuade management to sell off the quoted jewels and invest the proceeds in shrinking the share count – not always ideal if you are a long-term holder.

STOCK OPTIONS

The practice of issuing large volumes of stock options which were then ignored for earnings purposes attracted significant criticism in the dotcom era, notably from Warren Buffett. These are a valid and real expense, so should go against the P&L. Fully expensing the options is clearly the best way of reflecting the real earnings for shareholders, but the true value of the option is hard to calculate, and to understand the underlying operational trends, it is necessary to also look at the numbers pre-options.

One problem is calculating the real value of the option. Another is that the market may be looking at numbers pre-options. I use an alternative route, especially for companies in their early gestation – where the option value is extremely high relative to profit – so that a better measure of underlying profitability is required than simply ignoring the options. My technique is to use a fully diluted share count, as if all the options had been exercised (theoretically, adjusting the earnings for the notional interest on the cash, although practically of little relevance with today's zero-interest rates). I think it's in a sense double counting to charge the cost of the options in the P&L and then use the fully diluted share count to calculate EPS.

When doing a sum-of-the-parts calculation, I always use the fully diluted share count and add the value of the cash raised from the exercised options; a similar technique is appropriate in break-up or takeover situations.

CASH FLOW

There are a number of intricacies to the cash-flow statement, such as tax, which are too technical for the scope of this book. I illustrated above why a company's tax rate is so important, yet is a factor which is sometimes overlooked in analysts' reports. Just as the cash tax rate needs to be compared with the P&L tax rate, generally most items in the cash-flow statement should tie up reasonably with the P&L charges and any variance is cause for a question.

Two common issues which investors and even professional analysts seem to struggle with are working capital and capex. Working capital moves reflect a snapshot of the balance sheet on a single day, while capex in the cash flow is not the same as in the balance sheet. Therefore, fixed asset notes are a more fruitful area of exploration to detect the underlying trends; the cash flow merely reflects what has been paid for in cash, not the delivery of the physical assets.

I always relate changes in working capital to sales and average these over three-to-five years. I explained earlier that a review of working capital ratios is an important feature of the balance sheet analysis. Estimating future working capital needs is a critical element of cash-flow forecasting, but one which (with a few exceptions) is not generally done by Wall Street analysts with as much rigour as would be desirable.

As explained earlier, I relate capex to both depreciation and the average life of the assets, where possible, splitting the assets into property and non-property (although US companies offer poorer disclosure than European ones, for example).

One drawback of the cash flow is that it can be very difficult to reconcile the opening and closing net debt, unless the company provides this detail in the notes. Too often, I have noticed that sell-side analysts fail to reconcile the opening and closing balance sheets, sometimes leaving a large balancing figure hanging in the air. This is a serious deficiency, and if I cannot reconcile the opening and closing balance sheets with the cash flow, I always note the unexplained balance – if this is large and consistent enough, I will chase the IR of the company until they relent and give me the details or if they are unable to, I may even abandon the quest, if the missing gap is large enough.

RATIOS

I use the traditional working capital ratios and modify them to include analysis of inventory days into raw materials, WIP and finished products, as well as add unbilled revenue days and long-term receivables to debtor days. I also review the deferred revenue balances, which can be revealing. I have discussed above the returns, and my principal focus is pre-tax return on capital employed (RoCE), although I often use RoIC.

RoCE is the pre-tax return on the industrial capital employed in the operation, a measure of business quality, while ROIC is the post-tax return on total capital including goodwill, a measure of how effectively the assets are being sweated to generate earnings for shareholders. Both are useful in different ways.

Interestingly, I had a long conversation with an analyst at Bill Ackman's Pershing Square who used to look at return on equity (RoE) when comparing companies; he thought I was mad to use RoCE. In fact, the higher up the P&L you go, the more sensible the operating comparison, with RoCE effectively being an EBIT-related measure.

My method is to work up from RoE and to use RoCE as my benchmark, stripping out the impact of associates and joint ventures, and also perhaps somewhat controversially stripping out all cash and short-term debt from the calculation. I also look at RoCE excluding capital WIP (the value of factories etc. under construction) where this is significant.

While RoE is ultimately the test of performance as it affects the shareholder, a large element of a superior RoE, when comparing a company with its peers, could simply be down to one company having a more aggressive capital structure with a higher proportion of debt – in good times it will demonstrate superior returns, but in bad times, those returns will evaporate. Looking at RoCE gives a better picture of operational performance than RoE and, hence, is better for comparing two companies in a sector.

RoIC also gives a measure of how effective acquisitions have been; most people look at this post-tax, while I prefer to look also at the pre-tax ratio, as this removes the tax rate fluctuations from a trend analysis. I am not sure how important it is to define returns this precisely, as long as you use a consistent method for a company over time and when comparing companies across a sector.

There are a number of other ratios which I look at, including asset turnover – and more will be covered when discussing building the model later – but this is all quite basic analysis. Therefore, I focus below on some of the more unusual techniques that I use.

COOKING THE BOOKS

Many years ago, I built a sophisticated dashboard in Excel to identify areas at risk in an individual company – it consists of a series of charts which seek to highlight long-term trends and where a company is cooking the books. It's far too large to incorporate in full here, but it tries to break down trends in performance, and show how moves have been delivered and whether this might be due to accounting manipulation. For example, as with Montier's C-Score below, and long pre-dating it, it looks at the ratio of depreciation to the gross book value of assets to determine if the depreciation lives may have been altered over time to flatter earnings.

I discuss below some screening mechanisms which are generally available to identify stocks at risk of accounting manipulation. The main difference with my tool is that it is not a simple score which screens out companies at risk but a dashboard which highlights risk areas for an individual company. To do this requires a detailed analysis of a number of accounting ratios.

Some brokers and research boutiques have built scoring systems that draw attention to companies that have a large number of variables in danger zones. This then highlights that the stock may be at risk of accounting manipulation. Such tools are highly labour intensive to design and implement though, and the scoring systems I outline below have the virtue of being simple.

MONTIER'S C-SCORE

James Montier, when he was a strategist at Société Générale (SG), published a note containing his definition of the C-Score, "to help measure the likelihood that a firm may be trying to pull the wool over investors' eyes." The score has six inputs, each designed to capture an element of common earnings manipulation:

1. A growing difference between net income and cash flow from operations.

2. Days sales outstanding (DSO) is increasing.

3. Growing days sales of inventory (DSI).

4. Increasing other current assets to revenues. (Can be used to disguise accelerated sales recognition by not impacting the commonly used debtor and inventory days ratios.)

5. Decline in depreciation rates, relative to gross property, plant and equipment, indicating lengthening asset lives.

6. High total asset growth. Serial acquirers can use acquisitions to distort their earnings. High asset growth firms receive a flag.

Montier claimed that the strategy was highly effective, both in the US and in Europe, with stock-market performance over a ten-year period, from 1993–2003, being highest for companies with a score of 1 (companies with the least manipulation) and reducing steadily as the score increased.

Whether this works as a quantitative approach is debatable. First, there has been limited commentary on the execution by practitioners (of course, if it worked perfectly people would not necessarily advertise that). Second, I suspect that the sixth factor, eliminating serial acquirers, may play a big part in the performance by eliminating some big losers. Nevertheless, the issues he has identified are relevant and incorporating these into a screen might be a sensible way of avoiding traps.

I also may use the Beneish M-Score and, at a very high level, the Piotroski Score, which are good snapshots of company health and are worth looking at early on in the process. I tend to use them as a filter in various screens.

LEVERAGE

I pay close attention to company leverage and think of it not just as financial leverage, but also operational leverage and share-price leverage (companies with debt see magnified movements in their share prices for a given movement in the business valuation).

The first question is on financial leverage. I look at interest cover, cash-interest cover and fixed charges cover – the ratio of earnings before leases and interest, to the sum of the operating lease rentals and interest on both a profit and cash basis. I do monitor balance sheet gearing and debt to EBITDA multiples, but this is the key metric. I also look at the weighted average age of debt, and how this has changed over time, and monitor maturities closely.

But financial leverage is only one part of the picture. Besides this, I pay great attention to operating leverage. What will incremental revenues contribute in profit and what will be the impact of a decline in revenue. The ratio of fixed to variable cost in a business is a critical factor, although it's often hard to determine precisely.

A good illustration is a commodity producer. Many investors tend to gravitate to producers that have the lowest marginal cost of production and are highest up the quality curve. If you are looking at a 12–18-month position in a commodity stock, on the basis that you have reason to believe the price of the commodity will rise, it's usually more profitable to buy the lowest quality producer, as it will have the greatest operational and share price leverage.

This sounds slightly counterintuitive, but a simple example will explain how this works. Two gold producers, one with a cost of production of $400m and one with $800m, each producing 1m oz pa, and with $100m of HQ and finance costs.

With the gold price at $1,000, Company A makes $500m profit ($1,000m – $400m – $100m) while Company B makes just $100m ($1,000m – $800m – $100m). The gold price rises by 50%, to $1,500, and Company A now makes $1bn profit, i.e., double its former level, while Company B makes $600m, i.e., *six times* its former level. Company B likely also gets a rerating relative to Company A. In these circumstances, I therefore generally look for the lowest quality stock.

This is obviously an extremely risky approach, so I only tend to get involved when I have a high degree of confidence in the commodity's price trend. And buying the lowest quality stock generally means that the starting valuation is inherently depressed, which gives some support, if there is not significant financial leverage.

TIMING ISSUES

One favourite trick is to check for companies with odd period ends, 53-week years, or similar patterns which can distort the reported results or trends. These are not always picked up by analysts.

Supermarkets choose odd year ends, whether it's Tesco's February 23 or Sainsbury's March 19, in order that they can show a more favourable cash position at the balance sheet date. No supplier cares if they are paid on February 24 or 25, so the creditor days get stretched.

To be fair, the retailers would argue that they generally end the year on a Saturday, which allows them to provide more accurate like-for-like comparisons that are critical in this sector. I accept that this argument is valid, but the working capital is still affected.

An even more interesting example is Thomas Cook, which went bust in late 2019. The company had chosen a September year-end (although it was at least a normal quarter end, i.e., September 30) because this was a highly favourable point for cash – post the summer peak and before suppliers had been paid. A simple examination of its interest bill vs its average debt clearly revealed that its year-end balance sheet was not representative of the year as a whole.

The company reported net debt in its finance review of £389m at end-2018 and the total net interest charge was £150m! This included some bond refinancing and other costs, but the underlying charge was still extremely high relative to the average disclosed net debt.

Similarly, the timing of Easter is critical to the airlines as it represents a massive peak. Many airlines have a March year-end, so some years have two Easters and some none – it's essential for analysts to adjust for this when doing forecasts and it's important to recognise when reviewing the past performance record.

Surprisingly, analysts are far from perfect at making these adjustments. Good companies will tell you that they have a 53-week year, others will only comment afterwards when the 53-week year is in the base, and adjust the comparisons. I am anally retentive about all this and the impact of an additional week on a quarter's results should not be underestimated – it's about 8% on revenue and can have a greater impact on profitability, if a company has high fixed costs or indeed if it accrues expenses quarterly. Quarterly margins can therefore be heavily distorted, which is why I prefer to look at trailing 12-month trends.

OTHER SECTIONS OF THE ACCOUNTS

I generally would have a model for all major positions. I might have the odd, smaller, say 1%, short position without constructing a model, but this would perhaps be because the short is obvious, the financial shortfall is clear and does not need to be modelled, or because it's a hedge. Successful shorts have a short duration, whereas you tend to stick with winning longs for a much longer period.

Although in theory I would always much rather have a model to support every idea, in practice the return on the time spent building the model may not be sufficient for a short. I continue in the next chapter on the assumption that this is a long position which requires a model.

Before starting on my spreadsheet model, I should have read all the analyst reports, the results announcements, any presentation slides, transcripts of calls and the annual reports. I should also have read the MD&A section of the US companies' 10-Ks and some of the glossy material at the front of the accounts, at least the chairman's letter to shareholders and the CEO's review as well as the financial review.

In the chairman's statement, I am looking for possible warning signals, such as fallacious excuses, and hoping for an honest appraisal of the company's performance as well as a sensible explanation for any shortfall.

In the CEO's review, I look for consistency, honesty, and common sense. If I see continuous restructuring, or frequent mention of extraneous issues such as the weather in multiple years, these are warning flags. What I am looking for above all is a management team which is honest in their appraisal of the business and in their communication with shareholders.

The MD&A explains the reasons for fluctuations in performance from year to year, and is incredibly helpful as one can go back to periods of weak performance and examine the reasons – this is extremely helpful in understanding the robustness of the business to external factors.

In the financial review, there should be some transparency on the company's debt position, the extent of its facilities and how the company plans to refinance any upcoming debt maturities. Clarity on the level, type and purpose of capital expenditure is also helpful and its omission is another warning signal.

WHAT THE ANALYSIS HAS IDENTIFIED

By this point, I should have a decent understanding of the economics of the business, as well as a good picture of the overall economics, the divisional picture and, where appropriate, an idea of the economics on a per-product or unit-of-service sold basis. Of course, this is often something of an iterative process, because something which did not strike me as significant the first time I read the accounts will become of greater import later. Oddly, it's incredibly important to re-read the accounts at the end of the first phase of research, in case something has been missed first time round.

At this point, I would have hoped to have answered most of the following questions.

- Are accounting policies conservative and in line with their peers?

- Revenue – history, reasons for fluctuations, and how recorded. Have sales grown through volume increases (and relative to market growth), pricing, or acquisitions?

- Gross margin – what are the main raw materials and what are their costs, and cost drivers?

- Overheads – level, relative to history, appropriateness vs peers. What are the main elements of overhead – employee costs, marketing, advertising and selling costs, logistics, distribution, freight and transport, fuel costs, and any stepped changes in costs thanks to economies of scale. Fixed vs variable costs.

- Depreciation and amortisation, and relationship to gross capital expenditure over time.

- Interest and debt.

- Tax rates – how they change over time and the reasons for this. Comparison with tax paid. Balance sheet liability?

- Are EBIT/EBITDA margins reasonable, sustainable, and stable over time? (Is this because of barriers to entry, network effects, etc., and are these sustainable?) Where are we in the cycle? Review current margin vs five-year and ten-year averages. If the current margin is near its historic, or cycle, high or low, should mean reversion be assumed?

- Are incremental margins (i.e., margin delta over sales delta) stable over time and is this consistent with your understanding of the fixed vs variable costs in the business?

- Movements in working capital over time relative to sales – is the business working capital intensive and do the margins justify this? Have you understood the bargaining power between supplier and customer, and is this sustainable? What are the trends in inventory turns, days payable/receivable, and working capital?

- Capex trends, both gross and net. Is this a capital intensive business and has sales growth followed increased capital intensity in the past? Is there a high level of disposals in the business and does this make sense given the industry? How does it compare with peers?

- Free cash-flow trends – are these stable over time or highly volatile? Given the capital (capex and working capital) needs of the business, is this sufficient? If it is extremely high, are there barriers to entry which will protect the company from competition?

- Returns on capital – are the RoCE/ROIC/ROE ratios stable over time or volatile, high or low, and is this indicative of a quality business? Is improvement possible through faster capital turnover or increased margins or is a deterioration more likely? Have the returns been depressed by high cash balances or heavy levels of capital WIP and does this suggest potential upside in future? To what degree can the company reinvest in its business?

- Is the leverage sensible – how operationally and financially leveraged is the P&L and how indebted is the balance sheet? How does this compare with history and with peers? Do you feel any discomfort about cash cover, fixed-charges cover, interest cover, etc.? Any worries should be red flags at this stage. Does the capital structure make sense, and has leverage recently increased to fund share buybacks?

- How is the company investing its capital between maintenance capex, organic growth capex, acquisitions and buybacks? Is the company likely to need to access capital markets, either for debt (check maturities) or equity?

Having educated myself thus far, I now feel in a position to build a model, where it's appropriate to do so, and to look at the valuation in more detail.

CONCLUSIONS

A detailed analysis of the financial accounts is a key facet of my analytical technique. Every investor claims to read the accounts, but the evidence is that very few do, and certainly not thoroughly. My process is slow, painstaking and painful, and certainly not for everyone. But a line-by-line examination of at least the balance sheet would surely help every investor analyse a company more effectively.

9

VALUATION

I N T H I S chapter, I discuss how to build a model to forecast profit and cash flow. I then discuss the principles of valuation, considering the pros and cons of different valuation techniques. Although I generally initially use the valuation data produced by Bloomberg or a similar system, they are less reliable for EV-based measures than for simpler parameters like P/E and price-to-book (PB).

I therefore prefer to do my own calculations of EV. This can be extremely time-consuming for a complex company and there are all sorts of tricks to the calculation. It's beyond the scope of this book to go into detail here, but readers who are interested can find an online training course on the calculation on my website, www.behindthebalancesheet.com, under online training.

Suffice it to say, EV requires careful calculation before using some of the metrics below. Topics covered here are:

- Building a model
- Profit and loss
- Cash flow and balance sheet
- Forecasts
- Valuation
- Valuation techniques (I use a wide range)

Whole books have been dedicated to valuation techniques and there is a large school of thought which believes that profitable investment opportunities can be found in valuation discrepancies. In my experience, stocks are usually cheap for a reason. Valuation is important, but, in my approach, as a measure of calibration of the stock price, rather than being a reason to purchase a stock.

INTRODUCTION

Although many analysts focus a large proportion of their time and energy on valuation, it has always been secondary in my approach. My focus as a special situations analyst is on profit anomalies where the market has incorrectly predicted the outlook for a company. This is not to say that valuation is unimportant, of course it is. But a stock would have to be super cheap before valuation was my primary reason for buying it. Hence, my approach is not to seek valuation discrepancies and I tend to worry less about historic valuation trends than some of my peers.

BUILDING A MODEL

A simple model is all you need to value a business. Building a model of profit and cash flow is a critical step in ensuring that I am familiar with the financial drivers of a business. A line-by-line model requires me to be diligent about every line item in the P&L, balance sheet, and cash flow. It's beyond the scope of this book to outline the process in detail (and it's beyond dull!), but I outline some of the key processes below.

I usually build some long-term valuation criteria into the model, but the degree and complexity varies from company to company, although I always include some ratio analysis. Looking at trends in working capital ratios and, critically, return on capital invested, is extremely helpful in determining the likely quality of the investment. By going back several years, it is also possible to get a better understanding not only of the return in capital employed, but also the return on capital invested, because write-downs of failed investments in past years can be added into the capital base. Often

RoIC is measured on a net basis (after a write-down of goodwill), which gives a distorted picture.

When the model is completed – and it is often an arduous and lengthy process if conducted properly – I feel I have a much deeper understanding of the business, its history and its likely prospects.

Note that I have not even mentioned profit forecasts yet, as it's highly unlikely that you can forecast the future without a good understanding of the company's past performance. Hence, the first step is to record the company's history into the model. Some friends use Bloomberg or FactSet data, which I find slightly scary as I am not sufficiently confident in their accuracy. I actually *like* the process of entering the data though, as it makes me more familiar with the numbers. I am also much more likely to spot something than by simply reading the accounts.

My models generally span five years – I download the financials and look at ratios over a much longer time frame, but when I am manually entering the numbers directly from the accounts, five years takes quite a long time. On occasions, I have used two or three brokers' models for the history, but I verify that the brokers have consistent data, which reduces the risk of data errors. I then forecast three years out. I do not generally extrapolate over long periods unless I am doing a DCF, and I like to do three years as most sell-side analysts give two-year forecasts.

PROFIT AND LOSS

I start with the divisional analysis, but it's simpler to use a one-product company as an example and to work down through the P&L. The understanding of the historical trend informs the forecast for each line:

- **Sales:** What has been the long-term growth for the market historically, what have been the drivers and how are these expected to change going forward? Will the company's market share expand or contract? Do these estimated growth rates look out of line with past results? What is guidance? Is FX translation going to have an impact, and has it affected historical growth?

- **Gross margin:** What is the recent record, what has been the long-term history, and what has been guidance in the sector? Is the company benefitting from increased scale, is the company importing input parts or goods for resale, and will FX movements or commodity price changes have an impact? What assumptions are required for the cost of labour?

- **SG&A:** Are admin costs rising or falling as a percentage of sales, and is this reasonable? What is the depreciation charge, based on capex projections? Are advertising and promotional (A&P) spend forecasts consistent with the growth in market share? Are labour inflation and FX assumptions consistent with the cost of goods sold?

- **EBIT:** Do projected margins look sensible viewed in the context of recent trends, and five- and ten-year averages? Are the estimates consistent with trends in sales and costs, with FX moves, and with the sector?

- **Interest:** Calculated from the cash flow and net debt position, and the existing debt structure. Check for maturities, interest rates and FX rates.

- **Associates:** Use consensus or your own forecasts to calculate the associates line and ensure FX is not a factor. Are associates shown gross or net of tax (e.g., UK)?

- **Profit before tax:** An arithmetic calculation, and a point at which a sense check is possible.

- **Tax rate:** Check the company's past P&L tax rates, past cash tax paid, and any guidance. Is the tax assumption consistent with the geographic sales and margin assumption? For example, if European profits are the fastest growing part of the business, will the tax rate have to rise correspondingly as the tax rates there are higher? If capex is increasing, does the tax rate reflect the benefit? What is company guidance?

- **Profit after tax:** An arithmetic calculation, and another point at which a sense check is possible.

- **Minorities:** Is the minority calculation consistent with the top line assumptions?

- **Preference dividends:** A simple calculation, rarely applicable nowadays.

- **Earnings:** An arithmetic result.

- **EPS:** Check calculation of average number of shares in issue, have there been any options issued or buybacks during the year, or are they expected? It's important to be consistent and have the same assumptions here and in the cash-flow forecast.

CASH FLOW AND BALANCE SHEET

The cash-flow forecasts are often very revealing – it is surprising how few analysts produce these properly.

The cash-flow projections follow a similar line-by-line careful estimation, and the balance sheet is simply a function of the shares issued or bought back, profits retained (after dividends), and currency moves. One also ought to factor in any revaluations, notably, pension fund deficits, but these can be incredibly tricky to forecast. I generally only produce a summary forecast balance sheet (equity and net debt summaries), as I don't think a detailed line-by-line balance sheet adds much, but it's not particularly difficult to do. Sometimes it can be helpful to consider how the balance sheet looks three years out.

By doing the detailed projections first, the valuation is then a straightforward matter of calculation, and there is less risk of solving for the right answer in the estimates. If the valuation is done first, there is always a temptation to over- or under-shoot on the assumptions to fit the case, which is why I prefer to do the numbers first, then complete the valuation ratios.

The key issues are to understand clearly the drivers; the assumptions inherent in the forecasts and how these might change over time; and the sensitivity of profits, balance sheet and cash flow to such changes. That then allows you to form a view on the likely impact on the valuation if your forecasts are incorrect.

I place emphasis on the range of forecasts, the likelihood of being in that range, and the sensitivities that result. If there is a 10% chance that profits could fall by 80%, and consequently that debt would increase above covenants, then that is a much more serious proposition than a 20% chance of profits falling by 50%.

I cannot stress enough that forecasting is more of an art than a science. Having a model with a million lines of code is not necessarily likely to lead you to the right answer. In fact, I would argue that it's much more likely to be misleading and even worse to give you a false sense of comfort that you are right. In my experience, the back of the fag packet calculation almost invariably gives you a close enough answer, but the discipline of building a model with assumptions on a line-by-line basis through P&L and cash flow helps ensure that you have not missed anything.

Hence, for me, the construction of a model is an integral part of my research process. I always test the validity of my model's results, however, by doing my 'back of a fag packet' check, to make sure the assumptions are sensible. Bob Cowell, founder of Makinson Cowell, told me that he checked the top three analysts' models for one of his clients, an oil major. None of the three models worked. All three had inherent errors, significant ones – the companies were too complex and the analysts had models with hundreds of lines which were simply too unwieldy.

Keeping it simple is safest, unless you are prepared to devote sufficient resources towards keeping it accurate. The extra precision is, in my experience, simply not worth the effort and usually proves illusory. Indeed, academic studies suggest that most spreadsheets contain errors, a high proportion of which are serious.

FORECASTS

Analysts on both buy and sell sides often look at their forecasts relative to consensus. This is one of the more critical analytical parameters and one of the most important reasons for having analysts. But the forecasts are subject to a huge range of external factors. Very few companies accurately predict their own profit for the year, let alone their cash flow. What is useful as a supplement to the central estimate is the range of likely outcomes; a stock which will likely make £100m pre-tax +/– £10m is worth significantly more than one which will likely make £100m, or £110m if things go really well, but only £60m if things go badly.

RELIABILITY OF SELL-SIDE FORECASTS AND SEASONALITY

Sell-side analysts are time-pressured, much more so today, when they have a far wider coverage, than in the days when I started. This means they are on the lookout for quick wins and short-term trades, and have little time to devote to basic housekeeping when doing forecasts. One issue that frequently catches them out is the timing of Easter, which can play havoc with year-on-year growth rates when it moves from Q1 to Q2 or vice versa.

Another is basic housekeeping, like counting up the number of weeks in the year, or checking quarterly schedules. A good example is when Manchester United's Q3 2017 results slightly disappointed the market. Two bulge bracket firms reported that broadcasting revenue growth was lower than expected because they played one fewer Premier League home game owing to the timing of the schedule. These analysts had not bothered to count how many home games would fall in the next quarter when doing their quarterly forecasting. This is sloppy, but sloppiness is not unusual.

FORECASTING TRICKS, SENSE CHECKING

It's quite hard to construct sensible forecasts, and much more difficult for the private investor than the professional in an institution or an investment bank/brokerage. For the private investor, it's probably best to check the consensus (usually readily available from reading the press and stock-specific blogs like Seeking Alpha) and then asking if the forecasts make sense by cross-checking with comps and using common sense. That's a surprisingly effective strategy.

For the professional, it's a lengthy and tedious bottom-up process. I quite often take a selection of brokers' forecasts and do a line-by-line check to see how my assumptions compare with the sector experts. I also look carefully at the distribution of forecasts and that can sometimes tell you the degree of doubt in the market – especially if one looks beyond the current year, where sell-side analysts are heavily influenced by IR feedback.

Figure 9.1: EBITDA estimates range

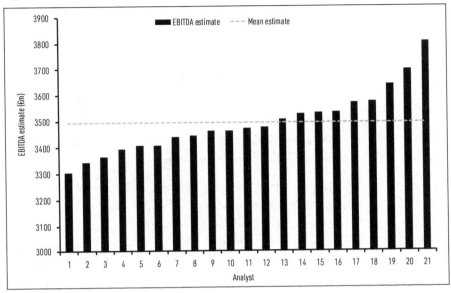

Source: Behind the Balance Sheet. Data from Bloomberg.

Figure 9.1 shows the distribution of estimates for a European industrial company's EBITDA. There has been no guidance from the company but there is a very tight clustering of estimates, with a mean of 3,494 (the constant light grey bars), a median of 3,471, a high of 3,305 and a low of 3,305. I download the estimates, sort them, and then look at the shape of the curve. There are three analysts with estimates significantly above the pack, and three analysts with estimates just 4% or more below the consensus, with the high having a significantly greater divergence from the mean.

I would then ordinarily examine the top and bottom forecasts in greater detail, examine the spreadsheet, and possibly question the analysts involved as to the rationale behind their assumptions. If you work for a large institution, you usually have the advantage of being able to talk to all the brokers, whereas for smaller investors, the identity of the outliers may not be known.

This divergence has become more profound since the introduction of MiFID II, a regulatory development designed to make the cost of research more transparent and reduce costs to the end-investor – it's likely, in my view, to have the effect of reducing research choice and ultimately making it more expensive, thus favouring large investors.

Because my investment approach is to focus on forecasts, I probably spend more time on this part of the research than others. Using the consensus is not a bad place to start.

VALUATION

The basics of valuation are to understand today's valuation relative to history and how this valuation will likely move over time.

I tend not to focus too much on the valuation until I am comfortable with the forecasts. I know that some investors, and some great value investors, only use historic numbers and think that forecasting is a waste of time. That might be an effective approach for them, but I think valuations are essentially forward looking, so I feel that I have to understand the outlook. And I prefer to divorce my forecasting process from my examination of the valuation, to avoid my thinking being contaminated and solving for the right result.

The most important question is how my forecasts compare with the Street, particularly in the case of EPS, but also EBITDA, free cash flow and from this, the progression of enterprise value (EV). If I have higher EPS, EBITDA and free cash-flow estimates than consensus, then clearly the valuation one or two years out will look much more attractive on my numbers as not only will the earnings and cash flow be higher, but the enterprise value will be falling more quickly, and the EV/EBITDA and EV/sales ratios will similarly decline at a faster rate. The EV equals the market cap plus the debt (plus other adjustments), so if the debt is falling, the EV will similarly fall.

How confident am I in those forecasts and what is the sensitivity range around those? Often, this will hinge on the likely growth rate in volumes for a new product, or the degree to which prices can be increased. Then it's a matter of deciding a central case and, on the basis of that, how much could the share price appreciate and what would it be in a bear and bull scenario.

HISTORIC VALUATION

It's important to put current valuation in the context of historical range, although I think that investors in the US are overly obsessive about this. Sell-side US analysts are fond of producing price targets based on past P/E ratios. In my view, this is overly simplistic, as businesses change, growth rates change and past multiples may no longer be appropriate.

Although the past context is certainly an important reference frame, the multiple is also affected by market valuation changes. Hence, I prefer to look at the P/E relative to the local market vs its historical range. Figure 9.2 illustrates that Procter & Gamble (PG) has traded in a fairly narrow range relative to the market.

Figure 9.2: Procter & Gamble historic relative P/E

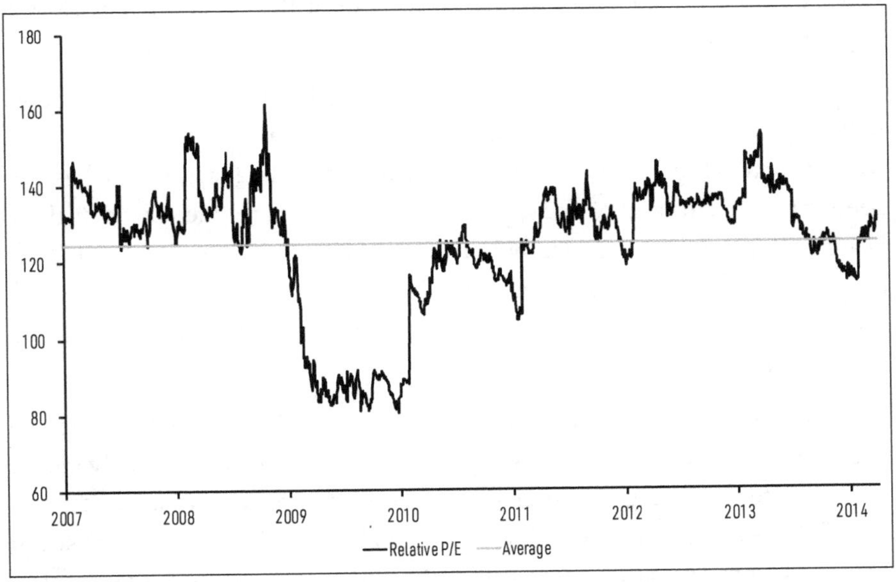

Source: Behind the Balance Sheet. Using IBES estimates from Sentieo.

For cyclical businesses, P/E ratios are not helpful at extremes and the EV to sales ratio measure discussed below makes a better tool, especially when used on a relative basis, but it has the important disadvantage of being extremely difficult to calculate. While US analysts tend to focus on the historic ranges for P/E and occasionally price-to-book ratio, I find the historic ranges more helpful for PE relative to the market, EV/EBITDA, and price-to-book ratio, as a longer-term reference point.

The simplest measure to look at is P/E relative, and I like to look at this for years zero, one, two and, if possible, three. Note that few people bother to do a year three forecast, but I like to make a stab at this number. Clearly, it's hard enough to produce an accurate forecast for this year or the next, so this is not much more than a stab in the dark; nevertheless, it is useful as it forces you to think a little further ahead and at the likely trends.

If the EPS is growing faster than the market, the stock will generally trade at a premium in year one. This premium tends to fade over time; the year one and year two numbers can then be put in the context of past history. It's important to remember that the P/E relative the market was looking at five years ago could have been in a similar context, that of above market growth – looking back, we know the actual results, but at the time, the market was relying on forecasts.

The better way of doing this is to compare the P/E relative one year forward with the same variable in the past, but this is not always available. I have worked with such a tool, when we built our own database, but it has not been replicated in any of the brokerage systems I have encountered; there is a useful, albeit quite crude, tool on Bloomberg though, called the EQRV (Equity Relative Valuation). Care should always be taken with the metrics on Bloomberg and FactSet, as the relative multiples may be calculated on different indices.

The comparison of forecast multiples with historic levels should be treated with extreme care. It's really best applied to companies with a fairly steady growth rate and a high predictability. The same constraints apply to EV/EBITDA – more usually considered on an absolute than relative basis, and hence subject to vagaries of market levels as well as changes in interest rates – and price-to-book ratios. The price-to-book ratio has the advantage that it usually trades in a narrower range and so the comparability factor is usually greater. But, again, its validity is subject to changes in the return generated on assets – if the return on capital is falling, you would not expect to pay the same multiple of book as the stock previously enjoyed.

There is one practical constraint with the EV/EBITDA calculations which is generally poorly managed by standard systems like Bloomberg, and which is not always factored in by analysts. Because you are using EV looking forward, it's necessary to roll forward the EV calculation as well as the EBITDA. Hence, if the business is highly cash generative, the debt will be paid down over time, shrinking the EV and reducing the EV/EBITDA ratio. I tend to use the average debt in the calculation and, where minorities or associates are significant, I forecast these and apply a constant multiple to roll forward for the EV calculation. This is perhaps overly technical, but the difference in valuation for a cash generative business can be significant and it's important to roll forward accurately.

PROBLEMS WITH TRADITIONAL MEASURES

The traditional valuation technique employed by a stockbroker is to focus on the current year P/E. This use of P/E ratios (or EV/EBITDA multiples), effectively as a shorthand for the DCF valuation of a company's cash flows, is inherently flawed, because too much emphasis is placed on this year one forecast. This valuation method tends to work quite well for companies subject to limited change, especially if they are widely followed, have been around for a long period, and have many comparables.

This technique tends to work less well for cyclical businesses. To understand the true value of these business, it is critical to have a good understanding of whether today's margins are high or low in relation to the long-term normalised margin. The industry or business may well have improved in quality, such that today's margins, even if they are higher than the average in the last 10+ years, are likely to persist in future. That is a perfectly valid hypothesis which can justify paying a high multiple for peak-looking margins. But it's dangerous because margins tend to be mean reverting in the long term (albeit US margins remained stubbornly high for ten years post the GFC).

Similarly, this technique is less reliable when looking at companies which:

- are subject to significant change

- have a shorter market history

- have fewer quoted comparables

- have a limited analyst following

- don't have consensus estimates

- have a longer-term view of profits because they are investing heavily in marketing in the short term.

I discuss the advantages and disadvantages of various measures below, but the understandable focus on the current valuation multiple is a potentially dangerous simplification.

VALUATION TECHNIQUES

I review below some of the standard valuation techniques and explain my personal preferences.

Everyone has their own favourite valuation ratios and different types of company often have their own ascribed valuation measures preferred by the market. I generally use a fairly consistent set of ratios, although I may give added weight to particular ratios depending on the company, the level of valuation and the particular circumstances.

P/E AND EV/EBITDA

If you were to have only one valuation tool, it should be P/E. The price/earnings ratio is the simplest and most useful tool for business valuation.

It's shorthand for a DCF valuation using current profitability levels. I always use it in conjunction with EV/EBITDA, as stocks can often look cheap on P/E because they have too low a tax rate or large amounts of debt, both of which are flagged up by EV/EBITDA (as EBITDA is before interest and tax).

I like to look at P/E relative to the local market, and look for a measure which is both low relative to history and falling (because its earnings are growing faster than the market). In current markets, it's rare to find an absolutely low level of P/E – they do exist, but can be value traps. As highlighted earlier, for forward EV/EBITDA calculations, it's better to have your own forecasts, so that you can factor in the level of debt one and two years forward etc., rather than relying on the consensus.

NORMALISED P/E

The Shiller P/E ratio, or CAPE (cyclically adjusted P/E), is quite commonly used when valuing markets – this is simply a valuation based on ten-year average earnings, which reflects the fact that earnings are cyclical and market valuations should be assessed on a longer-term basis.

The same is possible for companies – one can look at the ten-year average EPS and see how the stock is valued on that basis, or do a P/E on normalised earnings. I usually look at five-year and ten-year average margins as the context for the margin today. This is effectively the same measure, examined through a different lens.

SECTOR RELATIVE

Comparing the valuation measures with comparable stocks in the home and other markets, and comparing the company valuation with its sector averages, is a simple check which helps us to understand how the market views the company in context. Sometimes the earnings growth trajectory is completely different to the relative valuation, as in the example below which I have borrowed from a broker, whose anonymity I shall preserve to save embarrassment.

Table 9.1: Relative valuation of leisure stocks (mid-2016)

	TUI (p)	Growth	Thomas Cook (p x 10)	Growth
2016	78.6		71.2	
2017	101.7	29.4%	105.9	48.7%
2018	112.1	10.2%	133.5	26.1%
2019	122.4	9.2%	146.7	9.9%

Source: Broker whose anonymity is being preserved.

Thomas Cook, whose EPS is multiplied by ten in the table, had just had a profits warning and was considered a low-quality stock. Meanwhile TUI, whose earnings are shown in pence in the table, was considered a higher quality business. Thomas Cook had a 2017 P/E of 6.9× vs 10.5× for TUI.

Now, the market did not believe the Thomas Cook forecasts, but there was a significant amount of disbelief inherent in a 50%+ gap in the relative rating – especially as Thomas Cook was projected not only to bounce back faster in 2017, but to grow at a much faster rate thereafter. Comparison with peers is an essential part of the valuation process.

And, of course, it would be necessary to do this comparison on more than one basis, but this has been shortened for simplicity. I have only shown the P/E comparison. In spite of this valuation differential, Thomas Cook went on to underperform TUI significantly, until it finally collapsed in 2019. Therein lies the danger of relying on valuation.

THE EV-TO-SALES RATIO – AN UNDERRATED VALUATION TOOL

Enterprise value to sales is probably one of the most underrated valuation measures, partly because it is not so useful in isolation. It is most useful at extremes – a valuation of sub 0.15 is indicative of a very cheap stock, whereas a multiple of over 12× usually means an extremely expensive stock (obviously there are exceptions at both ends of the spectrum).

EV/sales is the third measure I look at, after P/E and EV/EBITDA. It's especially useful because of its lack of popularity. Even some quite sophisticated investors are relatively unfamiliar with it. I met Masroor (Mas) Siddiqui, now the managing partner of hedge fund Naya Management LLP, but then a partner at TCI, and we were discussing valuation ratios (OK, it was not that exciting a conversation) and he thought I was joking when I mentioned EV/sales – it was clearly not a tool he used.

Finding a tool which nobody else uses can be a really useful strategy in the investment world. There are a number of reasons why EV/sales is so helpful:

SALES DON'T LIE

It is extremely difficult, even for a crooked CFO, to fudge the sales number. Of course, it can be done, especially to draw future sales into the current year. This can be achieved by changing the cut-off date for year-end shipments, for example, by invoicing before goods are shipped over a year-end. You simply send out the invoice on December 31, although the goods are not dispatched until January 2.

But such cut-off tricks, as they are known, are really hard to implement over an extended period. Of course, if the sales are being manipulated, the earnings will be too, and by more. There are a limited number of ways of manipulating a sales number and they are mainly fraudulent, so it should generally be a reliable measure.

PRICE-TO-SALES IS NOT A USEFUL MEASURE

I use enterprise value in preference to the price-to-sales ratio, which for some unfathomable reason is more common. The price-to-sales ratio does not take into account debt and other forms of liability, for example, the sales may not be 100% yours if there are minority interests. Sales is a pre-interest number and hence the level of debt needs to be factored in. I quite often see the S&P price-to-sales ratio being quoted, and it makes little sense.

STABLE MEASURE

EV/sales is the result of the division of two large numbers – it tends for most companies to be an extremely stable factor. For some cyclical companies it can move quite a bit, but much less than EV/EBITDA and far less than P/E. It is therefore a relatively stable number with a limited range – that makes it incredibly useful for determining a company's valuation relative to history.

MOVEMENTS ARE MEANINGFUL

Consequently, if you have a relatively stable ratio, and if that then hits an extreme value, it is likely telling you something. If the stock has never been this cheap on EV/sales in the past, has something negative happened to alter its long-term fundamental outlook?

If the company and its fundamentals are relatively unchanged, a low level of EV/sales usually reflects a drop in earnings which may well be temporary. If you buy the stock for the long term, and the earnings come back, you should see a useful rerating.

TWO MOVING PARTS

One reason people find EV/sales tricky is that you need to encapsulate two moving parts in the ratio: you need to assess the ratio not only relative to history, but also in relation to its margin and sales growth. Having two drivers which are moving complicates the assessment, but it's straightforward with a little familiarity.

VALUING LOSS-MAKERS

You can't beat EV/sales for a company which is loss-making. You might be able to use EV/EBITDA if there is a positive EBITDA, but if you are valuing a start-up internet business, EV/sales is very useful. It's also incredibly useful when looking at highly cyclical companies, for example, the auto industry or airlines. Auto analysts frequently refer to EV/sales in their reports, although sadly they are an exception.

EV/SALES IS A USEFUL LONG-TERM MEASURE

Companies are sometimes rerated or derated over a period of several years. Because EV/EBITDA and P/E are more volatile numbers, EV/sales can be a useful signal of a longer-term derating or rerating trend. It is also a much better signal, especially relative to the market of bottoms or tops in a stock.

Unfortunately, this is quite complicated to calculate and therefore relatively rarely used. I don't think there are even systems generally available to calculate this precisely – tools like Bloomberg are, in my view, not sufficiently refined in their valuation calculations to use reliably for this purpose. One area where we may have gone backwards in the last 20 years!

NO ADJUSTMENTS FOR ONE-OFFS

Unlike P/E, EV/sales does not need sophisticated assumptions about the repeatability or otherwise of restructuring charges and similar one-offs. It is fairly simple to calculate, although the EV calculation can be trickier in more complicated companies.

EXAMPLE OF EV/SALES COMPARISON

Let me illustrate its utility with a practical example: I was surprised to calculate that Amazon was trading at a pretty modest EV/sales valuation, yet sales were growing really quickly. Indeed, when I projected Amazon's EV/sales in 2014, I found they would be at a discount to the US market two years out, which I thought was ridiculous for a company with its market presence, brand and growth prospects. So it proved.

Consider Table 9.2 comparing the historical valuations of Amazon and Walmart. Note that, for simplicity, I have not done all the adjustments to the EV calculation that I would recommend, and I shall return to the question of calculating EV separately.

Table 9.2: Amazon vs Walmart

	Amazon	Walmart	A:W relative
Trailing P/E	n/a	13.3	n/a
5-year average	562.5	14.5	38.8
Forward P/E	130.9	13.7	9.6
5-year average	178.9	13.5	13.2
EV/EBITDA	37.1	7.1	5.2
5-year average	40.3	8.0	5.1
EV/Sales	2.5	0.5	4.8
5-year average	2.1	0.6	3.5
Margin	0.9%	5.3%	6.1
5-year average	1.6%	5.8%	3.6
5-year sales growth	160%	15%	10.6

Source: Own calculations, Yahoo, Companies, Bloomberg and FactSet Consensus.

Amazon obviously then looked incredibly expensive on earnings-based valuations, as the company was investing in future growth which was depressing current profitability. Even on EV/EBITDA, the multiple is stratospheric at around 40×, or 5×, that of Walmart. On EV/sales too, Amazon is valued at 5× Walmart. But consider sales growth and margins:

- Walmart had grown sales 15% in the previous five years vs over ten times as fast at Amazon, whose sales had increased by over 160%. Five years prior, Walmart had sales which were 12× those of Amazon, and in the previous 12 months, that multiplier had shrunk to 5×. Look forward five years and if the same rates of growth prevail, Walmart will be just twice the size of Amazon.

- The margin picture is distorted by the development of AWS, Amazon's then-new cloud service business, which I assumed had negatively affected margins. On an underlying comparison of the retail margins, Amazon would have seen growth while Walmart would have seen its margins shrink. This picture seemed likely to continue.

Perhaps the most interesting conclusion from evaluating Amazon on EV/sales was that its valuation would fall below the US market on this measure in the following 18 months – if you believed that Amazon would never make a profit, then that would make sense, but if you believed that Amazon had the potential to be a much more profitable business than a conventional retailer, or anything close to the average US-quoted stock, that made no sense.

I will not buy a company with an EV/sales of over 12×, as I have not yet found a company whose growth or profitability of both justified such a high valuation – I am sure they exist, but they don't offer me a sufficient margin of safety. Conversely, it's extremely rare to find a company with an EV/sales ratio of under 0.15× which is not cheap.

EV/sales is therefore at the least a useful sense check as to whether you may be under/over paying for a stock with temporarily depressed/inflated margins. Tracking a company's EV/sales over time can often give a much clearer picture of where it lies in its earnings cycle than looking at more conventional valuation measures. Finally, absolute levels of EV/sales can signal an under or over valuation much more clearly than EV/EBITDA or P/E.

EV/UNIT OF CAPACITY

I like to use physical measurements of value wherever possible. I find it much easier to think of the valuation of a hotel chain or cruise company at so much per room or, as in the case of one notable Indian IPO, valuing the business at so much per employee (the IPO was totally hyped and investors had not bothered to check the number of people employed in this start-up – naturally, it crashed).

It makes sense, especially within a sector, to compare valuations on a unit-of-capacity basis. It's one of those simple reality checks, and it's somewhat surprising that investors don't make more of this. Of course, it works best when you have a simple homogeneous sector, electricity generation is a good example, but it can also give you a sense check in some surprising sectors, airlines and autos, for example.

Of course, a Mercedes sells for more than a Nissan, so it would be very surprising if Mercedes could not make more money per car. But it would be quite reasonable to compare two volume manufacturers. One may have low current production – and hence, low profitability – and could be very cheap on a unit-of-capacity basis, even though it might look dearer on a simple P/E measure; if you then have confidence that a new model introduction will push sales up, it could represent a buying opportunity.

Similarly, looking at the EV/car production capacity over time, forward and backward can give you a useful sense check – if capacity is growing, and the hump of capex has passed, the EV could shrink quite quickly with free cash flow while the capacity figure would be rising, and the EV/unit could fall quite sharply. Looking back, you can get a sense of how the market has valued the business and the implications for its future valuation.

EV RELATIVE TO REPLACEMENT COST

Electricity generators are another good example – I attended a breakfast meeting quite a few years ago with the CEO of Drax, at the Lanesborough Hotel in West London. To my surprise, I found myself sitting next to Ross Turner, CIO of Pelham, a then $3bn long short equity hedge fund, and his utility analyst. Ross is a personal friend (as opposed to a work friend), and chatting after the meeting, we found we were on opposite sides of the argument.

Ross was short – as I recall he felt that input costs were rising and the company could fall short of forecasts. I thought he was right, but that didn't matter. I was there because I had identified that the EV of Drax was just over £1bn (or around £4/share in the chart), which was a fraction of the cost to build that size of power station (Drax is a 4GW station, the largest in the UK). Fuelling my bull case, management were then switching part of the capacity from coal to biomass, so that the business would benefit from environmental subsidies.

Figure 9.3 tells the story – it was indeed a buying signal, even though the profits were on a downward trend in the short term. Note that, for power stations, it's essential to include the environmental liabilities as part of the EV calculation, otherwise nuclear capacity looks too cheap. Note also that the price of Drax has since collapsed, with the shares trading at a discount to book, because of fears about biomass capacity and its earnings power.

In early 2020, the company was valued at around £1bn again, which looks low in the context of replacement costs, but it has been hit by the withdrawal of a renewables income stream in the budget and by an EU state aid inquiry. One broker puts the liquidation value at over £1/share.

Figure 9.3: Drax share price

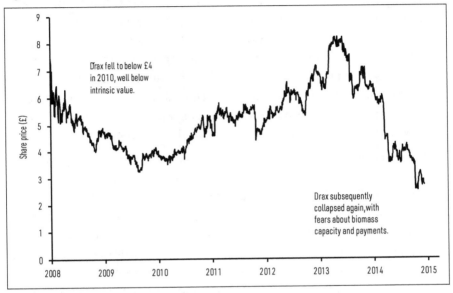

Source: Behind the Balance Sheet from Sentieo data.

This use of replacement cost is a useful tool, and one which is employed in some of the CROCI (cash return on capital invested) style analysis – there they use it to assess the trend in cash returns over time and how the returns will fade. But it's also a very good sense check, where it's possible to identify the replacement cost or the alternative value of an asset. Property assets, especially in smaller businesses, are a great example. See the panel for a discussion of how this might play out in practice, using the food retailers in 2014 as an example.

Gone are the days when corporate raiders like Jeffrey Sterling could buy a department store for less than the value of its property holdings, at least in theory. I wrote this piece in 2014, when supermarkets like Morrison and Sainsbury were trading at less than the value of their property. It was an interesting conundrum as, while it made little sense, Sainsbury had been trading at a discount for years and in spite of attempts to break it up. The market then thought that the property was probably not worth what the valuers said it was, and that Sainsbury (which then had quite a lot of leverage through debt, pension deficit and particularly off balance sheet debt in the form of lease commitments) would be forced into a declining cash flow spiral. A supermarket price war – with the encroachment of Aldi and Lidl from below, as well as Waitrose from above and Ocado laterally – would drive margins down and Sainsbury would be forced to cut the dividend.

The shares were trading 310–320p going into the results, and my simple view then was that there was a lot of risk in Sainsbury. The CEO, who was very good, had just left – I thought it could be rats leaving the sinking ship – a price war made no sense, but had happened many times before, and the property had been valued at a 4.7% yield, which looked much higher than the realisable value. What the company needed to do was to stop investing in additional stores and try to generate some free cash. Its problem was that growth in the sales line was needed to fund the business, as suppliers credit is a huge advance to the business.

As a complete aside, note how Sainsbury is one of those smart companies with a funny year-end – bet your socks that it's average working capital is a lot higher than the year-end position.

So, if the sales line shrinks, creditors will fall, and the cash required by the business will actually increase. And of course declining sales reduce purchasing power and the long-term gross margin, which is why all the grocers are hellbent on expansion.

A high level of short interest was a potential attraction, but one of the short sellers was Lansdown, who are among the smartest people in the market. In the long term, Sainsbury will not be trading at a discount to the value of its property. The shares will be rated differently when the competitive environment abates and the property will be revalued, likely downward.

Given the uncertainties, I passed on Sainsbury. Eighteen months later, I was actually betting against Sainsbury as a short at a lower price.

EV/EMPLOYEE

Looking at EV per employee is another useful measure. Tibbett and Britten, the UK logistics player, reached a low of £1,000/employee. It wasn't a great company and it had a lot of employees, but this seemed ridiculously cheap – eventually it was taken over. A low EV/employee ratio can indicate an opportunity either to cut employees, an overly cheap valuation, or a structurally challenged company.

A venture capital fund raising for Dropbox valued the business at $60m per employee – probably daft, although funnily enough, I could just about get my head round that calculation. My friends at RIT (Rothschild Investment Trust) participated in that one and actually made a lot of money – a good illustration that there are no set rules in the investment business.

When I was looking at professional services companies, I found the revenue per fee earner was a helpful statistic and, interestingly, one firms used internally. This further confirmed to me that EV/employee can be a useful measure.

Most companies indicate the number of people they employ; US companies are not required to do so, but a look at their graduate careers site will usually give you a rough idea. Looking at the EV/employee over time and relative to peers can give you a useful insight and sense check.

FREE CASH-FLOW YIELD

Many investors focus on a company's free cash-flow yield, i.e., the amount of cash it generates relative to market capitalisation. I like to think of it as EBITDA less working capital investment, less maintenance capex, less other adjustments (such as tax etc.). Each is explored below:

EBITDA

EBITDA is a fairly conventional measure of performance and requires little further elaboration here.

WORKING CAPITAL

Working capital is slightly more difficult. In theory, it's simple when looking at historic free cash flow (FCF), but beware of those companies with a miraculous release of working capital at the year-end. Looking forward, some analysts project working capital on the basis of last year's inventory turn and debtor and creditor days; I prefer to use the average over an extended number of years. The issue with a large multi-currency, multi-division company is that working capital is quite unpredictable and extremely hard to get right.

CAPEX

Capex is another parameter which can cause problems. Companies that are growing generally have to invest in working capital to finance sales growth, and in capex to deliver that growth. In assessing FCF, you should really adjust for this capex growth and look at maintenance capex – the level of capex required to keep the assets in a steady state. For the increasing number of companies with significant tech exposure, this should also include the necessary investment in intangibles.

It's difficult, however, to calculate maintenance capex. Sometimes the CFO may tell you the answer, which is fine if you are an analyst at a bulge bracket bank or major buy-side institution, but it's much harder to do this from the outside. And it's debatable how precisely even the CFO can estimate this. Most capital expenditure forms classify the spend as replacement, growth, development, or other, but the asset is often replaced with a better model, so there is an element of growth in the replacement, which is hard to calculate.

One of the best approximations is the depreciation charge (plus software and other amortisation as appropriate). Good companies will depreciate assets a little faster than they strictly need to, so depreciation less 10–15% can work as a sense check, especially if the company is in an industry which is seeing technological development where the cost of assets is falling. In companies where there is a high turnover of assets, e.g., certain asset-intensive leasing businesses, disposal profits should also be factored in.

This can be cross-checked by looking at average capex/sales and PPE/sales ratios over a number of years, say between five and seven. The depreciation charge and capex (plus additions to intangibles as appropriate) this year relative to sales can then be compared with the five-year averages. Another way of doing this is to take the average PPE/sales ratio and apply it to the sales growth this year; deduct the result from this year's capex to reach another proxy for maintenance capex. An average of a number of factors (depreciation, capex less estimated growth capex, average capex to sales times this year's sales) may give a better result for the maintenance capex estimate.

OTHER ADJUSTMENTS

- Calculating other adjustments is equally tricky. The historical tax paid can be derived from the cash flow, either read off in UK accounts or calculated from the US filings, but the forecasting is much more complex. For example, the tax paid next year will relate to the current year's tax charge +/– adjustments for deferred tax. There can be a number of other adjustments required in addition.

Calculating FCF is therefore quite a difficult affair, requiring a great deal of care. It's a number which can be quite far out, as it is a relatively small number in relation to the sales base or asset base of the business, and errors can accumulate at each level of the calculation. It's an essential tool, but not always a hugely reliable one.

Unsurprisingly, there is usually a much larger range of analysts' estimates of FCF than of EPS. Solving for a FCF yield is also a possibility, where one calculates the FCF yield that you think the stock should offer, translate that into a FCF value, and estimate how likely it is that the company can generate that sort of level of FCF on an ongoing basis

FAILINGS AND PRACTICAL USES
OF DISCOUNTED CASH FLOW

Conventional investment theory suggests that DCF is the best method of valuing a business – estimate the cash flows that a business produces, assign a terminal value at the end of the forecast period and discount back to today's value.

In practice, there are huge complexities in doing this – aside from the intellectual challenges of choosing the correct discount rate and the right valuation method to calculate the terminal value. And then constructing the cash-flow forecasts is inherently problematic, especially the further out you forecast.

Sophisticated investors often say that they focus on a company's FCF yield, i.e., the amount of cash it generates relative to its market capitalisation. This, of course, is the basis of the academic valuation, using a DCF. The only problem with this in practice is that analysts have a lot of trouble predicting the next quarter or next year's EPS, and they generally don't have a clue what the cash flows are likely to be in ten years' time.

There are a few rare times when I shall resort to using a DCF as an aid to company valuation:

- To value a business in its early stages. For example, Eurotunnel when it was a construction project. It was initially loss-making, indeed it had zero revenue, and the only way of assessing the likely value was to do a DCF. In the case of Eurotunnel, it was so clearly worthless that no DCF was actually needed. In the mid-1990s, I persuaded Julian Robertson's hedge fund, Tiger, to go short of Eurotunnel, to the tune of several hundred million – they made a 90% return and were able to use the cash to invest on the long side. James Lyle, the manager responsible, was persuaded to do the trade when I explained to him why I didn't need a DCF!

- A DCF can be helpful when doing a sensitivity analysis – the relative change in valuations when looking at two or three different scenarios.

- A DCF can be helpful in ascertaining what the value is of future growth potential vs the value of the existing business; when too much of the value is being ascribed to the growth opportunity, this is clearly inherently riskier. For example, where there is the prospect of a blockbuster new product, like a drug, one can look at the value of the next ten years' cash flows without that product and the terminal value. If too little of the valuation is supported by the next ten years' cash flows, then it may be an inherently risky investment.

- A DCF can sometimes be helpful in framing a valuation, for example, when looking at the valuation of the Universal music business vs Spotify, seen in the first chapter. But this is exceptional.

Hence, DCF is not a major part of my armoury, but it does appear alongside a range of much better tools.

DIVIDEND YIELD

I have never considered dividend yield as a particularly helpful method of valuing a business. Indeed, I don't consider dividend yield as a measure of business valuation, but as a guide to stock returns. The dividend is a product of earnings, pay-out ratio and cash available, and it's often used to support a valuation when it's not really justified – a good example is a Macquarie vehicle that tried to come to the UK stock market in the mid 2000s.

This entity had three great businesses – the Isle of Man Steam Packet Company, a cash cow with limited competition; the second largest car park owner in Manhattan, of course, that had to be a good business; and the US airport luggage trolley company, Rent a Car, which had been enjoying a bounce in volumes after a sharp dip in profits post-9/11. The valuation was not that racy and there was a massive dividend yield – the only tricky problem was that the dividend was only fundable because capex had dipped to near zero. As soon as they had to think about buying a new ferry, it would be goodnight dividend. Although the valuation proposed for the business looked attractive on the basis of a high yield, I valued the constituents at half the proposed price.

The range of dividend forecasts can be useful when looking at dividends and yield, and particularly where income is important, for example, a private client portfolio. This range can also be considered for a sector and sometimes indicates that management have not signalled dividend policy sufficiently clearly. It can of course also reflect a number of analysts forecasting a dividend cut. If income is important, opportunity can lie in a stock where the policy has not clearly been communicated and where, as a result of profit growth, dividend can surprise on the upside.

One European broker study suggested that companies without a dividend policy have, in the past, been able to outperform those with a policy by over 20% between 2012 and 2016. The broker deduced that markets are efficient at pricing in expected future returns from stated dividend policies. Conversely, where there is no stated policy, pricing is inefficient, creating opportunity for active managers. This would be consistent with my strategy of screening for high variations in dividend forecasts, but I think it could equally be fairly random.

Dividend income has been a huge part of stock-market returns for the last 100+ years and it clearly cannot be ignored. I generally prefer growing dividends to large dividends, although an important attraction of the latter is that management find it more difficult to go out and blow the money on a daft acquisition and tend to be more disciplined about capex. Dividends can also be a good indication of quality and management priorities – the dividend aristocrat screen is a good example.

Another issue with dividends is taxation. I am an advocate of the Jeremy Siegel proposal that dividends, if reinvested, should not be taxed as income, but only taxed on the sale of the stock, albeit this could be tricky to administer.

I don't believe that dividend yield is a useful method of business valuation (I would argue that it's not really a valuation measure), and if a business hits trouble, the dividend is often one of the first things to disappear. I prefer other, more fundamental, measures of value.

PEAK MULTIPLES

For cyclical companies, I find it quite helpful to think of multiples of peak earnings (and trough earnings). This protects me from over-enthusiasm and ensures that I am not paying an historically high multiple relative to past peak operating performance. A lot of my valuation work is designed to introduce checks into my process, to ensure there is a margin of safety in the valuation.

PRICE-TO-BOOK RATIO

Book values are generally so low these days and prices so high that this ratio has fallen out of favour. Its utility has also been degraded by the increasing relevance of intangible assets to business prosperity. It's still useful for financials – notably property, but also insurance and banks. Clearly it gives you a sense of whether there are real assets to support the valuation, especially if you use the adjusted measure of price to tangible book, which I prefer. It gives me no comfort at all to pay a multiple of goodwill which is probably overvalued in the balance sheet.

Book values are sometimes unreliable and often not comparable, for example, the differences in the treatment of intangible assets under US GAAP and IFRS. US companies generally expense R&D as incurred, while European companies are allowed to capitalise and amortise certain development costs. Although amortisation may approximate to spend over time, they are often widely divergent for extended periods and of course the EBITDA multiple for a US and UK pharmaceutical company could be wildly different.

The other problem is in valuing the assets and liabilities on the balance sheet. Where the market capitalisation is close to the balance sheet value, I may well look to get further comfort on how realistic that balance sheet value is – usually the liabilities will be worth what they sit in the accounts at. Current assets can generally be valued at balance sheet value. Valuing long-term assets is trickier.

Fixed assets can be thought of as property and other assets. For property, if the assets were bought a long time previous and have not been revalued, it may be necessary to do some further detailed work to ascertain if there may be some significant hidden value. For other assets, it is necessary to understand the nature of the assets and the industry. Usually, replacement cost will be significantly higher and the assets may enjoy an uplift, but for some capital goods industries, the replacement costs may have been falling and the assets are not worth carrying value.

Investments may be difficult to value, especially if they are in private companies (more common now, with many large groups having venture arms). Intangible assets are much harder to value. I consider goodwill as simply an accounting entry, so the issue is whether the balance sheet values are accurate – does the capitalised software or R&D have a real value? And are there any brands or similar IP which have a value but are not on the balance sheet? Generally, the rule I use is to think of book value as lying somewhere between liquidation value and replacement cost.

The price/book ratio has the advantage that it usually trades in a narrower range than, say, the P/E. Hence, the comparability relative to historical ranges is better, but its validity is subject to changes in the returns generated on the assets – if the return on capital is falling, you would not expect to pay the same multiple of book as the stock previously enjoyed.

MEASURING VALUE BY TIME HORIZON

To measure value, you can first look at asset value, then a value based on current earnings power, then on a value based on cash flow. One tool which can be quite useful in thinking about a stock is to look at how much of today's value is based on the foreseeable future, say, the next five to ten years. Not that this is foreseeable really, but you can have a gut feel for the most likely range of outcomes for cash flows and how much is based on the value beyond a reasonable time horizon.

You can think of the value over the next ten years as being a DCF of the next ten years' earnings based on either a sensible assumption of growth rate or, for a cyclical company, the average sales and margin. What proportion of the valuation today does this represent? If it's under 10%, or even under 20%, how confident are you that the company will be around in ten- or 20-years' time? I find such analysis to be most helpful when valuations are high and I am concerned about overpaying.

MULTIPLE OF INVESTMENT

Another trick is to relate the current EV to the sum of the last five years' capital expenditure and investment in R&D. An innovative company that has temporarily lost its way may be a bargain if within this past R&D spend there are a couple of winners. Occasionally, a screen will pop out a company which has been oversold and offers real value on this measure. More often, it is another way of gaining comfort that there could be some downside protection – obviously a false comfort if the money has not been wisely spent.

CONCLUSIONS

There is a wide range of valuation parameters, and not all are appropriate for every company and every situation. The most important thing is to find a range of measures that you understand and feel comfortable with, and not to use a single measure in isolation. It's also important to fit the measure to the stock. If there is a lot of leverage involved, I would recommend always using EV/EBITDA as well as P/E. If there is a strong asset backing, for example in a property company, then price/book is often a helpful guide to value.

I always do a sense check – am I paying the highest multiple in history for peak earnings? Similarly, wherever possible, I try to relate the valuation to a physical unit of capacity and ensure it makes sense – if all else fails, EV/employee can be a useful sense check. Equally, relating the value of the enterprise to its sales base and to other companies with similar sales bases will sometimes raise a red flag.

Multiple valuation techniques can be employed, but I tend to only use a few that are appropriate for the occasion – I always use P/E, EV/EBITDA, EV/sales and FCF yield.

10
COMMUNICATING
THE IDEA

I HAVE NOW exhaustively researched the stock. I know everything I can in the time allocated about the industry, the company, its management, and its shareholders – why they own it and why non-holders don't. I have a detailed set of forecasts which are significantly different from the market and a good understanding of the likely range of stock price outcomes with associated probabilities. I now have to produce a research note. This must contain all the necessary information, be clear, and not too long.

It's essential to communicate the idea properly. Many firms, certainly all the sell-side ones, have a standard structure for notes. Buy-side firms, especially the smaller ones, tend to be more flexible and analysts are often free to include what they like in a note. I have developed a standard structure, although the contents vary according to the investment style and to the capital required; a $25m short might only require a five-line email, while a complex $100m+ long might need a 30-page note – I would not produce anything longer than that though.

In this chapter, I therefore set out the best way of structuring a standard note and communicating your ideas. I highly recommend the practice of producing a note, even for private investors, because the discipline of setting down your thoughts on paper forces you to think through the potential investment outcomes. It's also a useful reference point later, especially if things start to go wrong, as you can clearly see mistakes in your assumptions – such reference points can be great for determining whether to stick with the stock or cut and run.

THE STANDARD NOTE

My note structure has several components which are quite different from the standard layout employed on the sell-side. Generally, all sell-side notes are very similar in structure and content, and are not as effective as they should be.

I showed a large selection of broker notes to a friend who runs an advertising and media agency; as a specialist in communications, he was flabbergasted at how bad they all were. Even the good ones were only 'less hideously laid out'. I would contend that they are not a good starting point, and most internal notes I have seen are not significantly different.

My first point of difference is the front cover, which contains the investment message. This is usually three main reasons to own the stock and a couple of risks. I developed this many years ago at the suggestion of my then boss and still good friend, John Holmes. The stock then was BTR and the investment message was:

- BTR has grown by acquisition and cooking the books

- it has £10bn in revenue (a big number then) and cannot grow revenue much faster than its markets – say 5% if you are lucky

- it already makes industry-leading margins of 15%, so margins cannot go up

- warrants about to be issued will dilute earnings

- BTR, therefore, cannot grow and yet it stands at a premium rating. This will contract rapidly when the market wakes up to the reality of lacklustre growth.

It was this simple but powerful story that appeared on the front page – three bullet points (slightly longer than the above) were all that was required, and all an investor really needed to know. I have tried to continue this practice. My favourite sell-side cover had a large chart of the British Airways price-to-book ratio. It clearly indicated that stock was probably about to bottom, where it had bottomed in previous cycles, and showed the message, "Don't read this note, this chart is all you need".

A clear exposition of the investment thesis is therefore all that is required on the front cover. Most buy-side firms will require some additional data, for example, on valuation, liquidity, and internal forecasts relative to consensus. This is primarily to ensure that the portfolio manager can quickly make up his mind if he wants to turn the page and read more, but the simplicity of the primary investment message is the critical component – if it's not that simple, perhaps you should go back to the drawing board.

The next page generally has a five-year share price relative history and an explanation of why the shares have moved in the past.

The next page has my forecasts and all the valuation parameters required (EV/sales, EV/EBITDA, P/E, price/book, FCF yield, dividend yield, plus any others, depending on circumstances); this is for the past two years, the current year and two further forecast years. The third forecast year is illustrative but necessary to show that some thought has gone into the long-term growth of the company. I show clearly where my forecast sits relative to the range of sell-side brokers (hopefully outside!) and the consensus. This table also contains stock ticker, location, and liquidity data (this last factor being essential to the sizing decision).

Inside, my commentary on valuation will include comparatives and historical trends. I usually give a graphical history of 12-month forward EV/sales, EV/EBITDA and P/E. I also like to include some different valuation measures, as discussed in the last chapter – for example, EV/unit of capacity, value relative to replacement cost of assets, value relative to the last three to five years capex plus R&D. I usually comment on why the market has valued the company wrongly, if this is part of the investment case, and what could make this change. Sometimes this may not be obvious, other than that the market has underestimated the likely rate of growth.

I then include the usual sections found in any broker's note, as well as some features that are less commonly seen in sell-side notes:

- Investment thesis. A full exposition of the rationale for the investment. This includes how much money we are likely to make out of the idea, the probable range of outcomes, and what the risks are. It also may cover the style of investment, how it fits within the portfolio, and the projected time horizon, including any catalysts.

- It's important that this range of outcomes includes the risks and what might happen if the thesis does not play out. Imagine you bought the stock and it goes down – how and why could this happen? This is even more important in the case of shorts, as reaction is more difficult and managing a loss-making short position is painful.

- A suggested position size is useful, in that it calibrates confidence in the idea. Do you want to bet the ranch?

- What does the company do? Characteristics of the business and industry, as well as their financial returns.

- History of the business.

- Management – their background, current and historical shareholdings, as well as some detail on the incentive schemes, including KPIs.

- Accounting policies.

- Profit forecasts, assumptions, and where we differ from consensus and why; I often give a distribution of broker forecasts, sometimes even on a line-by-line basis.

- Cash-flow history and forecasts.

- Balance sheet analysis and review of debt, maturities and market value.

- Valuation data and commentary.

- Sustainability comment.

- Shareholders and short interest.

- Sell-side coverage and which analysts are competent. This helps the portfolio manager (PM) to do his own work by reading some sell-side research.

- Due diligence completed – detail on the work I have done, the work I have omitted (and why) and further work I would like to do.

- I also like to attach an *Economist* article on the company or a piece from the trade press. At a pinch, if nothing else is available, I would insert extracts from sell-side notes. The idea is to offer an impartial, outside perspective. It's very easy to become attached to your idea and offer a less than balanced view; using external sources ensures that colleagues have not been seduced by your argument.

Any note should be under 30 pages. Obviously page length is dependent on how many charts are used, and if there has been a need to use pictures or diagrams to explain the product, but generally the PM needs just enough detail to understand the business and the investment proposition. In any case, the note is usually a prelude to a more detailed discussion. Although if it is convincing enough, a position may be initiated without a face-to-face meeting, but typically at a starting size.

Some private investors reading this may be put off at the idea of writing down the thesis in this way. I had an interesting discussion with a group of private investors at a training course in the summer of 2019, before I edited this book, who were shocked by my suggestion that they should write a note. But once we discussed it, and I explained how it would help them avoid behavioural traps, they all agreed that they would give it a try. I admit that I don't do it for all my personal investments, but when I do, I make fewer mistakes.

PRICE TARGETS

Many sell-side firms use price targets, but I think the practice (common on the sell-side) of having a price target 20% above today's price and then constantly pushing it higher is rather a waste of energy.

The best discipline is to set a realistic target without any reference to today's share price. Preferably, that is accompanied by a range of outcomes: central case is they make no acquisitions, grow revenues by 7% pa, margins improve by 50bps over the next two years, and the shares should be worth 60% more in the next 18–24 months. If they also buy XYZ, then the target would be 20% higher. The risk, however, if a new entrant comes in, is 20% downside. As a special situation investor, I would normally look at longs which had upside of over 50% on a two-year time frame in a flat market.

An important benefit of the multiple outcome approach is that probabilities can be assigned to each case. These probabilities can then be weighted to derive an expected outcome. If the downside risk is very large, even with a low probability, that can drag down the expected gain and help to ensure the position size is appropriate – it's natural when buying a stock to assume that the best case outcome will result, and assigning probabilities and looking at expected outcomes helps dampen over-enthusiasm.

It's really important to recognise that you have no control over the timing of the share price appreciation. The market can take a long time to revalue a stock and recognise a change in potential – once the results are delivered and the cash has been generated, it's usually hard to argue, and obviously tables setting out the forecasts and the inherent valuation create a simple picture of how the share price might develop.

I include a price/valuation target which usually takes the form of an argument that we expect the shares to trade at a 10% premium to the local market multiple of year two earnings in 18 months. If the market itself increases as expected by 10–15% over that time frame, this will give it a rating of 23 times. Couching it in relative terms is useful, while explaining the market outlook may be helpful if the stock is in some small emerging market in Asia which the manager has not looked at for some time.

I generally include a suggestion on sizing, although that is at the manager's discretion. Giving a conviction level is helpful – the manager has delegated this work and so needs to have an understanding of whether you would like to bet the house or whether there are still uncertainties to resolve. Hopefully this can help you avoid a situation I found myself in, when I was told that my bonus was dependent on the outcome of an IPO I had recommended – fortunately the stock went up.

I like to have an absolute price target and a valuation target, but I really focus on the earnings and cash flows rather than the multiples. Analysts often do the reverse, but it's extremely hard to predict the value the market will ascribe to an earnings stream, and I think you can have more confidence in a prediction of the earnings. I am always aware that even if I am right on the earnings outlook, I may be wrong on the stock – the market may not believe in the sustainability of an earnings improvement and the stock may simply be derated. These eventualities must be factored into the analysis from the outset.

PROBABILITIES

Behavioural economics explains that the prospect of making massive returns is highly seductive – witness the success of Bitcoin. I do not pitch long shots, and I focus on stocks with a perceived high probability of upside and limited downside risk. As explained earlier, framing these probabilities in the note is a useful discipline, ensuring that you remain grounded and do not get carried away with an idea – this can be easy to do if you have several weeks devoted to the research and think it's a brilliant idea.

When carrying out research for this book, I discovered the Kelly criterion, which offers a good indicator on the calibration of individual investments: the size of position is influenced more by the probability of success than by the expected returns. Private investors are often attracted by high-potential returns, while underappreciating their relatively low probability, but good returns with a high probability of occurrence are more profitable. Similarly, framing forecasts within a range rather than using single-point estimates is a good discipline because that readily translates into a stock price risk profile.

PORTFOLIO FIT

Style and fit within the portfolio are significant, as it colours the sizing decision. This is not just style, but covers factors such as geography, sector, economic exposure, and time horizon. If this is just another global consumer staple, and we have lots of them already, then I would include a lot of comparative stock valuation data, because this might have to displace an existing holding. If this were another value stock in a value-filled portfolio, I have to explain why it will be a positive addition to the portfolio. The same is true for geographical, sectoral and economic exposures.

CATALYSTS

Time horizons and potential catalysts are overrated in my view – catalysts are occasionally obvious, such as the IPO of a competitor, but usually you just don't know how long it will take for the market to recognise the opportunity identified. This is the classic psychological game – the Keynes beauty contest – and it's really a guessing game.

Nevertheless, when I entered the 2017 Sohn London Investment Idea Competition, it was a requirement to list the potential catalysts. As my idea was related to the growth of electric vehicles and the eventual transition to autonomous vehicles, I listed the likelihood that Waymo would publish new evidence of its AV experience in Q1, 2018. I had read such a rumour and I knew that it had driven further than its peers without incident, and such a publication would encourage markets to view AV adoption as coming earlier.

Waymo has not made any such announcement at the time of writing. All of my commentary was potentially true, but it was a classic sell-side ploy to dress up the story, rather than an objective appraisal.

It would have been better (although less likely to win the competition) to say that among the potential catalysts might be Waymo's publication of these statistics, but they have never published this data before and have good reason not to. This is a more accurate and less emotional statement, and that is what I would have written if this had been an internal report at a hedge fund.

PEER REVIEW/DISCUSSION

At one fund, we sent our notes to the other analysts. There were not that many of us and we did not produce many notes each, so this was less onerous on the readers than it sounds. In a properly functioning team this is a great discipline, as everyone is then on the lookout for issues which may affect the stock. It works even better if you discuss the stock before the note is written.

Talking through an issue is of tremendous benefit. Sometimes I may not even need a dialogue or debate, but simply rehearsing my argument out loud can be enough to convince or dissuade myself of the merits of a trade or theme. This is one reason why I think it's a good idea to go out with your colleagues once a week for a casual lunch. This worked really well at one fund where it was a small team; we enjoyed each other's company and, while we did not always have a full quorum for our weekly lunch (we all travelled a lot), it was a great way to exchange thoughts on the markets and get conviction on themes and individual ideas.

In a larger or less sociable team, asking a colleague to spare 15 minutes for a coffee to run through an investment hypothesis can be really helpful. The same is true for private investors – a coffee with a friend to discuss an idea is usually time well spent.

FINAL EVALUATION AND DECISION

Having got this far, usually the case is made for the investment or short. Sometimes the valuation is simply too high, and then the decision is to put the stock on a watchlist and hope that the share price retreats; a mental note of what might cause such a correction is useful. But the final evaluation encompasses the following:

- What are the risks? How likely are they?

- Is there an off-setting downside case, how can you lose money, and what are the probabilities?

- How attractive is this idea compared to other stocks in the portfolio, and are there any adverse impacts on the portfolio from its inclusion?

- What is the expected time frame for holding this position and are there any catalysts, positive or negative, to be aware of?

- What weight should this stock have in the portfolio, and should it be a gradual build-up?

Finally, it's important to establish at the outset what the right selling price is, and what might change that level. I usually express this as a share price, but couch it in a multiple – for example, 18× my forecast of 2019 earnings – recognising that my prediction of profitability may not be accurate and the exit must be based on the actual earnings. But by having a pre-meditated exit plan, it reduces the danger of falling in love with the stock. When that share price level is reached, the decision to retain the position has to be rationalised and a new exit level established. This is a great discipline for private investors.

Before I deliver the recommendation, or buy/sell the stock, I like to sleep on the idea. It's important that I am in a good mindset to make this decision and don't feel tired (or jet-lagged). Occasionally it's permissible to buy first and study later, but it's important not to make this a habit – especially to avoid feeling over-confident when doing so. It's also vital to maintain discipline – if it's not a good idea, no amount of sunk time will make the share price go up.

If necessary, if I don't feel comfortable or if there is a worry nagging away at the back of my mind, I may even park the idea for a week, for the duration of a business trip, or even a holiday, and return to it afresh.

And know that, even with a brilliant, properly researched idea and an excellent note, I still haven't managed to get anywhere near a 100% success rate in persuading my bosses to pull the trigger on every idea.

This might be because of my far-from-perfect record. I once recommended a stock which had not made it into the portfolio. It enjoyed a decent run and I assumed we would never return to it, so I took it off my watchlist screen. A few weeks later, the boss asked if I thought it was still OK and, without knowing the share price – a hideously dangerous action, but I was new-ish and didn't want to admit that – I acknowledged that the fundamentals remained positive. He bought a huge position that night, right at the top, and the stock fell 40% back to where I had recommended it in the next few months.

The moral of the story is that it's better to look stupid than lose money. Additionally, it pays to keep things on your watchlist for some time. Of course, once the decision is made and a position initiated, that is only the start of the work.

CONCLUSIONS

Writing the idea down is a great discipline. The risk, reward and probabilities somehow become much clearer when I put everything down on a page. A map of how you expect events to unfold is useful when things don't go to plan, as you can more rationally judge the potential risks/rewards without remaining wedded to the original thesis. This is critical to ensure that losers are cut at the appropriate time – loss management is in some ways a more important skill than picking winners. This leads us on to the topic of maintenance, which I cover in the next chapter.

11

MAINTAINING THE PORTFOLIO

MONITORING WHAT you own is the top priority in successful portfolio performance. This may seem obvious, but analysts can devote a lot of time to new projects to the detriment of the core. Investors need to keep track of news daily as economic factors don't often move in response to sudden changes, but rather signals developed over a lengthy period. It's necessary to be on top of these developments.

I look at the macro picture in the next chapter, both in terms of what is happening in the outside world and how the market sees this. The other half of the macro equation, apart from what is happening in the external economic environment, is what is going on in the company and how they communicate to the market.

In this chapter, I therefore look at the direct interaction between companies and the market, as well as monitoring how the market's attitude to companies develops over time. Direct interaction covers:

- how to deal with company interaction, including company meetings, analyst meetings and investor days, as well as assessing acquisitions

- monitoring financial announcements

- spreadsheets

- the use of technical analysis
- looking at what to do when things go wrong, as they of course often do.

INTERACTION WITH COMPANIES

There are many ways in which analysts interact with companies, be that face-to-face via meetings or indirectly through the perusal and analysis of company announcements. I deal with all of these here.

RESULTS

Results seasons are the busiest times for the analyst, and with the increased frequency of reporting, it sometimes seems that you never get any peace and quiet or enough thinking time. I wrote this section in the first week of January and a slew of retailers were reporting trading statements on how they had done over the critical Christmas period. These are very soon after the period end, so there is limited time to get intelligence on what is likely to be reported.

Most US companies, and increasingly European and Asian ones, report quarterly and companies that report bi-annually generally have a trading statement immediately after the period end. Hence, four times a year is a minimum schedule of important financial news. Some longer-term investors see this quarterly reporting as 'noise' – one such investor told me that they don't even look at the quarterly numbers. This particular fund has an excellent performance, and I would never criticise a successful approach, but I see each reporting point as additional information which allows me to refine my estimates of future profitability and, ultimately, of what a company is worth.

Company results are important and preparation is key. Statements tend to be pretty long these days, 30–70 pages, so you need to know what you are looking for in all key financial parameters and be in a position to pull the trigger. Sometimes this can be immediately after the market opens, as you will have had time to digest the data and determine the strategy – how much to sell depending on how far the stock moves. More often, there will be a question as to why margins in a division have fallen and it's necessary to learn from management the reasons for the result, either at the meeting/conference call or in a private call afterwards.

A set of results which disappoint you as the analyst, even if they are smack in line with consensus, may be a reason to trim a position. At one fund, we were far ahead of the market in understanding our positions. We might use a better-than-consensus set of results to trim a position into the strength on the day, if the results were not as good as we had hoped.

I generally prefer to wait until the following day to finalise my view, but in the past I have often initiated a trade before the open, after the open, or during or after a call. Surprisingly often, a finance director will say something on the call that makes you want to trade out of the stock. Usually you will not manage to sell many shares, but at a hedge fund you are charging 20% of the performance, so the team is acutely aware that every dollar counts.

In my view, the key to successfully navigating results is preparation, and this is one reason why I find it's helpful to have my own model. That enables me to calibrate variances (actual vs expected results) quickly and to identify any 'funnies', as well as refining my forecasts.

READING QUARTERLY, INTERIM AND ANNUAL FILINGS

For many investors and most of the sell-side, the quarterly earnings release and the call is the sole focus of attention. US companies are also required to file a 10-Q (a quarterly version of the annual report) with the SEC, which comes out some time later and usually contains some useful additional information. Similarly, all companies are required to produce an annual report following the preliminary results, which I read in detail.

Table 11.1 illustrates that US analysts must spend most of their time worrying about results, if each quarterly takes half a day to process. European analysts get away more lightly. I think the time estimates are optimistic – I take much longer to process the accounts, for example.

Table 11.1: Time spent analysing stocks

	Quarterly	Interim	Trading statement	8-K filing	Accounts	Total
Per company	4	2	2	3	1	
Time required (hours)	4	4	2	4	8	
For 20 companies						
US analyst	80			60	20	
US analyst hours	320			240	160	720
EU/Other analyst		40	40		20	
EU/Other analyst hours		160	80		160	400

Source: Behind the Balance Sheet estimates.

I generally download accounting policies statements into Word and review the differences from year to year; I compare the two documents for differences by using the 'review versions' function. Bloomberg and FactSet have redline functions and there are other free tools on the internet to do this for US filings, as they are filed in machine-readable format. This helps save time.

Doing this for risk factors in the SEC quarterly filings or in the comments to the forward-looking statements at the times of the earnings releases can also be revealing. For example, when there was furore in early 2018 about Russian influence in the election, after Mark Zuckerberg had been summoned to appear in front of senators, Facebook modified its language in respect of forward-looking statements, adding in respect of product risks, "maintaining and enhancing our brand and reputation; our ongoing safety, security, and content review efforts ... litigation and government inquiries". Had they not done so, it might have suggested they were not treating this seriously enough.

This is quite arcane stuff, but as artificial intelligence becomes more widely available, I imagine that this sort of analysis will become routine. I am sure that many quants and larger fundamental hedge funds are already practising this.

REPORTING DATES

Ahead of the company results, it's always useful to check the reporting date, but it's also useful to check the day – if the company has always reported on a Tuesday and it suddenly changes to a Friday, there may be some trouble ahead.

The distribution of reporting days is highly skewed. If you want to hide your results and reduce your coverage, Thursdays are the best days to do so, followed by Wednesdays. The best day to report is actually a Tuesday, as you will have the best coverage, the greatest attention from investors and there is a chance that they will have time to read the results notes the next day (although they probably will not bother).

Figure 11.1: Average number of European stocks reporting by day

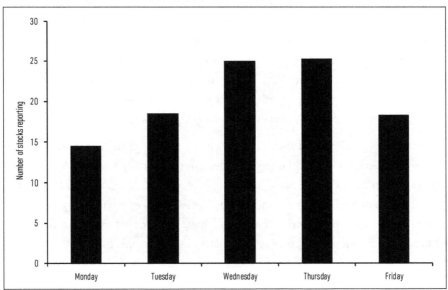

Source: Behind the Balance Sheet.

One trader I know believes that Tuesday is an odd day in markets and often sees a reversal of Monday's trend. I subsequently found evidence that my trader friend is wrong and Tuesday is actually the best day in markets! This illustrates how market participants are often superstitious. The fact of

Tuesdays being the best day in itself is one of those random facts that people like to trot out but which is unlikely to help much.

Berkshire Hathaway reports after-hours on a Friday, which gives time for proper analysis; that might not be a generally popular practice, but it's best for long-term shareholders and I am mildly surprised that it has no other proponents – although it does mean a busy weekend for the analysts.

ANALYSTS MEETINGS

If practical, and the position is significant, I prefer to attend the analyst meeting. All the sell-side analysts turn up to ask their questions and often you can assess the mood just from walking into the room, even without seeing the results. This is why I like to attend in person, as I can get a better feel of sentiment and the way participants, or at least the sell-side, are leaning.

Obviously this is not possible for every company, simply for reasons of geography – for example, most US companies only hold calls. But, if possible, it's better to attend in person. As a sell-side analyst, I specialised in asking awkward questions. Particularly if you are short of a stock, this can highlight an issue that management would rather leave undiscovered. After moving to the buy-side, I tended to be quieter, preferring to ask my questions in private.

When I have owned or followed a stock for a long time, I start to know it really well. After several quarters of listening to the calls I almost know what the sell-side analyst is going to ask before he asks it. At that point, I feel that I really understand the stock and the pervasive market psychology, and I am much better able to trade the shares, as I have a better intuition for the likely share price direction, and a sense of bottoming or topping.

CAPITAL MARKETS DAYS

There is an increasing trend, I believe mandatory in certain markets, for companies to hold capital markets days (CMDs) biennially or even annually. In my days as a sell-side analyst, these were a good excuse to head off somewhere nice for an overnight trip and have a couple of drinks after the dinner with your competitors, a few of whom were usually friendly. Life is a bit more serious on the buy-side, and now these events are scripted and choreographed down to the finest detail.

They are also usually webcast, so you don't have to attend in person, which is useful in that you can 'attend' meetings that you would otherwise miss – I watched the Walmart Investor Day from the comfort of my desk to learn about Asda, as we were involved with the UK supermarkets at the time; I was not interested enough to get on a plane, but happy to take a couple of hours out of my schedule. Attendance in person is preferable and usually worthwhile for serious positions.

Almost always with CMDs, it's a case of better to travel than arrive – the share price anticipates the event and the company has to produce something really special to make people more excited and the share go up. The number of attendees is also a good contracyclical guide. Overly popular CMDs can indicate a dearth of new buyers who have not yet heard the story.

I find these meetings can be a useful way of meeting industry contacts. At my first Tesco CMD they had invited along some of their top suppliers, while I met the media expert at one of the big accounting firms at the Sky Investor Day. The other advantage is that you get to meet employees lower down the food chain. Although they have usually been primed on the right answer to every possible question and routinely are the brightest graduate trainees, or top of the middle-management grades, so are probably not entirely representative. That Tesco CMD was notable in that they were real people, including the property guy who arrived for his presentation a few minutes late (we were in their head office, but were running ahead of time).

There is also the chance of a decent freebie – although my wife has insisted that I don't bring any more junk home, as she cannot face another solar radio, baseball cap with integrated earphones, or alarm clock cum barometer. For any IR practitioners reading this, my favourite was a picnic rug with a waterproof back, which even received Mrs C's approval.

COMPANY TRIPS

Company trips are somewhat similar to CMDs, but they are longer and afford a more detailed glimpse into a company's actual operations. Post-dinner drinks are an art which I have perfected over many years, but my initiation was at the hands of the great Dan White, then the number-one transport analyst. We spent the first night of a visit to BAA in the Holiday Inn at Aberdeen Airport, and Dan was not satisfied with his intake over dinner or in the lounge and bar after.

When the bar closed, he insisted that I accompany him for a nightcap and ordered a bottle of whisky; when the staff objected that they only sold miniatures, Dan was unfazed – and ordered the equivalent of a bottle in miniatures (think of a breakfast tray, full of miniatures).

When I started in the City, those older analysts really knew how to drink. Pete Deighton, the number-one-rated engineering analyst, and head of our 'box', took me and another newbie out for lunch a few weeks after we started. He ordered a bottle of claret and three rounds of roast beef sandwiches, and when we had finished the bottle, I felt fine and was ready to head back to my desk; he then ordered another bottle, and then a third – this was quite normal in the 1980s.

There have been some fantastic meals in this role – the opening of Eurotunnel was memorable – and some fabulous wines, for example, with Ronnie Frost, the founder of Hays, the recruitment company. Ronnie was a larger-than-life character, constantly on the mobile to the captain of his yacht in the South of France and often emerging from his chauffeur-driven Bentley, registration REF 55. We got quite drunk one afternoon in Paris, at the end of a company visit; the other analysts had gone back to the UK, but I was staying in Paris to see some French clients. A good indicator that his eye was not on the ball.

It has not all been gastronomic highlights. I once attended a visit to the European subsidiaries of a South African company, a competitor to one of our investments. I flew in late and headed off to the restaurant in the old town in Düsseldorf to meet the group. Company management had chosen a restaurant which specialised in pork and I arrived just in time for the first course – when I asked what it was, the MD proudly explained that it was raw pork. Mmmm…

You have to question their judgement. And it got worse – one of the investors from New York was Jewish and refused the food, while the South African analyst was a vegetarian but, out of a misguided sense of duty, ate her food. That was probably my worst culinary experience, although I felt similarly embarrassed when I hosted a lunch for several clients at Flemings, when the only main course on offer that day was liver.

While on the sell-side, I was quite close to Inchcape and unimpressed when they decided to hold an Investor Day in Hong Kong. They were the UK market play on emerging market growth and Hong Kong was a key profit centre. We started the day in Inchcape HQ, where they immediately decided to take the goods lift straight to the car park to save time.

It was quite a large group, but the goods lift was not the largest, nor was it air conditioned, as we soon discovered when it broke down. Unfortunately, it took well over an hour to extract us from there and of course it was boiling hot and we were all suffering – it was like a Japanese tube train in rush hour, except without air conditioning.

Inchcape didn't have much luck with its analysts' visits in those days. The following year, we had a one-week visit to South America. It was a fun trip, but as we were enjoying a visit to a vineyard in Chile, the Asian crisis broke. Inchcape, as the number one UK stock exposed, saw its shares collapse. There was very little interest in the missives from the trip.

TALKING TO MANAGEMENT

Private meetings with management, or even group meetings with other investors, can be really helpful. The more homework you have done prior to a meeting with a company, especially an introductory meeting, the more you will get out of the meeting. I changed role to become a conglomerate analyst in the 1990s, and I went into my first meeting with Tomkins' finance director armed with an extensive list of detailed points and questions; he was so impressed with my effort that he called in the CEO, Greg Hutchings, then one of the stars of the conglomerate era. (Like almost all such acquisitive companies, they later fell to earth.)

Detailed preparation shows respect to the management, they will then take you more seriously and will try harder to answer your questions. Interestingly, the long list of prepared questions is not usually what gives you the insight – the real insight comes from the off-the-cuff questions, usually the follow-ups. The best such question is "Why do you say that?" in response to a manager's answer – open questions asking for reasoning will generally give you an insight into their real thinking, rather than the glib, prepared soundbites that management (especially US management) like to offer up.

Anthony Bolton, in his book, *Investing Against the Tide*, suggests using a checklist for company meetings, designed to extract the quality of its economic moat related to the strength of its franchise, its competitive position, etc. This may well be an effective approach, but, as an analyst, I prefer to have done the detailed work beforehand.

At broker conferences, in contrast, I may simply be looking for ideas, or to determine if the company, its suppliers or customers, or its sector may be worthy of some more serious work. I sometimes go to meet a company for the first time with the bare minimum of preparation, especially if this is to fill in a gap in the schedule between companies that I really want to see. These meetings are generally group meetings, unless the company has few people wanting to meet management.

Before any meeting with management, I generally have a look at the stock, its track record and valuation, and try to get a view on its business. But I have slipped up before, like the time I went to see Cooper Industries, the industrial conglomerate subsequently taken over by Eaton. I ended up seeing a healthcare company by the same name, actually Cooper Companies – that was quite an awkward meeting, a one-to-one, and I don't think I entirely got away with my lack of knowledge. I have had hundreds, if not thousands, of company meetings over the years, so getting the wrong company once is probably not that bad a result.

One really important trick is to watch management's body language. Most CEOs and CFOs of large companies are highly political animals and highly accustomed to bending the truth to suit the audience. Occasionally though they will give a signal, or you can detect poor chemistry at the top table. In one IPO, the founder/CEO clearly disliked his CFO, as the body language was terrible; they didn't look at each other once through the whole one-hour meeting, but in this case, it didn't make any difference to the stock price.

One US broker used to indicate the companies' conference rankings by number of investor requests – I used to like meeting the companies nobody else was interested in, as if there is no interest, they will tend to be unloved and hence cheaper. Indeed, the number of people in the room is a great guide to the likely subsequent share-price trend – my meeting notes from broker conferences always include a comment on the number of people attending; if it's an annual conference, the trend relative to history is even more helpful and I have found exits from a position or shorts by detecting over-enthusiasm in this way.

The best meetings are those where you have owned the stock for a long time and know the management well and have a constructive, warm and positive relationship. Once you have earned their trust, you can have fantastically interesting discussions about the strategy of the business and how they should approach challenges. These are the meetings I enjoy most.

CURVEBALLS

When in a group meeting which is concentrating on the factors affecting the next quarter's earnings, I often try to change the subject – let's leave the issue of the next quarter and talk about where you see the company in five years and your vision for the company on a 10–15-year timescale. It's helpful to have a vision and a plan to get to where you want to be in five years. Meetings which focus on short-term results are usually not particularly helpful as companies are wary of giving inside information.

I sometimes try asking a few different questions to give a better chance of finding out what really makes this CEO tick, and of not giving him the opportunity to trot out rehearsed answers – good CEOs should have asked themselves these questions.

Talking about incentives can be quite revealing – "what is your incentive structure and is there anything that you would change? Would you like to introduce any different incentives for middle management or staff?"

"Are there any companies that you perceive as a threat that might not be in most investors' consciousness?" This can reveal that barriers to entry are not as high as you thought.

A great question which is difficult to answer is "what keeps you awake at night?" If it's nothing, the CEO can appear quite flippant, and the answer is often quite revealing.

"What is the most important attribute of your company's culture?" is a question which occasionally can elicit a revealing answer.

"What other CEOs do you look up to?" This can be a very revealing question, unless the CEO answers Warren Buffett, which is usually a hard one to argue.

"If you were in my shoes, what question would you have asked that I missed?" This is a good question to end on. Often you will get some platitude that you have done a marvellous job, but sometimes an honest CEO will tell you something important.

My opener to an IPO roadshow team is to have a quick scan through the PowerPoint deck, put it down, and interrupt their introduction – can we please start by you explaining why you want our money and why we should give it to you. This innocuous question can trap a surprising number of CEOs.

Going off script can create some amusing incidents. The chairman of one Indian IPO was the son of the founder and, clearly, knew very little about the business. When I dragged the questioning off script, he was totally lost, and the highly experienced CEO (and large supporting team) refused to say anything, presumably because they were more scared of making their boss look bad than they were interested in promoting the issue. This technique, of forcing the company to abandon the script and answer real questions, is incredibly effective. Jon Moulton, the hugely successful private equity practitioner, told me he uses the same technique.

The Charlie Munger technique of inversion can be helpful in extracting an answer to a question which management does not want to reveal. I was concerned about Sainsbury's property valuation and about the level of off-balance sheet finance in the form of operating leases. When I met the IR team, I naturally asked them about the property valuation. This would have been in 2014 or so, before things turned really bad. I framed the question, as I sometimes do in a private meeting, conversely to my position or intent. I asked them to defend the 4.7% yield-based valuation of their supermarkets, which they did stoutly.

A little later in the meeting I asked them what multiple should be used to assess the underlying capital value on the operating lease rentals – I suggested that a broker probably used 7–8× but if the right cap rate was a 4.7% yield then the correct multiple must be 21×. (Incidentally, I am still troubled by the operating lease capitalisation question, as I have been for some years. Unfortunately, the new accounting standard, IFRS16, which brings such leases on to the balance sheet, does not clarify the picture as well as might have been hoped.)

This strategy is often effective – asking direct questions makes it difficult for management to avoid giving direct answers, although they can sometimes become defensive. Asking a positive question and then reframing it around a liability can help to open the person on the other side. Another tactic is to ask very open questions or to ask very open follow-ups; and I always delay before the follow-up, allowing for an uncomfortable space between questions. The counterpart will often offer a rider, which he or she had not intended, and these can be really illuminating. Such meetings are a way of deriving an investment edge and although the company will never give you inside information, attitudinal insight can be revealing.

A good example was a bulge bracket firm's breakfast with the Vivendi management team – a slippery group. The analyst said we know that Canal Plus is doing a lot better than you have admitted and that you are going to come out with positive news at the Q1. This is the sort of question where you can learn a lot from management's reaction; they can either:

1. say nothing

2. smile and say they could not possibly comment

3. play it down by saying we have never said its going great, or be careful it will take some time for this to turn round.

The differences between these three outcomes are significant for the next quarter's view and the stock price in that time frame; but it is a good example of how the investor can make it uncomfortable for the management team to duck the question.

Even with the best framed questions, however, companies can be useless at responding. Solvay were presenting to a small group at a bulge bracket broker conference in 2017. They were telling the group, probably ten hedge-fund analysts, about how disciplined they were with a strong focus on cash flow and returns. They demonstrated this with a slide showing the HOLT methodology CFROI calculations (quite technical and not relevant to this story); I asked why the numbers didn't appear to add up – the divisional return calculations were significantly higher than the group average.

There were two members of the IR team present and neither could answer this simple question; their first response was that the numbers were correct, but I explained the calculations, and then various others present agreed with me. The IR team agreed to get back to me later with an explanation, but months passed by without contact. I was doing some filing which prompted me to follow up, and eventually someone came back to me with the answer that there were a pile of unproductive assets sitting in the HQ line. This was revealing as it meant that,

1. There could be some unproductive assets in central HQ which could be sold off, e.g., property.

2. The company was trying to push up its rating by obscuring the real data; it was parking low returning assets or investments, e.g., new business developments in a central line, and thereby flattering the divisional results. This is not a positive signal.

3. The IR team lacked a basic understanding of the financial drivers.

The key takeaway from this, however, is that it is **essential** to reconcile the data with the published financial statements. This is an absolute golden rule.

Meeting management is an essential part of my process. I don't do this because I think I am a great judge of management's ability – quite the opposite, in fact, I think headhunters are good at evaluating people and I think I am pretty useless – but I can get quite a good impression of a person, form a judgement as to whether they will make me money, and occasionally glean a titbit which will give me greater or lesser comfort about the investment. Not meeting management means sacrificing these opportunities and should only be the policy to follow if you believe that meeting them may prejudice your chances of making a rational decision – for example, post a profit warning.

I disagree with Terry Smith on this and believe that meeting management regularly helps spot strategy drift, and gives indicators of potential stock exit points.

ASSESSING ACQUISITIONS

As Peter Drucker pointed out, deal-making beats working. Many CEOs like acquisitions, and they can be a great way of adding shareholder value, although usually they are quite the reverse. There are a number of reasons for an acquisition and clear differences in the value accruing:

COST SYNERGIES

This is the single best reason and most likely to be successful. Buying a competitor and eliminating back office costs, for example, while consolidating a mom-and-pop industry, can be a highly successful formula, as practised by European players like Brenntag and DCC.

Low multiples are paid for the private company, there is limited risk and the real returns generated can be highly attractive. Small deals of this nature do not even need to be announced and this is the lowest risk/highest reward formula.

Note that I am generally wary of serial acquirers, as operating cash flow for these businesses is exaggerated as the working capital benefits of acquisitions are realised – debtor days and inventory in the acquired company are reduced, working capital is released, and cash flow boosted, which makes the operations *look* more cash generative than they really are.

REVENUE SYNERGIES

These can happen, but they tend to be more elusive and this can be a disappointing strategy. This is especially so in an industry consolidation, where customers will often want an alternative supplier and revenue dis-synergies result.

GEOGRAPHICAL OR INDUSTRY DIVERSIFICATION

Both are warning signals and success often proves elusive, as the new region or industry generally takes time to understand. Occasionally geographical diversification works, usually when the industry and customer base is relatively homogeneous. Industry diversification is extremely difficult. I followed the UK conglomerates sector in the 1990s and have developed a healthy scepticism about acquisitive businesses. The odd exception, like Melrose and Wassall under Jock Miller and Ian Roper, merely confirms this.

CHEAP DEALS

These do exist, but there usually has to be a motivation for the seller and this is the area to focus on.

Acquisitions, although often accretive in EPS and welcomed by the market, are usually a signal for the shareholder to re-examine the investment hypothesis. The exceptions are if the company is a serial acquirer of small businesses, and the deal is relatively small, or a professional acquirer with a great track record, such as Melrose (GKN is a different quantum of deal for them).

SPREADSHEETS

Believe it or not, when I started in the City, analysts did not use spreadsheets. I was regarded with suspicion, rather than awe, because I knew how to operate a PC!

I recall my former colleague, Mark Cusack, then the number-one conglomerates analyst, working out a very complicated and painful set of conversion calculations for the Hanson acquisition of Imperial Tobacco in 1986 (cash, cash and shares, shares and convertible options); his calculations were done in pencil on a landscape sheet of A4 and then photocopied and distributed round the sales desk (then doubtless faxed around the City). I offered to do it for him – it will only take me ten minutes, I said – but he preferred to spend a couple of hours doing it by hand on a calculator as he did not trust the PC (or perhaps he did not trust me).

I am, however, somewhat suspicious of spreadsheet jockeys where every assumption is tweaked into a final number. Interestingly, a few years ago one of the oil majors had the spreadsheets of the top analysts covering its stock audited – they all had errors, sometimes significant.

In my view, there are a few simple rules to using spreadsheets for investment analysis:

- Keep it simple; if it becomes too complex, you will be unable to audit it and you will waste time in pursuit of a spuriously correct answer.

- Reconcile the opening and closing balance sheet.

- Integrate the P&L, cash flow and balance sheet.

- Use standardised line items and headings, especially for the cash flow. This facilitates comparison, and unusual or odd items are then classed under other – often with a separate breakout.

- Don't value companies using DCF – as I discuss elsewhere, they are too sensitive to small changes in assumptions, and I really only use them to understand the valuation sensitivities to different factors, or for loss-makers.

Spreadsheets are obviously an invaluable tool for the analyst and I could not imagine life without them – in the old days, the pharma analysts used to calculate drug sales on a slide rule! But I do think there is a danger in becoming a slave to the spreadsheet and I always try to use my 'back of the fag packet' sense check to ensure that I have a roughly accurate answer.

TECHNICAL ANALYSIS

Technical analysis consists of analysing share-price charts for trends. Fundamental analysts are often critical of technical analysts who are a much-maligned bunch. One hedge fund manager I know was quite sceptical of a brilliant technical analyst – Richard Crossley, who sadly passed away a few years ago. He was a former salesman who brilliantly articulated how the mood of the market was being expressed in different stock and sector trends. This manager was vehemently opposed to paying for "drawing squiggly lines".

What Crossley did brilliantly, and some of his colleagues also do today, was to give a quantitative picture of the market's qualitative trends. The 'science' behind chartism is not something I personally bother too much about, but there are two simple premises which Richard and his peers taught me which make charts relevant for me:

- A stock making new 12-month relative highs is more likely to outperform in the short term than underperform (and vice versa for one making new lows).

- When that stock changes trend, it's an important signal and investors should check that nothing has changed.

Charts help you understand where a stock is in its market cycle. At one broker, we were required to write a commentary underneath a stock's five-year price relative chart, a practice I still follow. This simple discipline ensured that the analyst understood why a stock had gone up or down previously; and that knowledge helps considerably when understanding its likely future trajectory. Producing such a chart and understanding previous cycles is, I believe, an invaluable help when first looking at a new stock.

Richard Crossley was particularly keen on new **sector** (rather than market) price relative highs or lows, and in relatively homogeneous sectors like banks and food retailing. This is an important indicator that something is going right or wrong.

Watching which stocks are making new highs and lows is a daily maintenance task – I don't need to do it every single day, but I need to stay in touch. This tells you the market psychology. I prefer to do this globally, paying close attention to what is happening in the US markets as the European markets often follow. Individual stock action in emerging markets is probably less critical, although trends in markets like Korea and Taiwan with very export-oriented economies are good signals of likely macro trends. And of course, in certain sectors – for example, container shipping – the lead may be set by the larger universe of, say, Asian stocks in the sub-sector, which can give you an indication for Maersk in Europe.

As an example of this, the chart of Tyson relative to the US market (Figure 11.2) shows that the stock just reached a new 52-week relative high in August 2019, having troughed at a 52-week relative low in April 2018, less than 18 months previous.

Figure 11.2: Tyson relative share price

Source: Behind the Balance Sheet from Sentieo Data.

I also like to watch volumes – a change of trend accompanied by high volume or a new high on volume is much more significant than one in light trade. Above average volume activity can be an early signal that a stock or sector is about to change course.

My chartist friends, especially my old friend and former colleague Nick Glydon at Redburn, say to always buy 12-month relative highs, always sell 12-month lows, but this is probably too simplistic. I think that the price relative chart is definitely informative, and can be usefully supplemented by a sector relative chart and an assessment of volumes.

QUANTITATIVE RESEARCH

Related to technical analysis is quantitative research or 'quants'. This describes using quantitative rules to pick stocks. I use quants in the same way I use technical research, to help identify areas for attention or to help fine-tune exits from positions.

Quants research looks at baskets of stocks which fit a particular theme or style and also explain how different factors have driven the recent market performance. The quant baskets vary from firm to firm, and analyst to analyst, but a few examples would be:

- deep value stocks (price-to-book ratio, P/E, P/E deviation from average etc.)

- growth stocks (growth in revenues and sometimes in profitability)

- quality stocks (usually some form of return criteria, possibly with a volatility overlay)

- momentum stocks (stocks which are rising, occasionally also with rising estimates)

- risk stocks (usually those with a high degree of volatility or high beta)

- dividend/income stocks (stocks with a high or growing yield)

- small cap/large cap.

Some hedge funds, notably Maverick Capital, use quantitative rules to help limit their universe of potential investments. Lee Ainslie, the Maverick founder, is one of the Tiger cubs – managers who formerly worked for Julian Robertson, one of the gurus of the hedge fund world. He made the point at a London conference I attended, that imposing a quantitative discipline as an overlay on their fundamental selection was helpful, as it kept them out of some situations that just would not work and gave them additional confidence in others. He was the first fundamental person I have heard espousing such principles and I think it makes a lot of sense.

I use screens to filter ideas and quants as well as technical research to help me understand what markets are currently attracted to, or what they dislike. Using these tools helps categorise a stock into a particular style, which is useful not only in identifying possible investment opportunities, but to understand factor risk if the stock is eventually incorporated in your portfolio.

There are two main things I look at when reading quants research:

1. How each of these baskets or styles is performing – is the market looking for growth and momentum, i.e., are we in a risk on environment, or are quality and large cap outperforming a more defensive environment?

2. Which stocks are in which baskets – occasionally, an unexpected stock will pop up in a quality basket or a value basket. Stocks which are in unusual categories are generally a signal to take an interest.

Then the quants research will often discuss how different factors are performing. Again, the factors may vary from analyst to analyst, but some of the most common ones are:

- Valuation: NTM and trailing; EV/EBITDA, P/E, EV-to-sales, etc.

- Growth: EPS, FCF, RoE, EBITDA, etc.

- Ratios: gross margin, net margin, EBITDA margin, FCF to assets, etc.

- Volatility: EPS volatility (vol) five-year, beta various periods, price vol, etc.

- Momentum: price and return over one month/three months/six months/12 months, etc.

- Dividends: dividend growth over one year, dividend revisions, yield prospective etc.

- Other: EPS revisions, share buybacks etc.

There are a bewildering number of factors, and it can be extremely confusing to look at too many. Therefore, I tend to look at what is performing right now – is it growth or is it dividends? Within growth, what are the best performing factors? I also particularly like to observe the performance of factors like companies which are buying back shares, as, again, this helps to understand the market psychology.

Share buybacks have been a particular (although obviously not exclusive) phenomenon of the low-growth world post the GFC and in the US market especially. US companies buying back stock have been one of the biggest groups of buyers in the market, and there is no question that this has helped share price and market performance.

Revisions to EPS are, in my view, a key driver of share prices, and technical analysis shows which stocks are getting upgraded most. I like to look at earnings upgrades vs share price performance. One broker produces a 150-page report every month of the largest stocks in the world, with a quadrant analysis by sector and market, showing the upgrades on one axis and the share price performance on another – it makes it simple to see which stocks have lagged their relative upgrades (potential buys) and which have enjoyed a rerating (potential shorts). This type of scatter diagram is a helpful data visualisation for many types of analysis, and particularly this comparison between a factor and share price performance.

I find quantitative research most helpful when trying to understand current market psychology – over time, cheap stocks usually do better than dear ones, high quality beats low quality, and stocks with positive revisions will always beat those with falling profits etc. But, in order to understand what is in the price today, I try to understand the market mood now – looking at the performance of different styles and different factors is a convenient way of trying to achieve this.

WORRY ABOUT WHAT YOU OWN

Time management is an essential skill for investors and analysts, and after constructing the portfolio, the most important task is monitoring what you own. Watching for trouble and getting out before it happens is the single exercise most likely to add value to performance. Analysts often fall into the trap of looking for the next great idea when they should be prioritising the maintenance of what is already owned. A regular review process helps.

REVIEW PROCESS

Things change and it's necessary for most portfolios to weed out losers and find new winners. At one fund, we used to conduct a regular review of the portfolio and assess our conviction on every position on a formal basis, sitting in a meeting room at least monthly, more often on the dealing desk. Of course, some investors like Warren Buffett or Terry Smith pride themselves on barely changing their portfolios, but for most investors, especially hedge funds and those with clients with a shorter-term horizon, the discipline of assessing your conviction on each position on a regular basis is essential.

This is a difficult process, and inevitably some stocks are weeded out, sometimes with specific price targets (lets sell it when it reaches x), sometimes to make way for better opportunities. Quite often, the new position will only be a small exposure initially, for example, 1%, and this will be increased over time as conviction in the idea improves, or as relative pricing changes.

This book is focused on analysis, but a regular review of positions helps the portfolio manager assess the relative attraction of different constituents of the portfolio and helps with sizing positions – interestingly, I have seen very little written about this discipline, yet it's as important a factor in performance as picking the right stocks in the first place.

Recognising when you have got it wrong and cutting losses is probably the most difficult skill required of portfolio managers. It's necessary to admit the error and move on – none of us gets everything right and what is important is what will happen tomorrow, not what happened yesterday. Yet although we all know this, the behavioural finance heuristic of loss aversion is deeply ingrained and hard to shrug off – "lets keep it and hope it goes up" is a common attitude among private investors and is detrimental to performance.

One of my bosses was superb at this – he would cut a loss and would ordinarily never blame anyone for making a mistake, he only got really annoyed at opportunities missed. Another chap I worked with would get really emotional when a stock fell 5%, making him extremely difficult to work with.

When a stock goes against you, it's necessary to re-examine the investment hypothesis and ensure that it remains valid; if it does and the reason the stock has fallen is clear, then it is probably right to average down, although many money managers are reluctant to do so. As previously mentioned, this is more difficult for shorts.

Sometimes, however, you just don't know why the stock is moving against you. This only happened to me once, but it's a sure sign that you are not on top of things and are not in control. It's as clear a signal as an illuminated emergency exit sign. I discuss this at the end of the chapter.

WHEN THINGS GO WRONG

The portfolio manager generally gets much more closely involved when things go wrong with a position. I have worked with PMs who had fantastic market antennae and were highly attuned to stock movements in the market and tended to top up or take profit on positions on an ongoing basis, often to keep pace with fund inflows. I find it an emotional challenge when things go wrong, and I have to follow a prescribed path.

I found this to be the most difficult part of my job, but it is essential to be able to cope with things going wrong. At one firm, one of the PMs really needed help in this area and it created a lot of stress in the office. When I was advising on portfolios for the wealth manager, I made the add/reduce decisions myself, although as I was running very concentrated portfolios, this was in part forced on me by my personal risk tolerance. I make some observations on averaging down and taking profits below.

Traders like Paul Tudor Jones claim that you should never average down – "losers average losers"– which is the antithesis of the Buffett philosophy that if you loved it at $10, you should love it twice as much at $5. In reality, it's extremely difficult to call the bottom for a long-term stock, especially if you are in a large fund and wish to deploy $100m or more.

Of course, you should only average down if you are right. If you are wrong, you will lose a lot more money. The problem is, it's quite hard to tell, especially when things are going against you and you are stressed – the two go together in my experience. The circumstances will be different in every individual case, but I think the philosophy of averaging down should follow the same principles as when you decide whether to cut a short that has gone wrong.

When a short increases in value you already have a much larger position, so it's doubly difficult to increase. To do so, you need a lot more conviction, and you need to do dramatically more research and ensure you fully understand the buyers' psychology. I think the same discipline can be applied to longs.

My general rule is that if the stock falls 20% from my purchase price, i.e., the original purchase or recommendation point, it's necessary to revisit the hypothesis and ensure that nothing has changed and that I haven't missed something. At one fund, a 10% drawdown would require an in-depth review.

(An aside: I don't believe that practitioners can refine the value of a stock to the nearest 5%, although many traders profess that ability.)

When things go wrong, I follow these simple tenets:

1. Before averaging down, after a 20% or greater setback, retest the hypothesis and write a follow-up note confirming the original investment thesis if appropriate, and explaining why the stock has moved; if you don't really know why it has moved, then it's more difficult to buy much more.

2. Stick to the original limit in terms of risk exposure – so, if this originally was a 5% position and we have had 4%, even though it might have fallen 25%, so that it's now a 3% position, I would only add another 1%, unless there was absolute clarity as to why it had corrected and there was a much increased conviction level.

3. The downside risk assessment. If this is a long and it's a very stable stock – without significant contingent liabilities such as litigation or regulatory interference and with modest debt – the risk of severe loss is reduced and the additional purchase is less risky. But if it's a higher risk situation, then the odds of further losses are higher and my willingness to risk further funds is reduced.

4. If it's a short, it's much harder to average up; we would follow the same practice as with longs, but then it would be a common practice to speak to friends in other funds. If they were convinced of the idea, they might also short it and averaging in at the higher price would feel a little less uncomfortable. My worst experience of this situation cost me weeks of work, and I was then accountable not only to my boss but to the number two of a large and aggressive hedge fund in New York who would call me at home in the evening. We ended up making a decent return, 30% on the equity short, and they made much more.

5. I tend to avoid averaging down if the stock is making sector-relative lows. There is then a chance that your thesis is sound, that this industry is going to see an inflection in margins, but you have picked the wrong stock to play this through. Then it may be more sensible to increase your weight by buying another stock in the same sector. I also try to exercise patience if I do not have high enough conviction and to avoid increasing exposure in leveraged situations, as it becomes even harder to call the bottom.

This concept of retesting the hypothesis is not straightforward. On two occasions I have had to make a long-haul trip to meet management after a significant correction in a stock, the reasons for which were not adequately understood. Once, I had to fly to New York to meet various brokers, on the way to meeting the company and its principal competitor, then the cab driver could not find my hotel; that makes for a long day!

Far worse was when an Indian position went wrong. This was a mortgage finance company which had been raising new equity, much against the hopes of my boss, who was nevertheless committed to the story. But the shares kept going down and it was decided that someone had to go and check the company out. I should preface this by acknowledging that this has been a highly successful investment – any company engaged in the provision of mortgage finance in India was involved in a huge growth opportunity.

I flew out to Mumbai with a couple of colleagues to check out what was wrong. The CEO very kindly gave us his office to use, but the door was wedged open and a secretary spent most of her day watching us. There were some red flags:

- The founder was unfortunately unavailable, called to Delhi at short notice on urgent business. No reason was specified and his absence was clearly an issue – we had flown from London and were one of the largest shareholders.

- I asked to visit one of the branches, so that we could observe the initiation of a mortgage and follow the trail through. The CEO didn't think that was a good idea as the closest branch in Mumbai was a long way away and it wasn't convenient for us to interrupt the staff.

- The CEO's body language was all wrong. He took us to lunch in his very large Mercedes, a fortune in India, and it felt wrong somehow that he was driving such an expensive and flashy car, when he claimed to be very modest and focused on the business.

- We met one of the middle managers who was responsible for a new subsidiary for which they had hugely ambitious plans.

- We visited a property development, again, another venture outside the core, and it was a very expensive apartment block; it looked and felt like a top-class development in London.

I didn't feel at all comfortable about the position, but I could not get any hard facts – no data could be found to support us getting out, but we weren't confident enough to add to the position either. Given the size of the position, especially relative to the trading volume in the stock, we were stuck – I felt very uncomfortable about the position and especially our dealings with the management team. Fortunately, it played out over time.

MISTAKES

I could have written a whole book on my mistakes, but for two reasons: first, I am bound by confidentiality agreements from my hedge fund roles and, second, it's a natural inclination to try to forget one's mistakes. Being an analyst or a fund manager requires a certain degree of confidence in your own ability. It's ironic, because remembering your mistakes and keeping them front of mind helps to avoid repeating them.

I shall briefly discuss a couple of bad mistakes I made in the period when I was not restricted. One was Just Eat, the other Ocado.

I knew nothing about Just Eat, except that they had made an acquisition of the equivalent company in Australia for $800m. The company was loss making, had limited revenues, and the valuation made absolutely no sense – it represented $40 for every man, woman and child in Australia, which buys you an awful lot of advertising and free coupons. I talked to John Hempton of Bronte Capital about it and we agreed that it was a ridiculous price – we concluded that the management had lost their marbles, if they ever had any. I think John may have put on a small short.

Figure 11.3: Just Eat share price

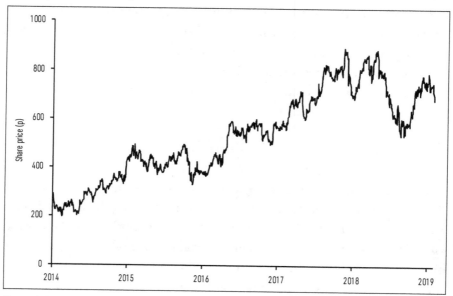

Source: Behind the Balance Sheet from Sentieo Data.

The stock pulled back initially but went on to appreciate significantly. There was little impact from the overpriced June 2015 Australian acquisition.

I looked at buying it in the hedge fund, but I could not get over the Australian deal. Several years later, I was talking to Graham Clapp, formerly an incredibly successful fund manager at Fidelity and then running his own hedge fund, Pensato Capital. He explained to me that he had bought Just Eat because management had told him a story about them buying out their principal competitor in Northampton or a similar smallish town. They could not dislodge the local incumbent, once it became established. That helped to explain the Australian deal.

In the mid 2010s, I almost recommended Ocado. The stock was heavily shorted, everyone hated it, but management explained that they were building a tech company and would soon sell their automated warehouse and food delivery technology to supermarkets around the world. Here was a rare case of a credible management team setting out a story and the stock market refusing to believe it... I thought this was a really interesting opportunity and I spent quite a bit of time looking at Ocado.

Unfortunately, the accounts made it look like the business was losing money. Indeed, it was losing money, but there was no way of understanding how much of the losses were down to investment in the business and technology, rather than an unprofitable trading operation. I talked to Dan Abrahams, the bull on the stock and an extremely smart investor, but I could not get any comfort on the numbers. I attended the analysts meeting and quizzed Sir Stuart Rose, the (non-executive) chairman – he agreed that it was a difficult company to value and he didn't seem excited enough.

I asked to visit the warehouses to see if I could judge the technology. I was given a tour of Hatfield and it was unimpressive. I asked to go visit their newest warehouse, which had the latest technology, and they said that I would need to visit at 4.30am, which would not be very convenient. When I agreed to the early visit, they then claimed they wanted to give existing shareholders priority. This did not alleviate my concerns.

I carried on spending time looking at the numbers, speaking to the sell-side and other investors, I met the finance director and watched him speak a couple of times, but I was at something of an impasse – to buy the stock, I would need to take it all on trust. Finally, I received an invitation from the company to a broker lunch with the CEO. He arrived late and was very circumspect in the way he answered, or indeed, failed to answer, questions.

So, I had an idea that the stock could be very cheap if management turned out to be telling the truth, but there was a record of consistent disappointment, failure to deliver their promised overseas contracts, the numbers did not stack up as far as I could see, and management were evasive and unhelpful. Ultimately, I could not buy the stock. Of course, what happened was they eventually announced a deal with Kroger and the stock rocketed up.

Figure 11.4: Ocado share price

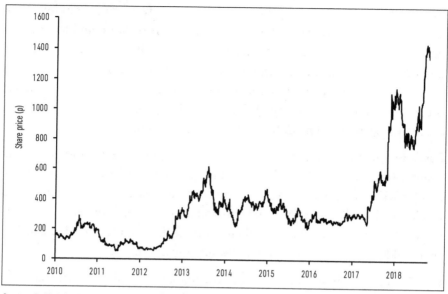

Source: Behind the Balance Sheet from Sentieo Data.

Still, it could have been worse – I could have been short like many hedge funds were. The only thing that saved me was that there was already a large short interest and management seemed convinced in their own story, although their attitude made me uncomfortable.

CONCLUSIONS

Maintenance is an essential part of the analyst's work and is at the heart of effective portfolio management. Unless you are on top of what is happening on a day-to-day basis, it is very easy to look one morning and find that the prospects for a stock you own have changed significantly – the world is changing faster than ever and it requires a lot of time to stay on top of a portfolio.

Many professional investors try to view their portfolios with a fresh eye every single day, and to re-evaluate the attractions of each stock as if they bought them that morning – assessing whether you would have the same positions is a great discipline and something even the private investor should do on a regular basis, if not every day. A number of hedge funds formally review the whole portfolio once a month, while quarterly is probably a sensible frequency for a personal portfolio.

12
MACRO-ECONOMIC ANALYSIS

Many investors spend a lot of time worrying about the overall valuation of the market. For example, a wealth management client of mine used to spend an inordinate amount of time at each monthly investment committee worrying about year-to-date performance, the interest rate outlook, and the likely direction of markets.

These are not the most productive things for investors to spend their time and energy worrying about!

In this section, I review why investors should pay more attention to companies than economic factors. Having said that, the macro environment, while highly unpredictable, is a huge driver of stocks and cannot be ignored. Hence, I discuss how difficult it is to extrapolate from macro knowledge to the outlook for stocks. I then explain why I think micro-economic factors, for example, the direction of travel for a commodity such as the oil price, are more critical areas to devote time and attention. (I use the term macro to describe broader trends in the whole economy and micro for trends in an industry, individual commodity or other section of the economy.)

I also explain why politics is not as important as people think, at least for your portfolio, before discussing cycles, economic and other, and concluding with some of the economic factors I use and monitor regularly.

MACRO-ECONOMIC INPUTS

While I am no macro analyst, I think it's important to have an idea of the general direction of trends and some understanding of where we are in the cycle. I try to look at the important variables in the major economies and get a sense of whether they are accelerating or slowing.

I deliberately keep this simple. For instance, China is the world's second-largest economy and few in the West fully understand what is really going on there, since its economic statistics are woefully inaccurate. Many investors spend too much time and effort worrying about small changes in US or German output, when such subtleties are much less significant than what is happening in China, where there is much greater scope for error. Whether China is going to grow more quickly or more slowly is a factor whose significance swamps almost any other factor.

In my experience, the macro factor that has the most important impact on equity portfolios is FX or exchange rate moves. They are also extremely difficult to get right.

Of secondary importance are oil prices in particular and commodity prices in general. These factors are critical in determining company profitability. But, once again, these are unfortunately also impossible to forecast with consistency and accuracy. The factor that people spend a lot of time debating, and probably shouldn't, is interest rates.

FOREIGN EXCHANGE RATES

Fluctuations in foreign exchange rates often offer excellent opportunities in equities, particularly in exporting companies or those with a complex currency exposure, e.g., airlines. Some examples of money-making opportunities from FX moves, such as a strengthening dollar, include:

1. buy BMW or similar Euro exporters, as there is a significant gearing to profitability

2. sell European or Asian airlines as their dollar costs (fuel, aircraft depreciation and lease costs) may be larger than their dollar revenues from transatlantic or transpacific routes

3. buy exporters which compete with US producers, e.g., Airbus, which has a largely Euro-based cost structure but sells in dollars.

A few years ago, a highly respected fund decided to sell Airbus because a large element of its backlog was orders from low-cost carriers in emerging markets, whose currencies were not tied to the dollar. The hypothesis was that the airlines would be forced to cancel aircraft as their cost base rose, forcing them to increase fares and choke off demand. I pointed out to the fund that this mattered far less than the fact that Airbus was locking in much higher profits on each new aircraft sold. I had been consistently positive on the stock for several years.

OIL

Oil is an input into everything. I met the Nestlé CFO in the lift at a conference in 2017 and in a quick chat he cited the commodity cost headwinds the company was facing:

- Coffee.

- The oil price, as an input into the cost of plastic for PET bottles in their water division.

- Milk.

Here is a consumer products company, revered for its earnings consistency, whose primary output is food and drink products, whose CFO cited the indirect impact of oil on the cost of plastic. This is a good illustration of the impact the oil price has on multiple sectors, both directly and indirectly. It's always important to watch the oil price, even if it's nearly impossible to forecast.

INTEREST RATES

Many investors spend too much time worrying about interest rates, whether they are going to rise and when. A wealth management client debated the topic of when the Fed was going to raise rates at every one of its monthly investment meetings in 2015. I pointed out in January, at the start of that year, that this was a waste of time because:

1. we had no idea when the Fed would raise rates

2. the Fed itself probably didn't know either

3. it was going to make no difference to markets, as this was the most telegraphed rate rise in history and was therefore likely already fully discounted.

In August, they were still having the same debate and were no closer to a correct answer than they were in January. This is an extremely common mistake – it's essential to focus on issues that can affect your performance.

Understanding what you need to worry about, and when, can save a lot of wasted effort. In practice, the first couple of interest rate rises generally don't make that much difference to the stock-market trends, as stocks carry on rising after the first rate hike, and for quite some time thereafter. A portfolio is not going to fall sharply if it is not defensively positioned ahead of the first rate hike, especially when hikes are 25 basis points at a time, so I question whether it is worth worrying about such issues.

James Montier at GMO believes that interest rates don't actually make that much difference to the real economy. That might be quite an extreme position, but I am not sure about the conventional wisdom of rates curing inflation. Rate rises in a highly indebted consumer society like the US mean people have less disposable income, but they usually arise when unemployment has fallen and people can push for wage rises or move jobs. With interest costs affecting mortgages, credit cards and auto loans, they can be a very big driver of disposable income and people may feel a need to ask for higher wages when rates rise. Is that disinflationary?

It might have been clear to some in 2007, for example, that it would be a good idea to bet against an overly leveraged US consumer. More often, the big picture can be astonishingly complicated. For instance, I have spent some considerable time debating in my mind the implications for inflation of an ageing population.

It might be thought that such a question would have an obvious answer, but I have read persuasive pieces that argue both ways. Some contend that it creates inflation, as there are fewer workers who can command higher wages, generating an inflationary spiral; while others suggest that it should create deflation, as people spend and save less.

Such theoretical arguments are likely to be outweighed by the influence of technological developments like AI. I try to understand these long-term issues and the arguments on both sides, even if it's sometimes impossible to draw a definitive conclusion.

Another major conundrum currently is China. Is it going bust? Credit growth has been increasing so fast and each incremental dollar of debt produces a lower amount of incremental GDP. It may even continue to grow if the authorities are adept enough to manage it, but this remains unproven.

WHY MACRO ANALYSIS IS PROBLEMATIC

Monitoring macro events is even harder than keeping an eye on stocks. There are a lot of variables involved, as was illustrated by a comparison someone made with chess. In chess, there are 72,084 move combinations after each player has made two moves, and over 288 billion scenarios after four moves each. Global markets and economies are infinitely more complex than chess, hence the difficulty.

Nate Silver, the US election pollster and pundit, in his book, *The Signal and the Noise*, suggested that the margin of error on the first report of US quarterly GDP was subject to revision in a range of +/−4.3%. This is larger than the reported number, yet investors nevertheless pay great attention to the GDP print. Given that it's a backwards-looking number, it's reported late, and you already know the quarterly results of the companies whose shares you own, I am not sure why is it considered so important by equity investors.

If analysing the past is difficult in macro, imagine how much more difficult it is to make forecasts. Hundreds of experts predict GDP growth for the next year or two, and hundreds of other variables, but they have limited success and it's dangerous to rely on them. The good news, as I shall explain, is that you don't have to – a basic understanding of the macro is useful to plot your investment course and not much more is required.

HOW I TAKE A MACRO VIEW

I focus on the direction of economic trends, paying particular attention to the outlook for exchange rates. This is difficult to get right but is critical to individual company profitability and stock performance. When evaluating the macro picture, I try to remember three rules:

1. USE DATA

I monitor multiple monthly data points – PMIs, car sales, housing starts, a wide range of transport stats (from rail loadings to airport passenger growth), electricity production and consumption, and average earnings and unemployment data, in the areas where I have specific interest. Government data tends to be less reliable (the US is probably best and China the worst) and subject to later revision, whereas airport passenger numbers and container imports are factual and not normally subject to revision.

2. DON'T LISTEN TO EXPERTS

There are a huge number of professional economists employed in the City and on Wall Street. They are reasonable at projecting on the basis of current conditions, but generally useless at predicting recessions, which is a main reason to have concern about the macro. Economic commentators are better at talking than making you money and are generally best avoided.

There is also a lot of macro analysis available for free – there are some good bloggers and even Twitter can be helpful – but much is consensual or wrong. David Rosenberg, previously of Gluskin Sheff, is a notable exception. I also enjoy the often-wild predictions of Steen Jakobsen of Saxo Bank.

3. ASSUME EVERYTHING IS CYCLICAL

We saw in the 1990s, and again in the 2010s, that there can be an unusually long economic cycle, but they always end. It's a safe working assumption. I talk more about cycles later.

Common sense and observation will give a sensible view of the cyclical position. For example, if I want to check the pulse of the UK economy, I look at how many houses in my street have scaffolding – is this the same, or more, or less, than at previous cycle peaks? Similarly, crane counts can be helpful.

The data cited above will give a very good sense of whether economies are growing and accelerating or slowing. The sectoral data are earlier and more accurate, as well as being a better indicator than the more commonly used measures of the wider economy. I have found transport statistics to be particularly helpful as the sector tends to be at the leading edge of the economy – generally a slowdown in air traffic growth precedes an economic slowdown. In the UK, for example, the London–Edinburgh air traffic statistics have been a reliable indicator of economic health.

MACRO VERSUS MICRO

I suspect that investors often waste too much time worrying about economic minutiae – the exact level of GDP growth, the number of rate rises this year, etc.

The direction of economic growth – and its second derivative, whether growth is slowing or accelerating – are the critical variables, but activity estimates only need to be broadly right to give the right framework for stock selection. This is true even for asset allocation, in the sense of the level of cash required in a long-only equity portfolio, or the critical gross and net exposures in a hedge fund portfolio.

Understanding the macro economic framework is most useful in order to identify areas that you want to avoid or to get exposure to. As an example, I might be seeking exposure to certain areas/themes/geographies and avoiding certain others. Say I liked the US, as the economy seemed healthy; I might be seeking exposure to infrastructure, as interest rates had been low for a long time, economies were well advanced in the cycle and I expected governments to use spending as a source of economic support when things slow down.

I might also be looking thematically for companies which have pricing power as, in a low-growth world, volume growth may not be sufficient to drive revenue growth at a scale which will improve margins, especially in a deflationary environment. This cocktail might lead me to a stock like Vulcan Materials, one of the US aggregate producers.

FOCUS ON STOCKS, NOT THE MACRO

My view is therefore that it is much more important to worry about the valuation of the stocks in your portfolio, than about the level of the market or macro-economic data, such as GDP growth rates.

In his 2016 letter to investors in his Fundsmith fund, Terry Smith claimed that he pays no attention to macro factors. In that letter he gave a list of factors which could affect companies and markets in 2017 – Brexit, China, 'demonetisation' in India, the French presidential election, the German election, interest rates, Korea, Trump, quantitative easing by the European Central Bank, Syria and the oil price.

Smith points out that even if you could guess the outcome of any or all of these events, it might not do you much good. "To usefully employ your predictions, you would not only have to make mostly correct predictions, but you would also need to gauge what the markets expected to occur in order to predict how they would react. Good luck with that," he says.

Imagine being told on 1 January 2016, with the S&P 500 Index at 1926, that in the next 12 months there would be a scare that China would have a credit crisis, over $10trn of government bonds globally would have a negative yield, the Japanese central bank would target 0% yield on its government bonds, the UK would vote to leave the EU, and that Donald Trump would be elected US president. Would you have expected the S&P 500 to rise by nearly 13%?

What about if you had been told that in mid-February 2016, in the middle of the China deflationary scare, the S&P was 1829? Would you have expected it to rise by nearly 20% from its low?

At a broker dinner for hedge funds in early 2016, after the worst start to the year for a long time, only one participant volunteered that the market would be higher at the end of the year. Interestingly, he was not working at a hedge fund but was a long-only investor.

Similarly, in emerging markets, suppose you knew at the start of 2016 that there would be a huge scare on growth in China in Q1, oil prices and commodities would collapse, both the Brazilian and Korean president would be impeached, and there would be an attempted coup in Turkey during the course of the year. Would you have expected emerging markets to be the best performing area in the world and to rise by double digits? In emerging markets, as with many cyclical areas and sectors, it only needs the news to go from terrible to really bad to engineer a big positive move in share prices.

Most pundits thought Clinton would win the 2016 US presidential race – in fact, I could not find one prediction of a Trump victory by a conventional forecaster. As a former colleague pointed out, even if you had predicted the Brexit and Trump votes correctly, you might not have drawn the correct conclusions. Most pundits thought stock markets would fall on Trump's election, yet they soared. It was actually clear at 9am UK time after Trump's acceptance speech that his win would be well received by markets, at least initially.

It's perfectly understandable that some equity managers profess to have no interest in the macro environment. I do not believe that you can entirely ignore the macro, however. You need to have a view on the economic outlook in order to shape your portfolio and to look for the most fertile areas of investment.

CYCLES

A key part of understanding the macro is looking at the cycle and, as Howard Marks puts it so well, understanding where we are in the cycle. Marks uses the prevailing environment to dictate his attitude to risk.

This is not straightforward because there are a large number of cycles, each with its own time frame, and it's a complex topic. I use the following framework of cycles, which I've borrowed from a number of smart commentators.

- Debt and deleveraging cycle – this was made famous by Ray Dalio of Bridgewater and is too long term to be of immediate application.

- Demographics – equally long term, but this is critical to an understanding of the direction of growth and to frame broad growth expectations. It's also critical to turnover assumptions – can growth this decade be higher or lower than last? There are several key elements:

  - Overall demographics and rate of population growth.

  - Number of people in the critical 16–64 age bands – i.e., number of workers.

  - Number of people retiring – from the mid-2010s, baby boomers are retiring in the US at the rate of 10,000 per month.

  - Fertility – the rate of births per 100 women aged 15–44 has collapsed to 0.8% in the US since 2000, versus 1.9% in the 1960s and 2.3% in the 1970s. This is critical to economic growth as babies create a large stimulus to economic activity.

  - A similar variable is household formation, which again creates a big economic stimulus. If it slows, economic growth will be less vibrant.

- The economic cycle – when was the last recession and how soon is the next one likely? This is almost never forecast accurately by economists, but it's the key question to address.

- The business cycle – an individual sector often has a cycle which is slightly out of phase with the economy at large. For example, the transport sector, which I used to follow, is tricky as it leads the economy.

- The stock-market cycle – where are we in the duration of a bull or bear market? Again, this can be slightly out of phase with the economic cycle – generally 18 months or so ahead.

A good way of identifying where we are in the cycle is to consider pent-up demand, which is an often-overlooked factor in economics. In the late 2010s, there were certain signs of cycle exhaustion in the US economy:

- Autos demand had been fading and indeed overall had only been supported by light trucks, not conventional cars.

- Used-car prices were falling.

- There were indications of overbuild in the apartment sector, arising from fading demand.

- Retail property was hard to rent, except in the most valuable locations.

When there are multiple signs like this, especially if the consumer is dodging big-ticket purchases in a consumer-driven economy like the US, it's unlikely that growth will accelerate. It's not impossible, but certainly more difficult without significant stimulus.

Trump's tax cuts and ever more buoyant consumer confidence led the US economy to accelerate in the first half of 2018, but the cycle in early 2020 looked to me to be extended.

POLITICS

When I started in the stock market in the mid-1980s, politics was considered an important influence on the market, and the UK Budget was a major event. Our entire research department was involved in producing a substantial book delineating the Budget measures and their implications for stocks.

I helped compile the book in February 1987. The colour cover was always pre-printed with a cartoon and the main measures were then overprinted on the cover during the night before Budget Day. That year I was set to travel to the US for my first overseas marketing trip and I was lucky enough to fly out with the Budget books on Concorde – this was a massive deal for me at the time. It was the time of the British Airways IPO and, as an airline analyst (one of very few in London), I managed to wangle a trip to the cockpit. Tagging along with me was my neighbour, Jim Randle, the engineering director at Jaguar. I remember the cockpit being small and, boy, were there a lot of dials.

I landed and handed the books to a colleague. We were first to distribute our research in Manhattan; this was long before email and I am not sure if the fax had been invented. Imagine! I then took a car to LaGuardia and flew up to Boston to meet the famed investment manager, Hakan Castegren.

Back then, the Budget was regarded much more seriously than today, when most of the measures are leaked beforehand in the press. More recently, politics has been a less significant factor in stock-market thinking, except for specific isolated instances, such as a change of power on an election. That was until 2016. Brexit and Trump brought politics, and political risk, front of centre.

THE US POLITICAL CYCLE

The US political cycle is often cited by strategists thus: the first year of the new president being positive, the best year generally being year three, and some uncertainty in the run-up to the election sometimes causing markets to fret in the fourth year.

Such political cycles are generally quite specific to local conditions, with uncertainty being enhanced in close-run contests or coalition governments. While they create a lot of noise on Bloomberg and CNBC, political events only rarely have a great impact on markets, and the difference in performance between, say, Republic and Democrat presidents is just noise. Stock markets have, in fact, fared better under Democrats in the last 100 years, with Democratic presidents returning nearly 75% over the cycle – or more than double the Republican average.

TRY TO UNDERSTAND THE RISKS

As an investor, you may not have a strong view on the political complexion. Even if you do, your clients are not really paying you to take those sorts of bets. Estimating the probabilities of political events is extremely difficult, as we have seen in recent UK and indeed US elections when almost all the polls got it badly wrong. But you need to understand the risks, all the same. That can frame the risk-reward judgement, even if the probabilities are impossible to calculate.

The June 2016 referendum in the UK, when the British people voted to leave the European Union, is a relatively rare example of a political event, rather than a change of political party, causing real economic change. UK domestic stocks sold off heavily then quickly bounced back. I approached the referendum with a degree of caution. The result was too close to call. My thinking was that the most likely outcome was a vote to remain, and that housebuilders like Berkeley Homes would likely bounce 10–15%. Although a gain of 20–30% from a housebuilder short was likely if the vote was to leave, and there was an asymmetric risk here, I didn't (wrongly) see 'leave' as being twice as likely as 'remain'.

In the Brexit vote, I knew that if the result was a vote to leave, then it was highly likely that sterling would fall significantly. I therefore looked for a company with substantial exporting capacity from the UK or significant overseas earnings. I then looked for something which would look undervalued even if the vote was to remain, as expected. I therefore recommended buying Diageo, which was depressed for various reasons, where there were good export profits; a large element of overseas sales, which could be translated back into a weaker sterling; and a high quality but fairly defensive business, which was already rather undervalued.

I knew that if the market ripped on a remain vote, then the stock would underperform but still go up. But it had the virtue that it was a good bet if there was a vote to leave, and a quick gain of 20% on the stock was possible. This was indeed how it panned out.

I learned from that vote and was wary going into the 2016 US election. None of us thought that Trump would win, but we didn't want to be caught out if he did. I made a small bet on the spread-betting markets the day before, buying Trump at 17 – odds of almost 6–1. I only made the bet because I thought it was the wrong price, rather than having any inkling that a Trump victory was likely.

Politics has become extremely complicated and confused in many jurisdictions. Portfolios need to be rebalanced going into an election, in order that you have protection against a surprise result. This means having some stocks which will do well in any outcome, and not a skew to a victory by one side or another.

CONCLUSIONS

Macro is really tough. You only have to look at the large number of macro hedge funds, run by really talented individuals, which have closed in recent years or made paltry returns. The best I hope for is a broad understanding of the macro environment and thus a feeling for when to take risk and when to be more wary. Even so, the macro does inform stock selection and remains an important factor for the equity investor.

13
LOOKING FORWARD

I HAVE UNTIL now explained how I used to do my job on the sell-side (working for investment banks) and on the buy-side (mainly at hedge funds). The nature of the work has been changing, and although the old techniques are certainly still generally valid, tech has been playing an ever-increasing role in company analysis, in three ways:

1. Disruption which affects most companies in almost every industry.

2. The analysis of tech itself.

3. The use of new methods.

In this chapter, I focus on disruption, which is by far the most important to the majority of investors. I then briefly discuss the analysis of tech companies and the use of new methods, before looking forward to the 2020s decade in my conclusions.

THE CONCEPT OF DISRUPTION

Commentators tend to scoff at the excesses of the 1990s tech boom and the idea of the value of eyeballs and similar nonsense. Yet Amazon has substantially outperformed the stock market since the peak of the tech boom in 1999 (even after Amazon initially fell 90%!). And for all the furore about Pets.com (a zero in the tech-boom fallout), few realise that chewy.com, the same business model, changed hands for over $3bn two decades later.

Figure 13.1: Amazon share price

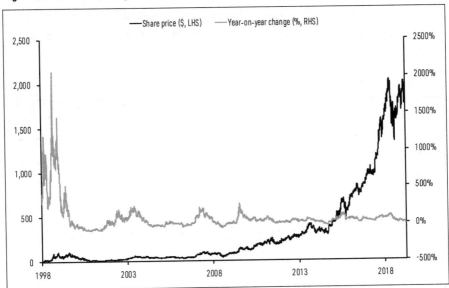

Source: Behind the Balance Sheet from Sentieo Data.

This is not to say that the peak of the boom was not a bubble; at least one stock in any bubble would have been bound to have outperformed since. But I would suggest that the 1990s was perhaps not *totally* mad. Certainly, many stocks were ascribed ridiculous valuations, but investors recognised the opportunity afforded by the internet, the disruption it would bring, and accorded it a large future value.

The issue of disruption is one of the most important areas for any analyst to consider today. This includes the opportunity afforded to new industry entrants as well as the threat to incumbents. I decided to cover disruption here in a separate chapter, rather than in the approach to researching the company, as it will be such a key factor in future analysis.

In this chapter, I do not cover the subject of how to invest in tech, which would be a book in itself, nor do I seriously address the issue of where and how disruption is having an impact. Instead, I discuss how I think about disruption. This is an area which is much more art than science and where there are no rules, but I hope that an illustration of some of my practical experience is helpful.

I discuss how difficult it can be to recognise a game-changing invention or development (for investors and industry participants alike), how hard it can be to assess the likely future impact of such developments and how to assess the threat to stocks in a portfolio.

Disruption has made heroes out of many investors who probably didn't deserve to be, at least in my view, for many have just got lucky surfing the wave. It has also made some really smart investors look quite stupid. I should admit that I have avoided looking really stupid through sheer luck and have dismally failed to look like a hero – I have been far too conservative in my approach.

THE NATURE OF DISRUPTION

Benedict Evans is a strategy guru and former partner at venture-capital firm Andreessen Horowitz, one of the most successful such firms in Silicon Valley. He has a blog and email list of over 130,000. He wrote a wonderful piece on Tesla in August 2018, where he assessed the company as a disruptive force and quite correctly dismissed its chances of being an equivalent of the iPhone in the automotive industry. This article is well worth reading, as it makes some very perceptive comments about what it takes to be a true disruptive influence on a market.[8] (Benedict has become a friend, but honestly he really is brilliant.)

In the article, he makes the point that Nokia dismissed the iPhone because it wasn't a very good phone. And, likewise, auto makers dismiss Tesla because of the panel fit and the production of the Model 3 in a tent in summer 2018. It remains to be seen whether Tesla will be a true disrupter in the sense of the iPhone. But it seems unlikely given both the sheer scale of the auto industry and the fact that while the incumbents may face a (diminishing)

---

8 Benedict Evans, 'Tesla, software and disruption', https://www.ben-evans.com/benedictevans/2018/8/29/tesla-software-and-disruption

disadvantage vs Tesla in innovation in electric vehicles, they have a massive advantage in every other area.

The concept of disruption is that a new entrant, idea or methodology changes the basis of competition within an industry. Using the iPhone as an example, to start with Apple was not great at making phones, but Nokia was really poor at creating software. This is a great example, as the incumbent had the superior phone, but making calls quickly became almost a secondary purpose of a phone. Such change is incredibly difficult to anticipate.

Sometimes a new technology or idea turns out not to be too disruptive, as the incumbents learn to adapt, although there are usually some impacts either up the supply chain or downstream in distribution or retail. Hence, the impact of a disruptive technology is extremely difficult to assess. Often the originator of the new technology or idea is not the company which gains the greatest benefit – Benedict points out that Apple invented the PC, but went bust soon after; the main beneficiaries were not the hardware producers like IBM or Dell, although both benefitted immensely for an extended period.

Instead, the biggest gainer from Apple's invention was Microsoft. This was impossible to predict at the outset. Notably, Microsoft won with software which was inferior. Excel was a poor copy of Lotus 123, and Lotus Notes was by far the best email software, yet not even IBM's deep pockets after its acquisition of the company could save Lotus.

This outcome would likely have been thought laughable for many years following the introduction of the Apple IIe. In some ways, it's still surprising that the superior products did not prevail (and to me, disappointing, as I much preferred the Lotus products to the probably still inferior Microsoft software I am using 30 years later). Yet the power of Windows and the pre-packaged or bundled software was much greater than the efficacy of the products. That's why such outcomes are really hard to predict.

I recall reading about the launch of the iPad in late 2010 in an article on the front page of the *FT*. I shouted out to the dealing floor, "Does anyone have any ideas what this iPad thing will be used for?" The only volunteer suggested that people who could not afford big houses in London would use it to read books (which they did not have room for at home). Not hugely constructive, but I mention this simply to illustrate that it was incredibly difficult at the time to imagine that a few years later, I would be one of the only people in the room at most analysts' meetings *not* using an iPad to take notes. Knowing this, I would have expected it to have been negative for sales of Moleskin notebooks, yet they still seem to be popular, notably as giveaways at conferences – disruption is difficult to gauge.

HOW DOES DISRUPTION IMPACT RETAIL INVESTMENTS?

Therefore, disruption is now one of the key risks for investors, as old business models encounter new competition from online players. Nowhere is this more prevalent than in the retail sector. And this is especially true of the US, which has too much space in bricks and mortar stores. Cowen estimated that there was 23,500 sq ft of retail space per capita in the US vs 4,600 in the UK, and just 2,400 in Germany in 2017.

With roughly one-in-ten workers employed in retail, the shrinking of the sector has profound implications for the US economy. For example, in the six months to April 2017, more workers lost their jobs in retail than were employed in the US coal industry, per 13D Research. Only 4.2% of the workers leaving retail moved to transport and logistics, the one obvious online substitute role.

Offline retailers have been forced to respond by moving online, but few are properly equipped to do so with the wrong supply-chain set-up. A survey by consultants PwC and JDA Software in 2017 found that only 10% of 350 global retailers were making a profit from online sales. This is a surprising metric, but perhaps understandable when one thinks about the free-returns policy operated by many retailers (think clothing, shoes, etc.) and generally thin margins.

This is coupled with a change in consumer spending as we become a more experiential society. For the first time, in 2016, more money was spent in restaurants and bars by US consumers than in grocery stores. Younger consumers in particular are spending more online, they are getting married later, they are having fewer children, later in life, and they are living in smaller homes. All this is conducive to lower sales of consumer goods.

Meanwhile, credit parameters in the Anglo-Saxon economies have been deteriorating as consumers borrow to spend. This is a trend which cannot continue indefinitely and indications in the US are that credit metrics have been deteriorating across the board, in student loans, automotive loans and credit card borrowing.

This makes investing in the retail sector incredibly difficult, especially as the sector bifurcates. At one end, old retailers like Marks & Spencer in the UK are shunned and have ratings which are a fraction of their peak; at the other end, online retailers have become market darlings and often enjoy stratospheric ratings, which are frankly hard to justify and may prove harder to sustain.

An example is ASOS, the UK online retailer, which fell 40% after issuing a profit warning and revising down its annual revenue projections from 20–25% to 15%. This is a significant change and the price drop is unsurprising for a retailer on a racy multiple (in September 2018, ASOS' P/E multiple reached around 80×).

THE IMPACT OF TECHNOLOGY

The stock market can be slow to recognise disruptive threats, but they can then impact stock prices suddenly and sharply, as more people become aware and momentum sends stocks down. We saw this, for example, in the automotive industry a few years ago when the twin themes of electric vehicles (EVs) and autonomous driving became a major concern.

I believe that autonomous vehicles (AVs) are a massive change, akin to the development of the internet, with huge ramifications across every investment sector, from property to transport.

EVs were perhaps not initially considered as disruptive in the conventional sense, with consensus in the mid-2010s predicting a penetration of sub-5% by 2025, with advanced players like BMW and Mercedes talking of a 20% share of sales ten years hence.

But such low levels of market share seemed unlikely given that the cost of an EV is dependent on battery technology developments and they seem likely to follow a tech industry evolution (assuming cobalt supply constraints can be overcome or circumvented). If batteries become much cheaper, EV will become cheaper than internal combustion vehicles, at least on a whole-life cost. At that point, much higher penetration is inevitable and already a plethora of platforms are being developed for pure EVs.

The precise penetration curve is less relevant than understanding the investment implications for more traditional cyclical sectors and also tertiary sectors, such as property, as car parking spaces are freed up when AVs become prevalent. Stock-market consensus also started to accept in the late-2010s that the rate of change was increasing, with autonomous driving starting to become more of a reality. In my view, the stock market has underestimated the penetration of EVs and has been too optimistic on the timing of arrival of AVs.

When I first met Benedict Evans, I took copious notes. I had not met him before, but he is a fascinating guy with an amazing insight into all sorts of tech trends; it was great fun to spend an hour over a coffee discussing what was happening in the world. I thought that these notes might help readers understand the difficulty and complexity of assessing the impact of future technological developments, and how this poses a significant risk to investors. Indeed, seeing how wrong you have been in the past is a great discipline and reduces the risk of overconfidence. This is a useful technique in the area of tech disruption, when commentary will quickly date.

At the time (2017), I wondered if the Street had it wrong in thinking that the big ad agencies were so at risk from Accenture, which had started buying digital agencies. I was also worried by Hyundai's move to cut out the middle man and design and place their own ads with Google. Interestingly, it transpired that the Street was thinking too short term and there were more serious longer-term issues to think about, namely:

1. Amazon – the Dash button is a good illustration of the trend. By installing a Tide Dash button on your washing machine, Amazon was not only disintermediating Procter & Gamble, but also the ad agency.

2. Mobile eats the world – as more advertising goes straight to social media, the ad agency becomes increasingly redundant, as happened with the travel agency.

3. The demise of TV – the amount of time watching TV is shrinking quite fast. For years, while the internet decimated print, TV held up, but now it seems to be going the same way. Netflix and Amazon have overtaken HBO in content spend. And they don't have ads.

4. Advertising is only 50% of the external marketing spend, with the other 50% going below the line on coupons, shelf placement and promotions in stores. As more spending goes online and more of that goes on Amazon, the amount of investment in A&P (advertising and promotion) by marketing departments will also shrink.

5. Advertising as a percentage of GDP has been flat for decades. That will surely shrink in the next ten years.

The counterargument is that in a world in which the traditional roles of advertising and A&P spend are no longer as significant in helping brands promote themselves to consumers, perhaps the ad agency and similar intermediaries will become *more*, rather than less, important to brands, as they need more creative ways of endearing themselves to consumers. The market may shrink, but TV advertising may become even more desirable.

TV ads in the UK are showing some such indications. There are more extravagant and even more creative ads – just look at the £5.6bn (+5%) spent on Christmas 2016 ads by the likes of John Lewis (£7m), Marks & Spencer (£7m), Burberry (£10m), and even Heathrow Airport.

Benedict and I also talked about autos, electric vehicles and autonomous cars. My view has long been that the OEMs (original equipment manufacturers – Ford, GM, etc.) are threatened as they have to spend a huge amount on new technology in two spheres: electric powertrains and autonomous driving. This is potentially a huge burden. Benedict sees EVs as being the greater threat, as do I.

Fully autonomous driving is ten or more years away, although in the interim there will be major advances in, for example, autonomous trucks. Freeways are much easier for autonomous vehicles. The driver will still be present, but will be sleeping in the cab. As a consequence, they will be able to travel much further. Platooning (stringing many trucks together) will reduce fuel consumption. This should happen quite soon in the US, which is a $800bn market. It's also where Amazon will focus its logistics effort. The 'Uber for trucks' is not simple and many have tried to conquer it, but Amazon has the advantage of substantial internal shipping requirements.

Although fully autonomous cars are further away, manufacturers and auto component suppliers will still have to spend significantly to develop the technology. This incremental R&D investment will not result in people wanting to pay more for cars and so margins will inevitably decline.

Development of AVs will be gradual – there will not be a big bang when everyone globally puts down their car keys and on 1/1/2040, switches to Uber's AVs. Rather, it will be a gradual and phased changeover, with cities like Phoenix, Arizona with a climate and geography more suited to AVs, likely being early adopters and others following later. Hence, we shall be able to observe the impact on a range of sectors like property and transport over an extended period. The ramifications will be immense, in my view.

THE AMAZON THREAT

In a similar vein to my coffee with Benedict, I summarise here a discussion with a former senior Amazon executive. This serves to illustrate the importance of thinking about technological developments and the difficulty in anticipating disruption, and why Amazon has been such a staggeringly successful business.

MARKET POSITION

Amazon in 2016 took over 50% of the US online market. The executive attributed this success to a combination of the following:

- A relentless focus on price – Amazon will not be beaten by a reputable competitor.

- Unrivalled breadth of selection – the UK site had an astonishing 180m SKUs, which I would guess is 100× the nearest competitor.

- Prime – the fixed price incentivises customers to amortise this cost over a broader suite of purchases and ensures they visit the Amazon site before all others. Prime benefits are constantly being extended to video, music, Kindle lending library, etc.

- Third-party sellers – these are critical as they make up half of all order volumes.

- Speed of delivery.

BRANDS

Amazon poses a huge threat to brands. While truly differentiated brands can resist this threat if they have sufficient marketing power, the surrender of Nike to Amazon is testament to the dynamics. Nike used to withhold its products from Amazon but was forced to give in and allow their sale on the site – Amazon was just too important. And for the majority of brands who sell similar products, they will suffer considerable pressure.

Consider a product made by a contract manufacturer in China, who can use an intermediary on the Amazon system to offer identical products with wafer-thin margins and incentivise the customer with a significant discount. Over time, customers will find that there is no difference and will move to the cheaper product. As has happened with electronics, brands too will experience commoditisation.

GROCERY

Amazon purchased Whole Foods for $16bn for its fresh-food supply chain – it would have taken them a decade to build that organically. This was also the motive for Amazon's deal with Morrisons in the UK.

Amazon cannot stay out of food because it is the number one spend for consumers; Amazon faces the law of large numbers, so it needs food to maintain its growth long term. Grocery delivery is an intrinsically unattractive operation, as you are competing with a store where the customer does the pick and delivery – Walmart and Tesco have refined operations after decades of experience, yet still only make thin margins. It may make sense to deliver groceries with a broad selection of non-fresh product, which is what Amazon had been trying to do without much success. It has struggled to get much traction with Amazon Fresh.

There may be no right economic model for grocery. It's a tough stand-alone business and supermarkets subsidise delivery. Supermarkets get returns, but instead of physically receiving the item, they tend just to give cash back, further depressing margins.

SERVICES

Kindle Direct Publishing has become a major platform for self-publishing, as the authors get to set the price and keep 70% of the retail price, compared to 15–30% for a bestselling author through conventional publishers. Of the Amazon Top 100 in 2015, 31 were self-published.

The music (a Spotify clone) offer is free, but Amazon measure very carefully to see if consumers who listen to a lot of music also spend a lot on retail and assess whether they can add value to the ecosystem, even without generating revenue from that individual product.

In video, Netflix and Amazon can afford to launch niche channels, e.g., food and wine, and if they can attract 20,000 subscribers they would not otherwise attract, that is good business for them – a conventional broadcaster cannot do that.

Watching Amazon's strategies in its various businesses is almost a full-time job, but it's important to monitor its developments, as the ramifications for other industries can be significant. Amazon simply mentioning that it might be interested in a sector is enough to crater share prices.

VENTURE CAPITAL

I mentioned earlier that a small part of my portfolio is allocated to venture capital and private equity. I believe that keeping in touch with the venture capital world is essential for the sophisticated investor in public equities, for two important reasons:

1. Information advantages are increasingly scarce and will decline further as investment becomes more automated – AI can read everything and in an instant. Hence, taking a longer-term perspective is likely to prove a better differentiator for professional investors. That creates a requirement to think further ahead.

2. Moreover, in a faster-changing world where technology is developing rapidly, it's essential to be aware of what may be coming down the road. Otherwise it will threaten your investments before you have had time to react.

I do this by keeping in touch with angel investors, venture capital firms like Founders Factory in London and analysts like Benedict Evans, and by investing myself in start-ups. Some of these start-ups have initiatives which can render traditional models obsolete if they are successful. Being aware of such threats is extremely helpful in evaluating the upside-downside scenarios for a stock.

Meeting with new start-ups is a useful discipline as you learn about the sort of things that people are dreaming up. Some of them, of course, are pure nonsense – socks-by-post.com was an actual business proposed to me as an investment. But sometimes you can gain insight into a development that would otherwise have gone undetected.

For instance, one proposal flagged to me an important development in the recruitment space – they had successfully built up a free job board as an alternative to employment agencies. (I did not invest in the company because the wife/partner of the founder lied in her CV about a role 20 years previous. I have no idea why, but she didn't seem worthy of my trust after that.)

Basically, by creating specialist sub-sectors, they offered the employer a complete list of candidates and the opportunity to advertise for free. For the 20% of jobs which are more complex, the venture offered the employer a cheap £500-ish service, whereby they searched both their own CV database and also other databases for appropriate candidates. With the development of AI, this process looked to me likely to be extremely effective.

They flagged up a test they had done for a potential client's search for a marketing director, at a salary of £80–100k. Because they subscribe to the CV databases of Hays and other agencies, they came up with an identical shortlist to the expensive headhunter who had been commissioned. Their cost was £500; the headhunter cost £27,000.

It seemed to me after this meeting that the recruitment agencies might experience a long-term secular decline in their fee levels. After running up 50% from its post-Brexit low, I thought Hays looked quite vulnerable to a deterioration in over-optimistic sentiment about Brexit and to this longer-term bow wave of potential fee pressure. Without this meeting, I would never have identified this potential risk and would not have had any reason other than valuation (not of itself sufficient) to consider such a trade.

CORPORATIONS AS THE SOURCE OF DISRUPTION

A longer-term factor to be aware of is the nature of profit margins. US corporate returns and profit margins have reached all-time highs and this has attracted a lot of commentary about the potential for mean reversion, etc. I believe that there are a number of coincident factors affecting this outcome.

First is an increase in high-earning tech companies, which require little capital and earn outstanding margins – think Google or Facebook. Of course, the corollary is that many disrupted businesses are earning lower returns and margins, so this is unlikely to be the sole cause.

Second is an increasing concentration in many industries – this is hard to measure but the number of publicly listed companies in the US has nearly halved in the last 20 years, so this likely reflects a higher industry consolidation than formerly. As an aside, this also reflects an increasing number of companies in private equity ownership, where there is less interest in long-term business health and more emphasis given to short-term cash generation. The issue of consolidation, its impact and possible backlash is covered in Jonathan Tepper's excellent book, *The Myth of Capitalism*.

The US airline industry is a classic example of increasing consolidation and its stocks have been significantly rerated. But the expulsion of Dr Dao from a United Airlines flight in April 2017 shows the social media backlash which can result when the public reacts to consumers being treated badly as industries become less competitive. In FMCG (fast-moving consumer goods), where the US consumer has been facing declining real income, consumer goods companies have responded with reduced packaging sizes.

When considering the long-term outlook for such an investment, one has to factor into the investment equation the risk that there will be a consumer backlash to this type of treatment; for example, the longer-term reaction might be greater regulation, whether that is the energy price caps envisaged by both Labour and Tory parties in the UK, or the potential for regulatory or consumer protection measures being introduced in the US airline industry.

This risk is perhaps most prevalent in the case of the major platform tech companies. Think of Airbnb, where cities like New York and Paris are imposing stricter controls on owners' rentals. Uber has become successful by destroying mom-and-pop taxi companies whose drivers may well end up working for Uber; its valuation might have been justified to some extent by the destruction of competition and the creation of a monopoly. At some point, however, politicians will engage with these platforms and introduce regulation.

THE ANALYSIS OF TECH STOCKS

It's clearly beyond the scope of this book to analyse tech stocks in detail. Tech bulls argue that we don't need to worry about profits and that the bigger the trading losses today, the greater the eventual market share gain. I fundamentally disagree with this view, but it's complicated. The focus on the relationship between the lifetime value of a customer and the cost of acquiring them is a valid technique. In my view, however, it does not entirely displace the conventional analytical techniques that I earlier covered at length.

In 2019, we saw the failure to IPO WeWork, a company which some of the biggest and most respected US investment banks valued at $50–100bn. It failed at $20bn and at $10bn, as investors did not believe the more ambitious valuations. In my view, it's not a tech stock and that was the primary reason the flotation did not proceed. We also saw household-name tech stocks like Uber and Lyft come to the market only to see their share prices decline when the broader market was making new highs.

Figure 13.2: Uber and Lyft share prices

Source: Behind the Balance Sheet from Sentieo Data.

Note: expressed as indices on starting values as of close on day of IPO

These internet-related stocks often behave like platforms and have winner-take-all characteristics – Uber has the most drivers, so it can offer the shortest wait time and hence attract the most customers. There is a virtuous circle in operation, which is highly attractive to investors.

The other major financial characteristic is that the companies often have a capital-light business model – Uber owns no taxis. Therefore, once the customer acquisition growth phase has peaked, these companies should be highly cash generative.

The problem with these investments is that they are incredibly difficult to value – it's hard to estimate how long the investment phase will continue. It's even more difficult to assess how profitable they will be once that phase is complete. And just because a company has built up an early lead, it does not mean that it will not attract competition, which often results in pricing pressure.

Netflix would be a good example – it has much higher spend on content than its peers and is much larger, yet a wave of new entrants are coming into the streaming market, attracted by its success. One study I saw suggested that in one year, streaming services' claims on customers' wallets increased from Netflix's $15.99 per month (Amazon Video being bundled with Prime) to over $250 per month, as multiple new services (HBO, Disney, Apple, etc.) entered the market.

When looking at tech stocks, I use LTV/CAC (customer lifetime value vs acquisition cost) in my analysis, but I also use EV-to-sales as one of my key parameters. The critical point, in my experience, is to use benchmarks which you know and understand – that keeps my feet on the ground and gives me a solid basis for valuation analysis.

NEW METHODS OF ANALYSIS

Analysis of big data will undoubtedly be a key factor in analysis in the coming years. I know of one European fund whose data scientists outnumber its conventional analysts. A friend runs a highly successful long-only boutique in London; he has eight analysts and has just employed his first data analyst. Such trends will certainly continue, and although I understand some of the techniques, much of the detail is beyond me.

I used to work with an analyst who had the idea of using satellite imagery to capture the number of cars in Walmart car parks – we shall see more of this. Unfortunately, it's beyond the reach of most institutional investors, let alone the private investor. It has been some time since I was involved with a large hedge fund which had sufficient resources and I am not therefore up to date with how such funds are harnessing technology. Hedge funds are likely to use technology in two main ways:

1. To identify stocks which will work – the quantamental approach is to deploy quantitative techniques in conjunction with fundamental techniques. Quant methods are becomingly increasingly sophisticated.

2. Using technology directly to extract information. This can be scraping websites and analysis of big data, for example, to determine pricing trends in particular sectors, or it can be using web data to inform a decision, as I discuss in an example below.

I once used Yipit, a tech provider, to determine the opportunity for a business undergoing a merger to strip costs out of the combined US operations. Technology was employed to read the addresses of all the shops and warehouses owned by the two businesses and plot them on a map – very simple and incredibly effective. This could, of course, have been done in the past, but it would have taken many hours, whereas today it requires limited time from one talented programmer. This detailed analysis of the stores overlap (using some clever software) showed a high degree of geographic fit, suggesting that there was scope for the company to beat its published targets.

Another area where, perhaps counterintuitively, computers are much better than people is language processing. Some funds and a number of research providers are using natural language processing techniques to identify trends. For example, Company Watch is a data provider which creates a modified version of the Altman score, a form of credit rating. For many years, it has had a 90%+ success rate in correctly identifying companies about to hit financial trouble. The analysis has been done purely on the company's financial filings.

They have recently started to use natural language processing to 'read' company reports and earnings call transcripts. Astonishingly (certainly to me), the success rate using language alone is 1% better than analysing the numbers. I find this a concern, as the computer can certainly do this more effectively than a person can.

SUMMARY

In this chapter, I have tried to conclude this book by looking forward. Clearly the role of tech is central to any assessment of the future of investment and disruption is one of the most important themes for investors today.

Changes in technology don't just affect our choice of stock, but the way we analyse companies. Larger funds can afford a high-quality technology research team, who are aware of the big picture and can advise their colleagues of new potential risks. Smaller funds and private investors, however, are surely at a disadvantage – they must work hard to keep up with technological developments and their potential longer-term consequences.

What is critical is that research notes, even for traditional businesses, should have a section titled 'Disruption – potential risks and opportunities'. Even as stable and dull a company as a pet-food producer faces the potential threat that Zooplus, the online pet-food retailer, could become a dominant purchaser. No industry is immune.

And although a private investor will never be able to generate huge data sets which calculate the number of cars in Walmart's car parks, they can use some common-sense principles and basic analysis to understand the most likely future prospects for Walmart and whether today's stock price properly discounts those fundamentals.

THE FUTURE

Tech and disruption is one important theme. Other themes that will dominate the investment landscape in the 2020s in my view are:

- climate change and the topic of ESG

- China

- emerging vs developed markets.

ESG/CLIMATE CHANGE

ESG is a buzzword in the asset management industry right now. The pressure to invest responsibly means that less investment will be directed into stocks like the oil majors – sheer flow of funds makes it likely that they will then underperform.

The topic of climate change will only increase in importance and analysts will therefore have to widen their understanding to include such issues as the use of plastics for a drinks company. This will be an integral factor in quality rankings, as I discussed earlier.

CHINA

The issue of China deserves a book on its own. But clearly the role of the country and its markets will be a critical factor to success for many companies in this decade. I am no expert, but it's something I pay a lot of attention to.

EMERGING VS DEVELOPED MARKETS

I am writing this in the first week of 2020, after a brief appearance on Radio 4's *Today* programme to discuss the year ahead. I thought we might also talk about the decade ahead and one thing seemed clear to me. When I sit down in the first week of 2030, I expect that developed markets will reflect three issues:

1. Demographics are working against most western economies. Immigration is a possible solution, but with fewer workers and more retirees, there could be less saving.

2. Interest rates are already extremely low. The opportunity for rerating may therefore be limited and there is a risk of a derating should interest rates ever climb to more 'normal' levels.

3. The US stock market has enjoyed fabulous returns since the beginning of the twentieth century. Only two decades, the 1930s and the 2000s, saw

negative returns from the US stock market. Both came after record highs in 1929 and 1999 and subsequent crashes. I am not predicting a crash after the 2019 market highs, but it will be harder to continue the past trend.

It therefore seems to me that the opportunities are more likely to be found in emerging markets. A country like India is emerging, has fabulous demographics, and appears to be addressing some of its past constraints on growth. Its stock market is highly valued, however, and is difficult for an individual foreign investor to access. There are many other opportunities in Asia and beyond, but risk assessment generally requires a more detailed understanding of macro factors than outlined earlier.

CONCLUSION

I sincerely hope that you have both enjoyed this book and found it instructive. I have tried to pass on the tricks I have learned in a three-decade career in investment, but at the same time make it interesting. Most importantly, I hope it helps you improve the performance of your investments. Thanks for reading this far.

14
COVID-19 POSTSCRIPT

INTRODUCTION

THIS BOOK was intended to go to press in May 2020, but the launch of my online course, the Analyst Academy, a 12-month programme for investors looking to improve their skills, made that a challenging deadline. Then the virus hit. I therefore decided to add this postscript chapter with some thoughts on how investing may transform as a result of the pandemic. So much had changed that it seemed almost pointless to write a book on investing and researching stocks without taking this into account.

I am sure that this chapter will age less well than the rest of the book, so please bear in mind that it was written in the midst of the initial crisis, when we were still in the April 2020 lockdown and forecasters were expecting earnings in 2021 to be above 2019. By the time this book is published, and by the time you read this, I am convinced that this will look like a fanciful assumption. I am far less sure about the other implications I discuss.

These are divided into two areas – the broader macro picture and what this means for companies. Under macro effects, I discuss financial repression and capital controls; why interest rates will stay low for some time and what this means; and some potential ripple effects, including the potential for inflation and the need for balance sheet restoration by both corporate and personal sectors.

I then discuss the ramifications for companies and equity investors, looking at the likely greater desire for stronger balance sheets by the corporate sector, the need to onshore elements of the supply chain, and the implications for equity valuation, working capital and income funds. Finally, I explore how this will lead to corporates *kitchen-sinking* reserves and why one result will be that more fraud is exposed.

1. THE MACRO PICTURE

The COVID-19 pandemic was obviously a massive shock to the financial system. One clear effect is that almost every government on the planet will have a lot more debt in June 2020 than they did in January, and likely even more by the end of the year. The situation at the start of 2020 was not looking particularly attractive as it was.

HIGHER DEBT

Advanced economies saw a significant increase in debt, above 100%, following the GFC. In their famous book, *This Time Is Different: Eight Centuries of Financial Folly*, Reinhart and Rogoff advocated caution that debt above 90% of GDP will slow economic growth. Their statistics and conclusions were undermined, however, when it was found that there was a mistake in their spreadsheet. It was always unlikely that two academics could predict future economic events on the basis of historical trends.

Figure 14.1: Government debt as a percentage of GDP

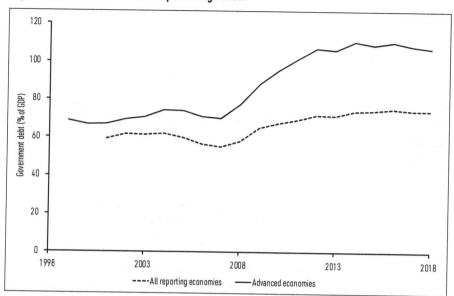

Source: BIS.

But simple common sense says that when the debt is larger than GDP, it's probably not great, and you should think about getting it down. It's certain that when this chart is redrawn at the end of 2020, there will be another huge increase. That surely is a cause for concern.

This may not be as much of a problem if every government has huge debts though. There will be no relative disadvantage and, hence, perhaps no real risk that they cannot be financed. I am a simple stock analyst though, this is above my pay grade.

My guess is that governments will, at some point, feel constrained in what they can spend and will seek to reduce their debt burden. Most will surely be forced to continue engaging with a policy of financial repression so that their interest rates are below inflation. This could be required for decades rather than years, which will undoubtedly have important implications for equity investors.

It's worth noting that this is not just a governmental problem; the corporate sector is also highly levered. Total debt excluding financial institutions is over 250% of GDP in advanced economies and it will certainly be a lot higher at the end of 2020, irrespective of a V-, W-, U-, or L-shaped recovery – or indeed any other type of recovery.

The best way of reducing the debt-to-GDP ratio is higher growth. Therefore, timely fiscal stimulus should be a priority for all governments. Correctly delivered, this will get us all out of a mess.

Figure 14.2: Total debt as a percentage of GDP

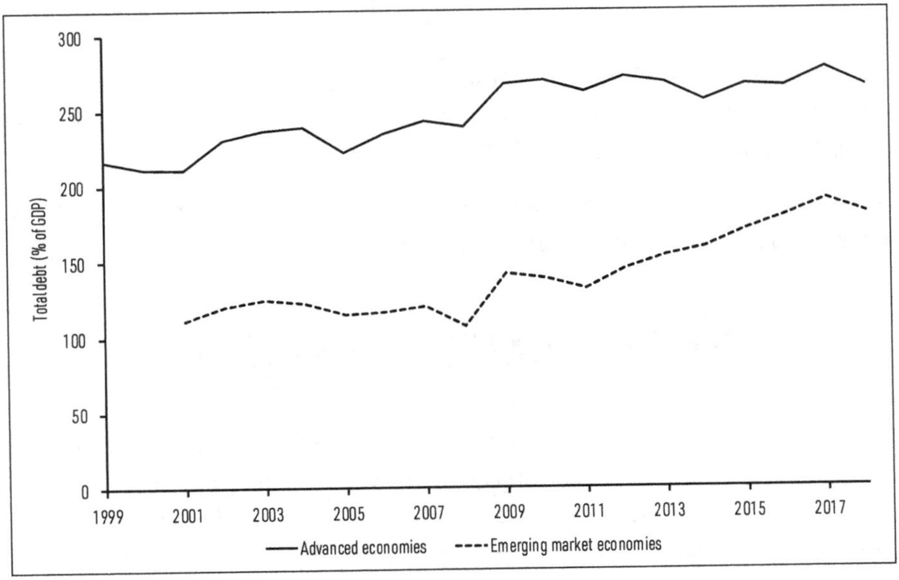

Source: BIS.

HIGHER TAXES

Another option for governments will presumably be higher corporate and personal taxes, although there is an economic impact here. Jim Chanos has opined that if government is to bail out businesses, then they will be forced to pay higher tax as an insurance premium going forward. He calculates that S&P 2021 consensus earnings of $170 (way too high an estimate in my opinion) will need to be revised down to $135 if the US return to tax rates of the pre-Trump era.

Other items cited by eminent financial historian Russell Napier include an unpalatable menu for investors:

- Wealth taxes

- Dividend controls

- Restrictions on investment

- Restrictions on ownership of gold (it happened in the 1930s)

- Capital controls.

The last one is the most interesting and raises all sorts of issues. It seems unimaginable in a global interconnected financial environment, but what would you do if you were president of, say, Turkey?

The solution for governments must be to engineer higher growth. Let's hope they can achieve this, as the alternatives are not attractive.

INTEREST RATES MAY STAY LOW

It seems highly likely that interest rates will stay low for an extended period. My base case assumption is that, as with the situation post the GFC, inflation will remain subdued for some time (this may well be the surprise of the decade if inflation eventually returns, as it did in the mid-1960s).

This will affect pension deficits, which I discuss below, but should, in theory, continue to fuel the valuation of growth stocks. With growth scarcer, it becomes an even more attractive feature. This would suggest that the last decade's winners – tech – should remain winners. I would just point out two caveats.

Can these valuations grow forever? Trees to the sky? Probably not. And relative valuations have already increased significantly. According to Star Capital, based on their composite valuation metric, by Q2, 2020, the growth-vs-value relationship had already surpassed the prior peak in the dotcom boom.

Even growth stocks are not immune to the general economic malaise. Internet advertising rates collapsed at the start of lockdown, which seemed likely to hurt Alphabet and Facebook for a period, for example.

RIPPLE EFFECTS AND INFLATION

The coronavirus crisis has created huge survivability issues for a number of sectors, notably airlines, travel, and hospitality. The duration may be variable. For example, as long as the threat of virus transmission remains, cruise lines may face a long struggle to persuade holidaymakers to take such voyages. But the risk of short-haul air travel may be perceived as lower. Although it should be noted that in May 2020 Carnival reported strong cruise bookings for late summer; so, somewhat surprisingly, cruising may recover quicker than expected.

There has obviously been an indirect effect across all sectors, even internet advertising, as I discussed earlier. A primary impact has been felt in the oil industry, where there appeared to be an almost existential crisis when Saudi Arabia and Russia co-operated, possibly to undermine US shale.

These were fairly obvious and direct initial impacts. What we had yet to understand, in the early stages of the crisis, were the indirect effects which reached beyond the general economic decline. This included food shortages; a break in manufacturing supply chains; an inability to pay footballers' wages; the collapse of secondary Formula One teams, leading to the death of the sport; and many other, potentially more serious, repercussions that we have not yet thought of.

My candidate for the most impactful consequence of the pandemic would be private individuals increased propensity to save, which will slow economic growth. Second would be the potential for the imposition of a police state, as track-and-trace measures are implemented at the expense of personal privacy. This was foreshadowed in an article which Yuval Noah Harari wrote for the *Financial Times*,[9] very early in the initial lockdown (in March 2020).

I alluded earlier to the prospect of a return to inflation. It seems impossible, given the depressed state of demand, but this was also true of the mid-1960s, when inflation returned and led to the dramatic destruction of wealth over the following 15 years. This would be the one surprise that would really help governments. Could it happen again? There may, after all, be some consequences of freely printing money.

---

9   Harari's FT article https://www.ft.com/content/19d90308-6858-11ea-a3c9-1fe6fedcca75

Inflation did not resume in the last decade, in spite of huge bouts of quantitative easing. It could happen this time, however, for two reasons:

1. The system has been flooded with more money, on top of its already liquid state.

2. Last time round, demand growth was anaemic and zombie companies being allowed to survive meant that the supply impact was lower than it would otherwise be. This time, it's highly likely that there will be multiple bankruptcies and some interruption to supply.

At first I thought that inflation could well return in the immediate term. My reasoning was that as oil demands rise, a sharp increase in oil prices would follow and feed through to plastic and chemicals, and to sectors of the economy that were hardest hit. Such sectors would see supply shrinkage:

- Airline seats will be scarcer, at least temporarily, as airlines fail and carriers are slow to reintroduce capacity.

- The restaurant industry may see a reduction in capacity as small restaurants and even some chains close down, while demand to eat out returns to close to pre-crisis levels (pent-up demand offset by lower affordability).

- Hotels, another mom-and-pop industry like restaurants, will similarly see a capacity reduction and eventually an ability to push prices up.

We will not have cost-push inflation, as labour will be in plentiful supply, nor will it be demand-led. It's possible that a new form of inflation, which is driven by supply shortage, will appear, at least in certain sectors. But the problem with inflation is that it's difficult to make disappear. It should be positive for equities, as long as it is contained to a limited number of sectors, but should inflation return in the medium term (not my central case), levels above 4% would severely impact valuation multiples.

2. COMPANIES AND EQUITY INVESTORS

BALANCE SHEET RESTORATION

Personal and corporate balance sheets need to be restored. This is likely to weigh on economic growth for a number of years. I initially pondered whether – in our new caring society *on the other side* – bling might become unfashionable. But after reading an article in an Asian edition of *Tatler* that the Chinese bought a record $2.7m of Hermes Birkin bags and assorted goods in one day post-lockdown, I wondered if the world would be that different.[10]

My takeaway was that there may be two types of post-lockdown consumer. Those wealthy employees, who have seen no impact on their earnings, may well have pent-up demand to spend in spite of the hit to their savings. They may go out and immediately buy big-ticket items and trade up in their restaurant choice – they cannot eat the lost meals out, but they can upgrade. My guess is that these will be the minority, and will be outweighed by the self-employed, the furloughed and the unemployed, all of whom will need to reduce their spending.

Even if luxury is partly immune, large swathes of the lower end of the income distribution and the middle class will be, and will feel, much poorer. If stock markets stabilise at higher levels, the rich won't feel as bad, but many will have suffered losses as business owners. If markets fall, there will also be a further reverse wealth effect.

Note that this will affect both corporate and personal balance sheets. Companies seem likely to rein in capex and discretionary spending for the 2020–2022 period. Consumers will buy fewer and cheaper big-ticket items. This seems inevitable, although the impact was hard to model on corporate earnings at the outset. We do know, however, that earnings will be lower than formerly forecast.

---

10   Asian Tatler article https://sg.asiatatler.com/style/post-covid-19-herm%C3%A8s-earns-2-7-million-in-sales-on-reopening-day-china-guangzhou-flagship-store

The one slightly odd exception to the big-ticket expense may be the leisure sector, where there will be a massive pent-up demand for holidays. Exhausted parents will demand holidays and this is the one luxury item which many middle-class households will be loathe to sacrifice.

FORTRESS BALANCE SHEETS

Andrew Smith, former KPMG chief economist, told me at the outset of UK lockdown that he was "quite shocked at how limited a financial cushion many businesses seem to have." Perhaps not so surprising, given that for the last 40-odd years investors and speculators have enjoyed a tailwind from falling interest rates. So long as you had the stomach for debt, you basically made money. This culminated in a veritable orgy of buybacks in the last decade.

One legacy of the pandemic may be a culture of greater conservatism and risk aversion. Boards are likely to adopt a more conservative approach – the shock we have just experienced will make even the less risk-averse director appreciate having more cash and more facilities *just in case*. Boards will likely want some security against another pandemic. This has two important implications for equity investors:

1. Corporations have been the single largest buyer of equities in the 2010s – buybacks may be much less fashionable, even after balance sheets have been restored post the pandemic.

2. Return on equity (RoE) will fall as a consequence – buybacks, even at high prices, usually boosted RoE, as money has been so cheap. It will remain cheap, but more conservative balance sheets will be one factor in lowering returns on equity.

As Michael Pettis, notable China commentator, put it in a series of tweets in April 2020:

"When an economy goes through many years of rising real estate and asset prices, surging debt, and loose monetary conditions, business balance sheets tend to get structured in highly speculative ways that effectively 'bet' on more of the same – 'inverted balance sheets'.

Over time the whole economy 'shifts' towards riskier balance sheets. This is likely to be a problem nearly everywhere, and especially in China, where decades of artificially high growth, soaring real estate prices, excess liquidity and surging debt have transformed the balance sheet structures of nearly all businesses.

Inverted balance sheets are highly pro-cyclical. Economies and businesses with highly inverted balance sheets tend to surprise on the upside when conditions are good, often developing a reputation for smart management, and then destroy this reputation when conditions reverse."

China may not have seen the last effects of the pandemic. And if investors in developed markets seek safer balance sheets, companies will be forced to respond.

Some investor reaction was underway even before this crisis. *Grant's Interest Rate Observer* of 7 February 2020 opened with: "The lowest interest rates, the most accommodating Fed, the shortest junk-bond durations, the highest corporate leverage and the longest business expansion frame the value proposition for junk bonds and the speculative-grade, tradable bank debt styled 'leveraged loans.' 'Hold on to your hats!' is the investment conclusion."

ONSHORING SUPPLY CHAINS

ING economist Mark Cliffe has suggested that "businesses are likely to shift from lean 'just in time' to bigger 'just in case' inventories. Businesses will be warier of single sources of supply or demand, allowing for a greater ability to switch activities or locations." Clearly there is an associated cost.

Similarly, Tim Harford wrote in the *Financial Times* on 18 April 2020, "It is tempting to fight the last war: we built up reserves in banking after the financial crisis, but we did not pay attention to reserve capacity in health."

The risk inherent in just-in-time and diverse supply chains has become more apparent and companies will surely want higher stocks, more diversity of supply, and will onshore more production as a protection against a recurrence. Again, this will have two implications:

1. Production costs will rise.

2. Returns will fall as inventory and working capital increase.

PENSION DEFICITS TO INCREASE SIGNIFICANTLY

The good news is that bonds have increased in value and, given the growth in deficits, governments have huge incentives to keep yields low. But the pension deficit (perhaps there is a surplus in the S&P 500 or the FTSE 100, but I haven't seen one for a long time) is the difference between two large numbers:

1. Assets have gone down significantly for those with a higher exposure to equity, less so for those funds with a larger exposure to bonds. And funds with heavy exposure to alternatives may find that the lack of a mark to market doesn't help if the private equity portfolio companies sink under the weight of their debt.

2. Liabilities have gone up significantly because they are discounted to present value based on bond yields, which have collapsed. This means that pension deficits will have increased significantly for most quoted companies. There is an indirect and less than 100% impact on equity values, but it's still potentially highly significant. I looked at one UK retailer whose equity valuation would theoretically halve if bonds were 2% lower at the date of the next accounts. Many companies with large workforces have a high sensitivity to lower rates through the pension exposure.

WORKING CAPITAL UNWIND

An unwind of working capital will occur on both sides of the balance sheet. I have observed a number of industrial companies which have improved working capital tremendously over the last 10–15 years. But many have done this predominantly by failing to pay suppliers on time. Unless their supply chains are extraordinarily robust, these companies will be hit by the need for increased inventory and by the need to start paying suppliers more quickly.

The following chart illustrates Electrolux's working capital over the last 15 years or so.

Figure 14.3: Electrolux working capital

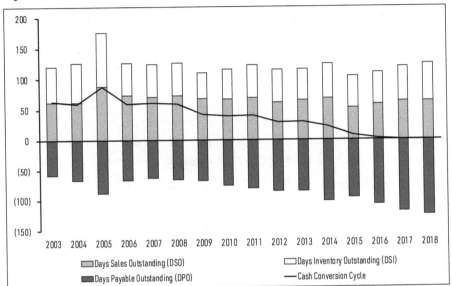

Source: Behind the Balance Sheet estimates from Sentieo Data.

The collection cycle (number of days' sales tied up in working capital) looks to have achieved a marvellous improvement, from 63 days 15 years earlier, and a peak of 87 days, to zero. But look at how this has been achieved – debtor days have been flat at 60-ish. Inventory days have actually increased slightly to around 60 days, while payables days have doubled from 60 to around 120.

Now, perhaps Electrolux's suppliers are all robust companies in great health after Electrolux has been so bountiful with its custom. But I doubt it. Rather, I suspect many of its suppliers will have been significantly impacted by the lockdown. Unless Electrolux not only pays its bills but pays them in *advance*, the suppliers may be unable to supply – cue a potentially massive working capital unwind for Electrolux. That's all assuming that housebuilders are back building houses, or homeowners are refurbishing and making big-ticket expenditure.

I have singled out Electrolux, but this would apply to any of a large number of quoted industrials which have been engaging in this type of financial engineering (spoiler – it's not uncommon).

WHERE NOW FOR INCOME FUNDS?

For many companies, the priority will be rebuilding balance sheets. Dividends will be a secondary issue. For those companies subject to government rescue, dividends are likely to be capped or forbidden until debts are repaid. Income fund managers will have an increasingly narrow repertoire. This is quite an important issue for many UK pensioners (not to mention fund managers). I have advocated selling holdings in this sector.

That British Telecom would use this as an opportunity to rebase dividend expectations was somewhat predictable. Less so for Royal Dutch Shell, which was seen as a stalwart in dividend payments and was perceived by many as the most secure dividend in the FTSE 100. When it cut its dividend, a perception could develop that no company is safe.

A corollary may be that some perennial dividend payers may be rerated as these funds are forced into a narrower group of stocks. I think this is more likely to happen in the US, where dividends are often paid quarterly and where companies may sacrifice buybacks but continue to pay dividends (which are generally much smaller). Stocks like Apple and Microsoft have seen strong share-price performance for a long time, but this has been less so for stocks like Johnson & Johnson and Procter & Gamble. All four have been consistent dividend payers and will attract renewed attention, as these types of stocks may be perceived as safer bets for income investors than some traditional dividend stocks.

THE 'BEZZLE' AND THE GREAT RESET

John Kenneth Galbraith coined the term the 'bezzle' in his book, *The Great Crash, 1929*.

> "In many ways the effect of the crash on embezzlement was more significant than on suicide. To the economist embezzlement is the most interesting of crimes. Alone among the various forms of larceny it has a time parameter. Weeks, months or years may elapse between the commission of the crime and its discovery. (This is a period, incidentally, when the embezzler has his gain and the man who has been embezzled, oddly enough, feels no loss. There is a net increase in psychic wealth.) At any given time there exists an inventory of undiscovered embezzlement in – or more precisely not in – the country's business and banks. This inventory – it should perhaps be called the bezzle – amounts at any moment to many millions of dollars. It also varies in size with the business cycle. In good times people are relaxed, trusting, and money is plentiful. But even though money is plentiful, there are always many people who need more. Under these circumstances the rate of embezzlement grows, the rate of discovery falls off, and the bezzle increases rapidly. In depression all this is reversed. Money is watched with a narrow, suspicious eye. The man who handles it is assumed to be dishonest until he proves himself otherwise. Audits are penetrating and meticulous. Commercial morality is enormously improved. The bezzle shrinks."

Throughout 2019 and 2020, I have been preaching that too many companies were cooking the books. This has been the 'bezzle'.

Figure 14.4: S&P 500 operating profit margin and after-tax corporate profit margin

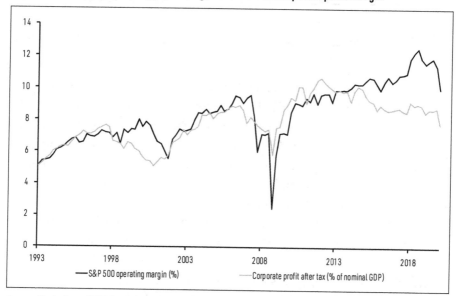

Source: Yardeni.com (IBES (Refinitiv) and profit after tax with IVA and CCAdj from Bureau of Economic Analysis).

The chart shows the gap between the S&P profit margins and the NIPA margins, an economic measure. The S&P number has been moving straight up, while the economic margins have been in steady decline. This is exactly what happened in the late 1990s and it indicates that margins are being goosed. Back then it corrected when S&P margins fell to the economic margin level and this will happen again. There are some technical reasons why the S&P should be somewhat higher, but not to this degree.

Now finance chiefs have an opportunity, presented by the virus, to engage in a great reset. Earnings will be reset and the pandemic will be the excuse.

Even if there were no lasting effects from the virus, earnings for the vast majority of quoted companies would be reset down. They have been stretching the elastic of earnings for some years and now they have the opportunity to get their books in order. Forecasts will go down, even before you factor in the virus effects.

One final point regarding company profits. The Japanese earthquake in 2011 is the best analogy for an economic halt such as we are currently experiencing. It took industries there a long time to restart the supply chain and return to normal. We are told that China is already nearly there, but that process may take longer in other economies.

CONCLUSIONS

I confess that I don't know where the market will end up. Even doing a forecast for an individual company was incredibly difficult at the start of the crisis – more difficult than it had ever been in my (long) career. As difficult as it was post-9/11 when I was researching airline stocks, for example. The good news is that I saw many great opportunities in markets then on both the long and short side. Rarely does such an opportunity set present itself.

Structural trends like climate change, an ageing population and the emerging middle class will continue regardless.

But we may also see impacts that we don't expect. For example, ice cream sales collapsed by 44% in the 1930s depression, as Figure 14.5 illustrates. It took seven years to regain the 1930 peak and a further four years to surpass it.

Figure 14.5: US ice cream production (12-monthly million gallons)

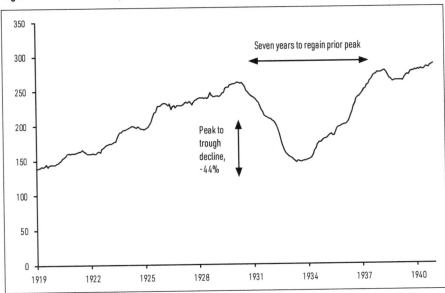

Source: St Louis FRED.

What we now know, however, is that the impossible can happen. Who would have thought that forward oil could trade at a negative price?

The single conclusion to take away from this postscript is that you should assess the resilience of your portfolio against every eventuality. Probabilities may be low, but look at the impact that those extreme events at the left tail of the normal distribution can have. Analyst teams should sit down and brainstorm what they think could happen, assign a probability, and assess the impact on portfolios.

One simple example: let's assume that this is indeed a point like 1965 and we see a return to inflation. Interest rates reached 15% in 1982. Now, it may not reach that quantum, especially starting from effectively zero, but what would happen to your portfolio if rates reached 10% in 2030, or 2035? Most young investors probably cannot imagine a world in which rates are 15%. Thinking the unthinkable is one of the lessons I am trying to take away from this crisis.

Which is quite a good way to end this book.

ACKNOWLEDGEMENTS

NO BOOK is written single-handedly, and I have had some fantastic help and support through this one's long gestation. You would not be reading this had Matthew Goodman not encouraged me to write it over breakfast at Cecconi's in Mayfair. He then introduced me to literary agent Robert Dudley, whose interest persuaded me to persevere. My particular thanks to Craig Pearce, commissioning editor at Harriman House, who saw the book's potential and then did a brilliant editing job.

I would also like to thank the whole team at Harriman House and web agency, Buzzbar, especially Anna Downey, whose marketing brilliance helped shape the presentation of the book. Joseph, in-house copywriter for my training business, Behind the Balance Sheet, effortlessly came up with the title – well done.

Andrew Smith, a close friend and confidant for many years, read an early draft and made constructive comments, as did Dominic O'Connell and Mahgul Ansari – my sincere thanks to all of them.

There would be no book without the people who have helped me so much in my career. There are far too many to list, but I should single out for special mention Roy Dantzic, who suggested a career as an analyst; Bob Cowell, who gave me my first job and was a great teacher; and John Holmes, who took a chance on me and has been a dear friend ever since. As has Keith Hiscock – we have worked together multiple times and are now in business together.

I must pay particular tribute to Martin Hughes, who created a role for me at Toscafund. This was the best job I ever had – I learned more, and more quickly, than in any other role. Similar thanks to John Webster, former CEO of Altima Partners, and David Scott, founder of Vestra Wealth, the wealth manager where I taught myself about quality investing. And special thanks to Russell Napier, whose early help and encouragement contributed significantly to the success of my training business today.

I should also acknowledge my debt to my late parents, who would have been so proud to see their son's name on a book cover (although they would not have understood the contents, they would not have cared). Finally, I must thank my wife, Julie, and my sons, Max and Finn, who allowed me time to shut myself in my study and write.

INDEX

12-month relative highs and
lows 210, 211
*23 Things They Don't Tell You About
Capitalism* 51

A Wealth of Common Sense
website 18
AA (Automobile Association) 87–88,
129
AB Ports 61
ABB 138
Aberdeen Asset Management 99
Abrahams, Dan 70, 221
Accounts 112–149
accounting policies 119–123
acquisitions 123
audit report 112
balance sheets and reconciliation
of 123–130
contingencies and
commitments 112, 116–118
investments 127
profit & loss (P&L) 130–145
related party transactions 118
tax rates 137–138
Accounting for Growth 116
Ackman, Bill 100, 108, 140,
Acquisitions, assessment of 94, 95,
123, 141, 142, 207–208
Ontex 117
Adidas 81
Aena 16
Aeroports de Paris 44
Ahead of the Curve 40
Ainslie, Lee 212

Airbnb 251
Airbus 16, 26, 27, 226
Airlines 61, 64, 145, 166–167, 169, 250
and COVID-19 263–264
and foreign exchange rates 225–
226
AKO Capital 67
Aldi 10, 68, 172
Alfreton Capital 70
Allan, John 97
Alphabet, investments in Google,
Waymo 135, 262
Amazon 17, 64, 71–72, 78, 80, 105,
238–239, 244–248, 253,
and tax 137
compared with Walmart 167–169
management 104
Amortisation 120–122, 126, 133, 147,
175, 179
Analyst recommendations 36
Apple 31, 68, 137, 241, 253, 270
Arnott, Rob 131,
Artificial intelligence (AI) 196
Asia 105, 106, 194, 226, 256
Assets under construction 124
Associates and joint ventures 137, 141
ASOS 243
Asymmetric pay-offs 9, 32
Aurizon 16
Auto Trader 69
Automotive Original Equipment
Manufacturers (OEMs) 67–68,
70–71, 245
Autonomous vehicles 71, 189, 243,
245

Australia   10, 50
   Just Eat acquisition in   219–220
Averaging down   87, 216–217
Ayling, Bob   102

B2B   44, 51
BAA   16, 61
Bain & Co   105
Bank OZK   92
Bannatyne, Duncan   108
Barriers to entry   57, 58, 65, 72–73,
   78, 147, 148, 204,
Behavioural economics   188
Behavioural finance   215
Beneish M-Score   143
Bezos, Jeff   71–72
Big data   98, 253
Billionaires   50, 90, 106–107, 109
Bitcoin   188
Bloomberg   18, 37, 87, 94, 113, 114,
   119, 150, 152, 160–161, 167, 196
BMW   225, 243
Body language of management   100,
   102, 202–203, 218
Bollore   45–47, 105
Book value per share   123
Bolton, Anthony   202
Brands   65, 69, 80–81, 180, 245
   threat of Amazon to   247
Brexit   49, 70
   and Diageo   236
British Airways   16, 61, 102, 183, 234
British Gas   16
British Telecom   270
Bronte Capital blog   18, 62, 81, 219
Broker ideas dinners   13
Broker research   36, 142, 152, 183, 214
BTR   183
Buffett, Warren   58, 60, 62, 64, 79, 92,
   138, 214, 216
Bus companies in UK   12–13, 61
Buybacks   123, 148–149, 154, 213,
   266, 270

C-Score   141, 142
Capacity, entering or leaving an
   industry   57, 77, 79–80, 101, 170,
   264
Capital equipment suppliers as sources
   of information   43, 44
Capital expenditure (Capex)   139–

   140, 146–149, 174–175, 178, 181
   and COVID-19   265
   and tax   153
Capital markets days   198–199
Carlson, Ben   18
Carnival   263
Cash flow   6, 41, 63, 71, 91, 131,
   139–140, 151–155, 158, 176–177,
   180, 209
   and C Score   142
   and serial acquisitions   207
   at Sainsbury   172
   at Thomas Cook   116
Cash return on capital invested
   (CROCI)   171
Catalysts   6, 189
CK Hutchison   1–2
Chan, Ronald   106
Chanos, Jim   261
Charting   84
Chartwell Capital   106
Checklists   47, 52, 53–55
Children's Investment Fund   16
China   51, 225, 228, 229, 256
   and COVID-19   266–267
Chipotle   16
Circle of competence   50–51
Clapp, Graham   220
Cliffe, Mark   267
Climate change   255, 273
Coca-Cola   62
Commodity price movements   21, 25,
   225
Common Stocks and Uncommon
   Profits   45, 75
Communicating investment
   ideas   182–192
CompanyWatch   254
Compass   73, 103
Competitors as source of
   information   42, 43
Compounding returns   62, 63
Confirmation bias   48, 99
Consolidation   56, 207, 250
Constellation Software   92
Cost synergies   207
Cote, Dave   103
Counterarguments to investment
   case   33, 37, 42, 52
Cousins, Richard   103
COVID-19   258–174

and corporate balance sheets   265–267

and dividends   270

Cowell, Bob   155

Credit card businesses   65

Credit Lyonnais Laing   84

Crescat Capital   24

Crooks, investing with   108–109

CRH Irish construction conglomerate   21–22

Crossley, Richard   209–210

CSX US rail operator   45

Cunningham, Lawrence   67

Current and fixed assets   120, 124–127, 142, 179

Curveball questions   203–207

Cusack, Mark   208

Customer captivity   66, 72

Customer loyalty   65

Customer-switching costs   66

Cyclicality   36, 38, 70, 71, 131, 134, 136, 159, 161, 166, 179, 180, 230, 232

cyclically adjusted P/E   163

and inverted balance sheets   267

Dalio, Ray   233

Darden   95, 121

Davis, Ned   29

Debt   56, 122, 124, 127–128, 137, 141, 143–145, 148, 158, 161–163

and COVID-19   259–261, 266–268

and family businesses   105

and priced-to-sales ratio   165

and quality stocks   60

debt and deleveraging cycle   233

Deferred income   129

Deferred tax   128, 137, 175

Deighton, Pete   200

Demographics   20, 233, 256

Depreciation   120, 125, 131, 133, 140, 141, 142, 147, 175

Diageo   127, 236

Discounted cashflow (DCF)   176–177

Disney   65, 106, 253,

Disruption   238–257

and Amazon   246–247

and retail   242–243

Diversification   208

Dividends   178, 213

Dixon, Mark   86

Drax   170–171

Dreman, David   84

Dropbox   173

Druckenmiller, Stanley   85

Drucker, Peter   207

Earnings estimates   35

easyJet   55, 101

EBIT and EBITDA margins   130–131, 147–148, 153, 157–158, 160–163, 181

constraints on calculation of   161

Economic commentators   229

Economies of scale   64–65, 73

Einhorn, David   42

Electric vehicles   71, 189, 241, 243, 245

Electrolux   67, 269–270

Electronic Research Interchange   20

Element Solutions   see Platform Speciality Products

Emerging markets   27, 63, 138, 210, 226, 232, 256

Enterprise value (EV)   158

Enterprise value to sales ratio   164–165

EPS   154, 160, 163, 176

and acquisitions   208

growth targets   94–95

revisions to   214

Eskom, South Africa utility   40–41

ESG   see Impact Investing

European low-cost carriers   101, 226

European media sector   29–32

Eurotunnel   176–177, 200

Evans, Benedict   240, 244, 249

Exchange rate movements   25, 27, 225–226, 229

External confirmation of hypothesis   33, 42

Facebook   69, 85–86, 137–138, 196, 262

Factset   152, 160, 196

Family businesses   83, 105–106

Felder, Jesse   18

Ferrans, Dougie   137

Ferrari   68–69

Fidelity Magellan Fund   11

Fisher, Philip   45, 75

Fixed assets   120, 124–125, 179
Florange law in France   46
Forecasts and Forecasting   155–158
Forward-looking statements   196
Founders Factory   249
Founder-led companies   39, 82, 83, 86, 94, 97, 105–106, 109, 111
Franklin, Martin   14
Free cash flow yield   174
Frost, Ronnie   200
Fundamental ideas   15
FundSmith   62, 77, 231

Galbraith, John Kenneth   271
Geopolitical trends   21, 23
Gerson, Lehrman and Coleman Research   43, 45
Gilbert, Martin   99
Gillette and Dollar Shave Club   69
Gluskin Shef   230
Glydon, Nick   211
Goodwill   121–122, 124, 126, 179, 180
Google   67, 135, 137, 244, 250
   Google Alerts   98
   Google Maps   124
Government subsidies to an industry   57
Gross margins   131–133

Ha-Joon Chang   51
Harari, Yuval Noah   263
Hardman & Co   29
Harford, Tim   267
Hargreaves Lansdown   70
Harley Davidson and Trump's protectionism   23
Hays   200, 249, 250
Hempton, John   18, 62, 81, 82, 219
Historical valuation of a stock   36, 84, 167
History of a business   80–82, 185
Hohn, Chris   16, 35, 45, 88
Holders of a stock, are they 'smart money'   36
Holmes, John   183, 275
Honeywell   103
Hong Kong   2, 106
Horowitz, Andreessen   240
Hosking & Co   57
'Hourglass' sweet spot   78

How Can Smart Beta Go Horribly Wrong   131f
Huber, Phil   40
Hugo Boss   45
Hyundai   244

'Iceberg' principle   125
Idea generation strategies   8–32
   Instant ideas   28–29

Impact investing   66
Inchcape   201
India   50, 80, 218–219, 256
Initial public offers (IPOs) and privatisations   16–17
Independent research providers   19–20, 36, 40
Information edge   26, 38, 39–41, 112–113, 118
Insider buying   86
Intangibles   120–121, 126–127, 174, 175
Intellectual property rights   65
Interest rates   139, 153, 160, 227–228, 256, 258–259, 260, 262, 266, 267, 274
   too much time spent on   225, 227
Internet and business models   63, 65, 69
Investing Against the Tide   202

Jakobsen, Steen   230
Jarden   14
Johnson & Johnson   270
Juniper   16
Just Eat   219–220

Kelly criterion   188
Kindle Direct Publishing   248
Kirrage, Nick   98
Kodak   80
Kolhatkar, Sheelah   40

Landlords, as source of information   43, 44
Laterals   10
Lauren, Ralph   92–93, 105
Leahy, Terry   103
Lees, Andy   20
Leverage   60, 128, 143–144, 148, 181, 217, 267

at Sainsbury   172
Li Ka-Shing   2
Lindsell Train   80
Liquidity
  corporate   18, 127–128, 267
  of Woodford funds   70
  of stocks   11, 35, 88, 184
London-Edinburgh air traffic
  statistics   230
LVMH   105
Lyft   251–252
Lyle, James   177
Lynch, Peter   11–12

Macro-economic factors   25, 27, 38,
  224–237
  as a time trap   49
  COVID-19 and   258–264
Micro-economic factors   39, 224,
  230–231
Microsoft   66, 72, 133, 241, 270
Makinson Cowell   155
Management   14, 90–102, 182, 185
  and dividends   178
  share transactions of   86
  worth meeting management?   195,
  201–207
Manchester United   156
Marathon Asset Management   57
Market psychology   38, 198, 210, 213,
  214, 216
Market sell-offs   17
Marks & Spencer   243, 245
Marks, Howard   233
Marshall, Colin   16
Maverick Capital   212
Melrose and Wassall   97, 208
Micro environment   39
Microsoft   66, 72, 133, 241, 270
MiFID II   157
Miller, Chris 'Jock'   97, 208
Minorities   138, 153, 161
Mistakes   15, 35, 115, 186, 219–222
Moats, economic   63–73, 78
  digital   67
  longevity of 69
  checklist for   72–73
Models, used by analysts   136, 152,
  155
Momentum   212, 213, 243
Montier, James   99, 141, 142, 227

Moulton, Jon   204
Munger, Charlie   58, 204
Music-streaming business   30

Napier, Russell   20, 262, 276
Natural language processing   254
Naya Management   165
Nestlé   226
Netflix   245, 248, 252–253
Network effects   65, 69, 72, 147
Next   92
Nike   81, 247
Nokia   240–241
Nomad Foods   14
Novy-Marx, Robert   131–132

Ocado   133, 172, 219–222,
Oil prices   10, 18, 21, 25, 225, 226,
  264,
One Up on Wall Street   11
Overheads   147

Pareto Rule   1
Parvus Asset Management   88
Peak multiples   179
Pearson, Mike   100
Peer review   189–190
Pelham   170
Pensato Capital   220
Pension deficits   50, 128, 154, 172,
  262
  and COVID-19   268
Pershing Square Capital   108, 140
Personal contacts   13–14
Personal observation   11–13
Pettis, Michael   266
Pets.com and chewy.com   239
Phoenix Asset Management   55
Piquadro   11–12
Piotroski Score   143
Planning of use of time   49–50
Plant and machinery   120
Platform Speciality Products   14
Playtech   108
Politics   224, 234–235, 237
Portfolio fit   188
Portfolio maintenance   192, 210, 214,
  222–223
PPHE Hotel Group   29
Price-to-book ratio   150, 160, 179–
  180, 212

Price-to-earnings ratio   159–164, 181, 184
  Shiller P/E ratio 163
Price targets   159, 186–187
Pricing power   68–69, 72, 133, 231
Prioritising ideas   34
Procter & Gamble   80, 81, 159, 244, 270
Pronovost, Peter   54
Puyfontaine, Arnaud de   107

Quaero Capital   105
Qualcomm   65
Qualitative analysis   64, 74, 79, 93, 114, 210
Quality Investing   67
Quantamental investing   253
Quantitative research   11, 60, 90, 74, 119, 142–143, 210, 212–214

R&D   126–127, 134, 179, 180, 181, 246
  and OEMS   71
  and scale   67–68
  at Aston Martin   122
  of competitors   43
Ralph Lauren   92–93, 105
Reading, importance of   8, 17–18, 82
  reading accounts   113–114
Regulation of industries   57, 73, 251
Regus and IWG   86
Reinhart and Rogoff   259
Reinvestment rate   63
Reporting dates   197–198
Rerating opportunities   6–7, 132, 214, 256
Research Affiliates   131–132
Results seasons   194–195
Return on capital employed (ROCE)   136, 140–141, 148
Return on invested capital   61–64, 70, 72, 140, 141, 148, 152
Revenue synergies   107, 207
Richemont   105–106
Rightmove   69
Robertson, Julian   176–177, 212
Rolling Stones   54
Ronson, Gerald   93, 108–109
Rose, Stuart   221
Rosenberg, David   230
Rothschild Investment Trust   173

Royal Dutch Shell   270
Rupert, Johann   105–106
Russia   51, 196, 263
Ryanair   64, 101, 115,

SAC Capital   40
Sagi, Teddy   108
Sainsbury   108, 144, 172–173, 204
Scottish Amicable   137
Screens   10–11, 141–143, 212–213
'Scuttlebutt'   45
SEC EDGAR search tool   87, 113
Seeking Alpha   37, 156
Segments of a business   69, 76, 85, 134–135
Sell-side analysts   15, 114, 140, 156, 159, 186, 189
  meetings   198–199
  and price targets   186–187
  sell-side brokers   19
  sell-side notes   182–185
Share price history   84–86
ShareSoc   103
Shareholder base   36, 74, 84, 87–89
Shorting stocks   19, 87, 112
Siddiqui, Masroor   165
Siegel, Jeremy   178
Siemens   44
Silver, Nate   228
Smith, Andrew   266
Smith, Terry   62, 77, 98, 231
Société Générale   142
Sohn London Investment Idea Contest   87, 189
Solvay   206
Sorrell, Martin   95
Southwest Airlines   64
Spain and solar panels   57–58
Special dividends   91, 94
Spin-offs   16–17
Spotify   30–31, 177
Spreadsheets   131, 155, 208–209
Stock options   138–139
Strategas   20
Sum Zero specialist ideas exchange   20
Sunak, Rishi   45
Supermarket chains   79, 133, 144, 172–173, 247–248
Supply chains and COVID-19   263, 267–268

Sustainability   *see* impact investing

Talent attraction   67
Taleb, Nassim   102
Tchenguiz, Robert   108
TCI hedge fund   16, 35, 87, 165
Technical analysis   209–211
Tepper, Jonathan   250
Tesco   43, 79, 97, 103, 144, 199, 247
Tesla   71, 98, 122, 240–241
The Analyst   20
The Great Crash, 1929   271
The Macro Strategy Partnership   20
The Myth of Capitalism   250
*The Quality Dimension of Value
   Investing*   121
The Signal and the Noise   228
Thematic investing   20
   opportunistic   21–22
   structural   22–24
*This Time Is Different: Eight Centuries of
   Financial Folly*   259
Thomas Cook   116, 145, 164
Tibbett and Britten   173
Tiger hedge fund   176–177, 212
Time as constraint   8–9
Time horizons   39, 40, 180, 185, 189
Timing issues   144–145
Trade suppliers as information
   sources   43
Train, Nick   73, 80, 82
Trump, Donald   23, 232, 234, 236–
   237
Tudor Jones, Paul   216
Turner, Ross   170
TUI   164
Turnaround situations   14, 80

Uber   10, 65, 69, 251–252
Unilever   79, 80, 138
Universal Music   30, 31, 107, 177

Valeant   100, 108
Valuation   2, 9, 10–11, 35–36, 56, 62,
   130–131, 158–181
   and COVID-19   262–264
   EV to sales ratio   164–169
   for loss-makers   166–167
   for Sotheby's   125
   for Spotify   30–31
Value investors   158
Visual Capitalist   97
Vivendi   30–31, 107, 205
Venture capital and private equity   31,
   75, 127, 173, 240, 248–250
Volatility   15, 212, 213
Volkswagen   82–83, 97
Vulcan Materials   231

Walmart   104, 167–168, 247, 253, 255,
Warburton, Peter   20
Wassall   97, 208
Waymo   135, 189
Webster, Ray   101
Western Union   65
WeWork   251
White, Dan   200
Whole Foods   247
Wolfson, Lord   92
Woodford fund   70
Working capital   127, 139–140, 144,
   148, 174, 207
   and COVID-19   268–270
   at Amazon   104
   at Sainsbury   172
WPP   29, 95, 107

Yardeni, Ed   19–20
Yipit   254

Zodiac   26–27
Zozo   93

THANKS FOR READING, PLUS A SPECIAL OFFER

Thanks for reading this book. I hope you enjoyed it.

If you did enjoy the book, could you please leave a review on Amazon? It would really help.

Before you go, I have two suggestions for you:

If you would like to see the training course based on the book, please visit: bit.ly/smart-money-X.

Use the coupon code SMART-MONEY to get 20% off.

And if you would like to see more of my writing, make contact with fellow enthusiastic investors and access my library of over 1500 investment articles, fund letters, and stock research reports, please join our club/community at bit.ly/smart-money2. It's free!